Slingshot

Slingshot

The Defeat of Eric Cantor

Lauren Cohen Bell
Randolph-Macon College

David Elliot Meyer
Randolph-Macon College, Class of 2015

Ronald Keith Gaddie
University of Oklahoma

Los Angeles | London | New Delhi
Singapore | Washington DC

Los Angeles | London | New Delhi
Singapore | Washington DC

FOR INFORMATION:

CQ Press

An Imprint of SAGE Publications, Inc.

2455 Teller Road

Thousand Oaks, California 91320

E-mail: order@sagepub.com

SAGE Publications Ltd.

1 Oliver's Yard

55 City Road

London, EC1Y 1SP

United Kingdom

SAGE Publications India Pvt. Ltd.

B 1/I 1 Mohan Cooperative Industrial Area

Mathura Road, New Delhi 110 044

India

SAGE Publications Asia-Pacific Pte. Ltd.

3 Church Street

#10-04 Samsung Hub

Singapore 049483

Printed in the United States of America

ISBN 978-1-5063-1196-8

This book is printed on acid-free paper.

Acquisitions Editor: Sarah Calabi

Editorial Assistant: Raquel Christie

Production Editor: Libby Larson

Copy Editor: Amy Harris

Typesetter: Hurix Systems Pvt. Ltd.

Proofreader: Ellen Brink

Indexer: Sheila Bodell

Cover Designer: Candice Harman

Marketing Manager: Amy Whitaker

Certified Sourcing
www.sfiprogram.org
SFI-00453

15 16 17 18 19 10 9 8 7 6 5 4 3 2 1

Contents

About the Authors

Lauren C. Bell is Professor of Political Science and Dean of Academic Affairs at Randolph-Macon College, in Ashland, Virginia. She holds a Bachelor of Arts degree from the College of Wooster and Masters of Arts and Doctor of Philosophy degrees from the Carl Albert Congressional Research and Studies Center at The University of Oklahoma. Bell previously served as an American Political Science Association Congressional Fellow on the United States Senate Committee on the Judiciary and a United States Supreme Court fellow at the United States Sentencing Commission in Washington, DC.

Dr. Bell is the author of *Filibustering in the U.S. Senate* (Cambria Press, 2011), *Warring Factions: Interest Groups, Money, and the New Politics of Senate Confirmation* (The Ohio State University Press, 2002) and *The U.S. Congress, A Simulation for Students* (Thomson/Wadsworth, 2005) as well as co-author of *Perspectives on Political Communication: A Case Approach* (Allyn & Bacon, 2008). In addition to these books, she has published single- and co-authored articles in several peer-reviewed journals, including *The Journal of Politics, Political Research Quarterly, The Journal of Legislative Studies, The Journal of Public Administration Research and Theory,* and *Judicature.*

Ronald Keith Gaddie is President's Associates Presidential Professor & Chair of the Department of Political Science at the University of Oklahoma, associate director of the OU Center for Intelligence and National Security, and editor of *Social Science Quarterly.* He previously taught at Tulane University and Centre College. Keith received his Ph.D. from the University of Georgia (1993) and his undergraduate degree from Florida State University (1987). He has published over 20 books on campaign politics, election law, sports, and fiction, including *The Rise and Fall of the Voting Rights Act* (2016); *The Three Governors Controversy: Skullduggery, Machinations, and the Decline of Georgia's Progressive Politics* (2015); *Politics in America,* 10th & 11th eds (2014, 2016); *Georgia Politics in a State of Change,* 1st & 2d eds. (2009, 2013); *Ghosts on Vintners Landing: A Novel* (2010); *The Triumph of Voting Rights in the South* (2009, winner of the V. O. Key Award); and *University of Georgia Football* (2008).

David Elliot Meyer serves as a Special Assistant in the Office of Governor Terence R. McAuliffe. He graduated from Randolph-Macon College with a Bachelor of Arts degree, majoring in Political Science. Elliot participated in the 2014 Schapiro Undergraduate Research Fellowship and presented his research paper, "Crashing the Tea Party: The Effects of the Tea Party on U.S. House of Representative Elections" at the 2015 Southern Political Science Association Conference.

Preface

This book should not exist because the events it describes should never have happened. Eric Cantor was not supposed to lose his primary election in 2014. But despite the majority leader spending nearly $6 million and completely dominating every conventional form of campaign media, he was defeated. An inevitable march toward the Speakership of the U.S. House of Representatives was derailed by an economics professor from a small liberal arts college who leaned in and challenged one of the most powerful people in Washington.

Our project began with a bit of good fortune in the unlikely form of Elliot Meyer's undergraduate research project, conducted under the direction of Lauren C. Bell. The emerging trend in undergraduate political science education in the twenty-first century is to arm undergraduates with research skills, some basis in the literature, and then aim them at empirical questions in politics. Students are supposed to take to the streets and engage in research that allows them to see how the scholarship they read reflects the larger political world we study. Lauren Bell and Keith Gaddie come from a strong tradition of field observation, interviewing, and mixed-methods examination of empirical political puzzles. In particular, both of the faculty contributors to this book were deeply invested in field observation techniques such as those employed by Richard Fenno Jr. in his book *Home Style: House Members in Their Districts* and later by political scientists such as James Glaser in *The Hand of the Past in Southern Politics*. Gaddie's previous book *Born to Run* and Bell's *Warring Factions: Interest Groups, Senators, and the New Politics of Senate Confirmation* make use of these techniques as well.

For his part, Meyer spent the spring and early summer of 2014 immersed in the *quixotic* campaign of David Brat, who was running in the 2014 Virginia Seventh District primary election against Eric Cantor, the majority leader of the U.S. House of Representatives. When Brat lost—because, of course, he could not win—Meyer was to spend the remainder of the summer analyzing the tea party's declining fortunes, using the primary election as part of a broader research project.

That was the plan. But as the spring progressed, Brat's campaign gained momentum. And then on June 10, 2014, the unknown economics professor defeated Eric Cantor by a double-digit margin. In just five months, Brat transformed himself from a wonky, classroom lecture-style speaker with small groups of constituents to a man capable of rousing hundreds of people at rallies headlined by nationally renowned conservative elites. This, along with many other reasons, culminated in a stunning political upset. In this book, we expand on Meyer's efforts, using them as a starting point to test the validity of arguments advanced for Cantor's defeat by journalists and pundits in the wake of the defeat. We bring science to bear on the political *schädenfreude* that was the coverage of his fall. In so doing, we demonstrate that many of the analyses offered were just plain wrong.

In the end, this book is less about David Brat and more about Eric Cantor. After the polls closed and Brat was declared the winner, Cantor's loss reverberated throughout Virginia, on Capitol Hill, and around the world. The notability of the case was in the fall of the incumbent. Incumbents don't lose, especially not in primaries. When they lose, it is most likely through their own fault. Eric Cantor became leader of the GOP in the House because he was, in part, an architect of the majority who could identify and recruit attractive candidates as well as propel them to victory. How could it have happened?

This book tells that story. Cantor's loss was unfathomable to most people, but it was not without warning. Public opinion polls heralding Cantor's electoral vulnerability were ignored by Cantor's political advisers and by Cantor himself. Efforts by party loyalists to manipulate structural impediments to certain victory—district boundaries, the nominating process for local party chairs— backfired on Cantor and did more harm than good. Even his campaign strategy of attacking his challenger had the paradoxical effect of building name recognition and support for the opponent. Given that Cantor placed millions of dollars into the campaign effort, this ironically amounted to substantial exposure for the challenger.

The examination of this case allows us to elucidate the reasons why good politicians lose. Students of politics have exhaustively examined the politics of defeat, in part because it is so lopsided. When rare losses by incumbents do happen, there are reasons why—and most often they manifest in a loss of faith from the voters, who will throw out the occasional bum in the spirit of former political consultant Dick Tuck's observation, "The people have spoken, the bastards."[1]

At one level, Cantor's loss is a story about taking his constituents for granted and about a basic failure of representation. At another level, however, his loss is about the difficulty of governing in an era of hyperpartisanship, about the public's increasing mistrust of government, and about the public's shortened patience for political leaders. In an environment of sensational media and political drama, the other party is the enemy. Political parties don't bargain or argue;

instead, they obstruct and make war. The lack of political solutions reduces confidence and trust in Congress, which is registering at such low levels that one is amazed that anyone is reelected to the chamber. Leaders have a special challenge because they can become targets if they fall out of step with the party rank and file. When any transgression is viewed as political treason, all that is left is the execution.

Cantor's loss demonstrates the extent to which the Republican Party in the South—ironically, fueled by centrist leaders over the last half decade—has now come to be dominated by the conservative wing. The crafting of racially and politically homogenous districts has changed the game in Republican politics. Instead of holding the center to win, Republicans often must bank right to avoid getting outflanked in the primary. In all these respects, Cantor's loss is a cautionary tale about the importance of constituency service and representation and about the limits of control that politicians have over an increasingly restive body politic. In a way, this book serves as a warning: If it can happen to Eric Cantor, it can happen to any incumbent. As we will demonstrate, however, Cantor's failure to attend to the most basic elements of representing a constituency was the necessary precondition to what occurred in the 2014 primary. His lack of attention was so complete that it is hard to believe that other members of Congress could make the same mistake.

This book will be of particular interest to those who want to learn about representation, congressional elections, political parties, and southern politics. Each of these broad areas of study is informed by the Cantor loss and by the events that led up to it. What follows is a detailed look at the defeat of Eric Cantor. His loss was certainly not inevitable, but it resulted from a tidal wave of forces that were in part of his own making and in part beyond his control. The seeds of his undoing were sown years before the 2014 Republican primary election in the Seventh District. They germinated in the six months that preceded the election, but there is no indication that Cantor ever took seriously the warning signs that emerged during the campaign.

A BRIEF NOTE ON METHOD

The study of politics is often consigned to numbers; vote totals, polling data, and dollars determine much of the shape of politics, and they are the alterable part of the political equation. But to understand how things get moved and why things don't break with the numbers, you have to look at politics on the ground.

Down on the ground in Virginia's Seventh, Elliot Meyer was paying attention. With the full permission of the candidate, Meyer shadowed the Brat campaign from early April 2014 through June 17, 2014, engaging as a participant observer at the campaign office, at campaign events and activities, and at meetings of tea party groups that supported Brat. He recorded many of the speeches, engaged in conversations with supporters, and had the opportunity to meet and talk directly with many of the key players in that race, including Dave Brat himself and Zachary Werrell, Brat's 23-year-old campaign manager. Meyer also attended meetings of local tea party groups and had the opportunity to talk with several active members, whose insights also inform our understanding of how some of the Seventh District's most conservative members came to distrust Eric Cantor.

In addition, because Brat continued to teach at Randolph-Macon College throughout the spring term, this meant that both Meyer and Bell had the opportunity to talk with him about his campaign. Throughout the research and writing of this project, other congressional staff members were consulted about various elements of the story. Consistent with guidance from Fenno and best practices of social science research, private citizens that were interviewed by the authors for this project have been granted anonymity; throughout the text, the names of the private citizens that consented to interviews are kept in confidence. When interview subjects are identified, it is with their permission.

Beyond the firsthand accounts and behind-the-scenes details that are an important feature of this book, no account of the Cantor loss would be complete without a detailed look at the important role that the grass roots' mobilization played in unseating the House majority leader. In preparing to write this book, we undertook an extensive inquiry into the grassroots sentiment, especially within the tea party movement in the Seventh District, which was such an important part of the dynamics of the 2014 primary election. There is a robust political blogging culture in Virginia, particularly on the right, and collectively we have spent countless hours combing these blogs for insights into the Republican grass roots' activities and opinions in the months and weeks leading up to the primary election. These posts, while certainly not scholarly, provide important information about the grass roots' mobilization efforts against Eric Cantor.

ACKNOWLEDGMENTS

Inasmuch as the events leading up to this book are almost impossible to fathom, it is unfathomable as well to think of this book being completed without the support and assistance of many people. The authors wish to acknowledge the staff at CQ Press, especially Sarah Calabi and Charisse Kiino. In addition, we are grateful for the wise comments of several reviewers: Gibbs Knotts, College of Charleston; Kirby Goidel, Texas A&M University; and Seth McKee, Texas Tech University.

U.S. Congressman David Brat and his campaign staff—both paid and volunteer—were important resources for the original project that informed this research. Brat's general election challenger, Jack Trammell, was also an invaluable resource. In addition, the Schapiro Undergraduate Research Fellowships program at Randolph-Macon College provided financial support to Elliot Meyer and Lauren Bell, which permitted their spring and summer 2014 study of the Seventh District primary election.

Each author also benefitted greatly from the support and assistance of many others. Lauren Bell wishes to thank Randolph-Macon College and particularly Provost William T. Franz for supporting this work and Professor Elliott Fullmer for his wise counsel and colleagueship on multiple aspects of this project. Bell also acknowledges her family, especially her husband, Dr. Jim Doering, for tireless support and understanding while the work to complete this volume was under way.

Keith Gaddie thanks the University of Oklahoma Department of Political Science for research support in the completion of this manuscript. He also thanks Centre College in Danville, Kentucky, and especially Professor Dan Stroup for their support while he was in residence during winter 2015 and where much of his writing on this project took place. He also thanks and appreciates his lovely wife, Dr. Kim Gaddie, for keeping him organized through the writing of another book and for continually reminding him over the past 15 years that "campaigns do matter."

Elliot Meyer thanks the people that contributed to this project and helped to make this research experience possible, especially the political science faculty at Randolph-Macon College and the faculty and staff associated with Randolph-Macon's Schapiro Undergraduate Research Fellowship Program. In addition, Meyer thanks Thomas Morgan for his assistance with data collection and analysis. Most of all, Meyer wishes to express his gratitude and love to Mom, Dad, Louisa, and Mikhaila for their unwavering support and encouragement to explore his potential.

CHAPTER 1

The Cantor Case in Context

"Cantor may have not known or cared, but in his quest for national power he had burned one too many bridges back home."

—Jeff Singer, *Daily Kos*[1]

On June 10, 2014, Eric Cantor was beaten in the Republican primary for the Seventh Congressional District in Virginia. Lots of politicians lose primaries. But Cantor was the majority leader of the U.S. House of Representatives. He was a young, active, well-funded incumbent. No majority leader had lost reelection or renomination since the position was created in 1899. It was a historic defeat.

The defeat of Rep. Eric Cantor for renomination by economics professor David Brat defied the conventional assumptions of American politics. An incumbent lost. An incumbent lost a primary. The floor leader and architect of a durable GOP majority was ousted in his own primary. And it happened in a safe district that had been drawn to keep the incumbent in power for at least the next 10 years. Cantor's defeat was foreseen by no one and was subsequently explained by everyone.

As a case, the primary in Virginia's Seventh is an example of "the cautionary tale," an illustration of how a good thing goes bad in politics. As such, it attracted the excessive use of hyperbole and analogy that dominates journalistic and pundit "studies" of elections. It tells us about how the media and new class of immediacy analysts engage an event and generate explanations for the public in the short term, when the glare of attention is most bright. The cautionary tale is nothing new in the human experience. We recount our history and mythology in epic tales. Great leaders emerge. Empires fall; others rise. There are villains and heroes. Giants are slain by the most humble of opponents, and underdogs prevail in the face of long odds. When powerful leaders fall, people seek metaphors and analogies to lend context to events that unfold before their own eyes. The fall of Eric Cantor pulls part and parcel from all of these—the vanquishing of the king in waiting, felled by his arrogance; the political giant felled by the slingshot stone of an insignificant and unarmored David; the man denied because he misjudged political circumstances and thus fell on the wrong side of history and its forces.

JOURNALISTS VERSUS POLITICAL SCIENTISTS

Traditional journalists and the instant pundits of new age media engaged in a variety of speculative theories of why Cantor lost. Their speculations were often the typical "single-factor" explanations that are popular in journalistic circles, the effort to boil an unusual outcome down to a pithy 15-second cable news utterance or a 300-word Internet posting or a 140-character tweet. Eric Cantor was politically dead, and inquiries into how he died quickly concluded. Politics and journalists moved on to other primaries, other stories. For political scientists and political operators, the question of *why* a rich, powerful, well-heeled political leader fell remains to be answered.

Richard Fenno Jr. engaged the difference between journalists and political scientists regarding how they access a political story. In his book *Watching Politicians*, Fenno observes that journalists have inherently different goals than political scientists when they observe and write about politics. The journalist is often concerned with the immediacy of the story, of the topic as it appears on the surface. Journalists are there to test the candidate, to test the environment, and to not only inform it but also illuminate and shape public choices. There is the need to be first, to command the attention of the public. Journalists recount and explain the particular case before them, or, in the case of the punditry, try to explain an outcome and also derive from it broader lessons. Those efforts too might be accompanied by a desire to shape the choices of the broader public.

In contrast, political science approaches problems like Cantor's defeat differently. American political science is concerned with the application of systematic methods to improve our understanding of democratic politics. Often this involves using large numbers of cases to explain politics. We survey the public or collect information on many elections or examine numerous decisions to try to determine the relationship between explanations and outcomes. But American political science also finds value in the illustrative case study. It is possible to drill into a case and find evidence that is representative of things that are generally true or to build theories for later testing with additional data. We can take data from the case and then see whether the data behaves as expected in similar cases. American political science places different explanations for an outcome into competition to see which offers the most leverage on the problem. Often those competing explanations to be tested are advanced by journalists, pundits, politicians, and the lay public. The political scientist is there to understand, to explain what is happening or what has happened in order to identify and craft more generalizable and testable propositions of politics.

The defeat of Cantor presents an opportunity to apply political science tools to a rare event in order to illustrate important aspects of American politics. Political science can test competing explanations and home in on both the indicators and explanations of the Cantor loss as well as its representativeness of contemporary politics. In this book, we interrogate the Cantor case in the context of other cases and data to see how typical or unusual it is. In doing so, we shed light on the state of American politics in the middle of the second decade of the second millennium.

PLACING CANTOR'S DEFEAT INTO CONTEXT

To understand the Cantor loss, we need to ascertain whether the case is exceptional. Most often, political science seeks more data through multiple cases in order to create general models of politics. In this instance, we confront a different type of question—is the Cantor defeat unusual, or is it typical of incumbent defeats within their own parties. If the latter, then existing theories of politics are likely sufficient to understand what happened. If the former, however, then extant theories may be revealed to be insufficient, and the Cantor case can help us to refine them.

Before getting too much further into the Cantor story, however, it is necessary to provide some background information about candidate selection in general and how the nominating process works in Virginia more specifically.

Nominating Candidates

The specific structure of a state's candidate selection system determines in part the nature of the primary electorate. The combination of institutional constraints and the makeup of the primary constituency can have significant effects on who is selected as a party's nominee for the general election. In general, there are three types of nominating processes: caucuses, which permit small groups of party elites to select the party's candidate; open primaries, in which any registered voter may participate and cast a vote for his or her preferred candidate; and closed primaries, in which only members of a party may cast ballots to determine that party's nominee. Modifications to the open primary abound as well; for example, blanket primaries put all candidates for office on a single ballot regardless of party affiliation, while some primaries that would be otherwise closed allow for same-day party registration so that the voter may ultimately select whichever partisan ballot he or she prefers on that day.

It is well documented that voters who participate in the nomination phase of a multistage election are different from general election voters, but the particular form of nominating process adopted by a state also has implications for the numbers and types of voters who participate in the nominating of party candidates. Voter turnout is highly variable in primary elections. The extant literature on primary elections suggests that voter turnout in these contests is affected by perceptions of the competitiveness, with more voters going to the polls when they perceive the election to matter or when one party is so dominant in a county or state that voters recognize the primary as their only opportunity to affect the election outcome.

In circumstances in which the primary election may be the only opportunity to affect the result of the general election, crossover voting may occur and may affect turnout rates. Research demonstrates that voters from the nondominant party may desire to nominate a candidate closer to their preferred ideological or partisan position, recognizing that the candidate selected in the dominant party's primary will likely be the winner of the general election contest. As one study of California's blanket primary notes to the extent that voters cross over, "In general it seems that the decision to cross over in primary elections is largely motivated by sincere and not sophisticated motivations."[2] That is not to say that there are not partisans from the out party that are interested in sabotaging the other party's nominating contest, but in general, the literature on crossover voting has concluded that such calculated behavior is unlikely to have a significant impact on election results. As political scientists Elisabeth Gerber and Rebecca Morton note, "While both strategic and sincere crossover voting are possible in these very open primary systems, sincere crossover by moderate voters dominates and leads to the election of moderate candidates from both parties."[3]

Who turns out may also be affected by the particular arrangements of the nominating phase. Caucus participants tend to be highly motivated and engaged partisans, and caucuses produce the most ideological candidates.[4] Open primaries are expected to produce the most moderate candidates, owing to their broad and inclusive nature. Crossover voting by partisans from the other party is also possible and most likely in open primary systems. By comparison, closed primaries tend to produce more ideological candidates since the voters selecting them are themselves likely to be more ideological.[5] Furthermore, who votes in primaries is often determined by candidate-specific factors. As Fenno noted nearly four decades ago, since party labels are neutralized in most primary elections, primary election voters tend to have a deeper attachment to the specific candidates in the race than do general election voters, who may be motivated simply by partisan considerations. As political scientist Barry Burden notes, "Because primary voters are often partisan diehards who care a great deal about policy positions, they prefer candidates with noncentrist positions."[6]

The Rules of the Game in Virginia

The Commonwealth of Virginia provides few rules for political parties with regard to nominating their candidates for public office. Section 24.2-509 of the Virginia Code makes party leaders responsible for determining how to select their nominees for office.[7] This means that from election to election, the method of selecting the party's candidate may vary. Contributing to the parties' indecision about how best to nominate candidates is the fact that Virginia does not register voters by party. As a result, the incentives for the state and local parties to hold nominating caucuses are increased because when a party does hold a primary election, any registered voter in the relevant jurisdiction may participate. At the same time, caucuses are expensive and must be paid for by the party itself, whereas the party does not pay to nominate its candidate through state-run primary elections; this argues against caucuses when party coffers are running low or when the party's nominee is a foregone conclusion. Complicating matters further, when only one candidate expresses a desire to run for office, the party may simply nominate this person through whatever internal means it wishes, such as during the party's own convention or by a vote of the central committee for the relevant jurisdiction.

Even within the same election, the process to nominate a statewide candidate may vary from the process to nominate a local candidate. And since the two major parties in Virginia make decisions about the candidate selection process independently, they frequently choose different selection methods, such as one party but not both will hold a primary to select a candidate. The fact that the parties often use different procedures in the same election cycle to select their candidates can be confusing for voters in Virginia, who sometimes are called upon to participate in primary elections but often are not.

The result is that Virginia selects its candidates in a hodgepodge of caucuses and primaries. In 2005, for example, Republicans nominated Jerry Kilgore for the 2005 gubernatorial election via primary. In 2009, the Democrats held a primary election to allow voters to select their preferred candidate from the three who had filed to run. But that same year, Republicans nominated Bob McDonnell as their candidate during their convention; McDonnell had been the only Republican to file for the office. In 2013, Virginia Republicans again opted to use a convention to nominate the then attorney general Ken Cuccinelli over the then lieutenant governor Bill Bolling. Bolling likely would have won the nomination had a primary election been used to select the party's candidate, but conservatives packed the party meeting where the nominating procedure was decided. The choice of the convention by the party leadership in 2012 was itself widely perceived as a victory for Cuccinelli, the more conservative candidate in the race, and indeed the convention almost certainly assured his nomination.[8] Cuccinelli's nomination over Bolling, who was favored by establishment partisans, contributed to the efforts by establishment Republicans to keep conservatives from influencing the outcome of local nominating contests during spring 2014. These establishment efforts, led by Cantor supporters and campaign staffers, galvanized conservatives against Cantor.

Beyond the varied methods used to nominate candidates, Virginia's lack of party registration has been a perennial issue, particularly for the state's

Republicans. Since the mid-1990s, the state's Republican Party has from time to time required voters in Republican primaries to pledge their support to the Republican candidate in the subsequent general election. These highly controversial "loyalty oaths" have been widely panned whenever they have been proposed or implemented, but their use speaks to the desire of the state parties, particularly the Republican Party, to find workarounds to the commonwealth's open primary system. In 2012, Republican members of the Virginia state legislature began introducing bills to allow voters to register by party and to restrict voting in primary contests to those who share the party label; to date, none has been successful. Those who favor party registration claim that they are certain that crossover voting in Virginia is widespread, although supporters of measures to register voters by party or to close Virginia's open primaries have relied primarily on anecdotal evidence to support their claims. Nevertheless, in recent years Virginia's open primaries have provided many commonwealth voters from the nondominant party with their only real opportunity to affect election outcomes, particularly in local elections, since the number of uncontested seats in general elections to the Virginia state legislature has been high. On average, nearly half of the seats in the Virginia General Assembly have gone uncontested since 1999.[9]

Understanding Virginia's election rules is important for understanding the 2014 Seventh District Republican primary election. The Seventh District Central Committee could have elected to hold a convention or nonprimary nominating process, but it did not. In December 2013, the party notified the State Board of Elections that it would nominate its candidate in a primary. Within a few weeks, Brat formally announced and launched his campaign.

INCUMBENT DEFEATS

Cantor's loss is not explainable simply as the consequence of Virginia's unusual nominating rules—although as we will discuss in Chapter 2, the rules of the game affected party elites' decisions internally and therefore were at least a contributing factor to Cantor's defeat. Many incumbent members of Congress face challengers in their quests to be reelected, regardless of what process ultimately is used to nominate a candidate. But we would be remiss if we did not point out that incumbent defeats are rare. Incumbency rates in Congress have been 90 percent or better for decades, which suggests that regardless of the myriad ways that candidates can be selected, when an incumbent runs, he or she is very nearly always the nominee and the winner of the general election. But from time to time, incumbents do lose elections for reasons that have been well documented: changes in district boundaries, partisan "waves," scandals, and the like.

As a result, we turn now to looking at primary losses by incumbents generally to see whether we might gain some purchase on Cantor's loss specifically.

Since 1992, there have been only 59 defeats of incumbents in general primaries for the U.S. House of Representatives, excluding contests where redistricting forced incumbents together in the same primary. The majority of incumbent defeats in primaries since 1992 have affected Democrats, who make up 35 of the 59 incumbent losses. On the GOP side, there have been 24 incumbent defeats.

Starting with the 2002 primary elections, 25 incumbents have lost renomination for the U.S. House. We identify them in Table 1.1, which demonstrates that a slight majority of incumbents who lost renomination—13 of 25—were Republicans; however, since the slight majority of lawmakers since 2002 are also Republicans, this is not out of line.

As we consider the defeat of Eric Cantor and attempt to place it in its proper context, it becomes clear that the factors that typically lead to incumbent defeats

TABLE 1.1
Incumbent primary defeats, excluding redistricting matchups, 1992–2014

Year	Republican defeats	Democratic defeats	Total primary defeats
1992	5	12	17
1994	1	3	4
1996	1	1	2
1998	1	0	1
2000	0	2	2
2002	0	3	3
2004	0	2	2
2006	1	1	2
2008	3	1	4
2010	2	2	4
2012	6	7	13
2014	4	1	5
TOTAL	24	35	59

Source: Data compiled by authors.

largely are not present in the Cantor case. Redistricting, party identification, wave elections, scandal, advanced age, and the like, do not play significant roles in Cantor's loss, and in fact, Cantor lost in spite of electoral conditions that should have favored both his renomination and his reelection. We briefly address each of these in the following paragraphs.

Post-Redistricting Loss

According to elections scholar Robert Boatright in *Congressional Primary Elections*, most incumbent primary defeats come in cycles immediately after redistricting. The most recent redistricting cycle of 2011 demonstrates this; there were a large number of incumbent defeats in 2012. But of the 13 incumbents who were bested, eight lost to other incumbents of the same party who were redistricted into competition with one another, leaving just five incumbents defeated by actual challengers. We lay aside incumbent-versus-incumbent primaries in our analysis. By definition, someone will lose, and therefore the conditions for a true incumbent upset are not met, as neither is bested by a traditional challenger.

We explore the redistricting impacts on Cantor's Seventh District in Chapter 1 and Chapter 5, but suffice it to say here that his primary loss came two years after redistricting and did not involve an incumbent-versus-incumbent pairing, so his defeat is not a direct consequence of redistricting. But as we will show later, redistricting contributed to one of the factors that led to his eventual defeat, a rightward shift in the aggregate ideological makeup of the Seventh District.

Waves, Parties, and Incumbents

Cantor's defeat was also not a consequence of the year. When incumbents lose, it is often part of a partisan wave that sweeps aside people in general elections. The largest incumbent defeat waves of the past half century have ranged from 50 in 1974 (a Democratic wave) to 58 in 2010 (a Republican wave). But party does not explain incumbent vulnerability particularly well, if at all, since 2002. Of the 25 incumbent defeats in primaries since 2002, 13 were of Republicans, 12 of Democrats. Moreover, the 2014 congressional midterm elections benefitted Republicans generally. The party increased its majority in the U.S. House of Representatives, recaptured the U.S. Senate, and won three new governorships. There is no macro- or microlevel reason to believe that party identification explains Cantor's loss.

A close analysis of 2014 incumbent defeats reveals some interesting patterns. The 2014 elections claimed 18 incumbents in total. Five lost in the primaries; of these, four were Republicans. Of the four Republicans defeated, three were in Louisiana, Texas, and Virginia. Of the 13 incumbent general election losses, just two were by Republicans. Republican incumbents were more likely to lose within their party than outside and in the South rather than outside the South. Republicans generally lost primaries, and Democrats generally lost general elections, but losses in general were rare. Of the dozen Democrats defeated, only one—John Tierney in Massachusetts—lost his primary. The 11 Democrats who fell in the general election were largely outside the South. Democratic incumbents John Barrow (GA), Joe Garcia (FL), and Pete Gallego (TX) lost general elections in the South. Most of the Democratic losses were in the Midwest and Northeast, where Democrats have been generally dominant since 1992.

The difference in the pattern of incumbent losses between Republicans (who lost primaries in the South) and Democrats (who lost general elections in nonsouthern states) provides a hint at one of the factors affecting Cantor's loss—the willingness of Republicans to mount challenges to their own in primary elections since 2010; but as we will see, the presence of a conservative challenger to Eric Cantor is just one of the factors contributing to his defeat. On the Democratic side, seven of the 12 defeated incumbents were either African American or Hispanic, suggesting that race played a role in their defeats. One of these incumbents, Rep. Cynthia McKinney of Georgia, was defeated twice for renomination in four years.

Southern Volatility

Approximately 30 percent of all U.S. House seats are in the 11-state South. However, of the incumbent defeats since 2002, just over half (13) were in the South. At first glance, this might suggest greater volatility in the South than in other areas; if so, Cantor's loss might simply be part of a broader pattern of southern instability.

Indeed, the evidence demonstrates that incumbent losses in the South do seem to fit certain patterns. In the elections following the 2001 decennial redistricting, it was mostly Democrats in the South that lost their seats; in contrast, since the 2011 redistricting, it has largely been Republicans who have lost their seats. To some extent, then, Cantor's loss—coming, as it did, alongside the losses of several other southern Republican colleagues—might simply be the result of increasingly restive constituencies in the South. At the same time, however, many of the recent incumbent losses in the South can be explained by idiosyncratic factors: Rep. Parker Griffith was a Democratic party switcher in Alabama who lost his first bid at renomination as a Republican. The only non-Hispanic white Democrat to be defeated, Rep. Chris Bell (TX), sought renomination in a Houston district that was substantially altered by a mid-decade redistricting in 2003. Although Cantor's loss fits this southern bias pattern in that he is a Republican who lost a post-2011 primary that took place in the South, it is impossible to contextualize it within other Republican losses in the South because, as we have shown, there is no typical southern loss in the GOP. Certainly the evidence does not suggest that Cantor's loss resulted from the slightly reduced southern incumbency rate overall.

Quality Challengers

One indication of the vulnerability of an incumbent is quality of the competition the incumbent faces. As the political science literature on candidate emergence demonstrates, the best candidates for Congress are state legislators or other state and local elected officials. They have run successful campaigns before, and they understand the legislator's job. They have a base of support and organization in the congressional district because they represented part of it as a state or local official. They bring fund-raising abilities and an existing financial network. And when they run for open seats or as challengers to incumbents, they do better than all other nonincumbent candidates.

Two other potentially good types of candidates are lawyers and people who previously ran for a congressional office or other major office. Lawyers have long been overrepresented in elective office. This is in part because legal training provides avenues for political advancement that may not be available to candidates without such training. Lawyers, for example, qualify to work in posts within legislative assemblies or in the legal system, such as in prosecutorial or judicial roles, which may be important stepping-stones to running for office.[10] Lawyers may also have important contacts within bar associations and other professional organizations that provide access to campaign funds. In addition, these candidates also bring public speaking abilities and networks of connections to their candidacies, as do candidates with prior experience running and winning elective office.

Then there are the amateurs. These are the folks that Canon described as the "actors, athletes, and astronauts" who bring a form of celebrity or notoriety outside the political realm through experiences that are generally popular in the public.[11]

Table 1.2 lists the 25 incumbent primary challengers who bested incumbents from 2002 to 2014. Of these challengers, 12 were lawyers, 14 had held prior elective office, and four had sought office before. A total of 18 of the 25 had at least one of these experiences. Of the remaining seven, one had been a football player at the major university in the state, and three were recent military veterans.

Just three of the challengers in Table 1.2 lacked any of the experiences or characteristics that would make them quality challengers by the standards of the literature on congressional elections, and David Brat was one of them. Brat, an economics professor at a selective liberal arts college in the Seventh District, had never run a campaign and had little more than volunteer experience working in

TABLE 1.2
Characteristics of successful primary challengers to incumbents, 2002–2014

Year	State	District	Incumbent	Challenger	Multiple primary challengers	Challenger is officeholder	Challenger ran before	Challenger is lawyer	Other challenger distinctiveness
2002	AL	7	Hilliard (D)	Davis	Yes	No	Yes	Yes	
2002	CA	18	Condit (D)	Cardoza	Yes	Yes	No	No	
2002	GA	4	McKinney (D)	Majette	No	Yes	No	Yes	
2004	TX	9	Bell (D)	Green	Yes	Yes	No	Yes	
2004	TX	28	Rodriguez (D)	Cuellar	No	Yes	No	Yes	
2006	GA	4	McKinney (D)	Johnson	Yes	Yes	No	Yes	
2006	MI	7	Schwarz (R)	Walberg	No	Yes	Yes	No	
2008	TN	1	Davis (R)	Roe	Yes	Yes	Yes	No	
2008	UT	3	Cannon (R)	Chaffetz	No	No	No	No	BYU Football
2008	MD	1	Gilchrist (R)	Harris	Yes	Yes	No	No	
2008	MD	4	Wynn (D)	Edwards	Yes	No	Yes	Yes	
2010	MI	13	Kilpatrick (D)	Clark	Yes	Yes	No	Yes	
2010	WV	3	Mollohan (D)	Oliverio	No	Yes	No	No	
2010	AL	5	Griffith (R)	Brooks	Yes	Yes	No	Yes	

(Continued)

TABLE 1.2
(Continued)

Year	State	District	Incumbent	Challenger	Multiple primary challengers	Challenger is officeholder	Challenger ran before	Challenger is lawyer	Other challenger distinctiveness
2010	SC	4	Inglis (R)	Gowdy	Yes	Yes	No	Yes	
2012	PA	17	Holden (D)	Cartwright	No	No	No	Yes	
2012	TX	16	Reyes (D)	O'Rourke	Yes	Yes	No	No	
2012	OH	2	Schmidt (R)	Wenstrup	Yes	No	No	No	Iraq Veteran
2012	OK	1	Sullivan (R)	Bridenstine	No	No	No	No	Naval Aviator
2012	FL	3	Stearns (R)	Yoho	Yes	No	No	No	
2014	MA	6	Tierney (D)	Moulton	Yes	No	No	No	Iraq Veteran
2014	VA	7	Cantor (R)	Brat	No	No	No	No	Professor
2014	TX	4	Hall (R)	Ratcliffe	Yes	Yes	No	Yes	
2014	MI	11	Bentivolio (R)	Trott	No	No	No	Yes	
2014	LA	5	McAllister (R)	Abraham	Yes	No	No	No	

Source: Compiled by authors.

politics. He was not, by any measure, a quality challenger—save, of course, for the fact that he ended up winning.

Nomination Format

One set of pundit explanations for Cantor's loss homed in on the outcome of a relatively low-turnout June primary in Virginia as representative of a broad based national trend. It was argued in the aftermath of Cantor's loss that open primary formats are more likely to lead to incumbent primary defeats due to low voter turnout rates and the lack of control over the composition of the electorate by the party. Presumably, independents and other partisans can engage in strategic behavior and cross over to cause mischief in the other party's primary. But evidence of such strategic voting is hard to find. Academic studies that have explored whether open primaries lead to greater electoral volatility have generally concluded that they do not.[12]

Further, our examination in Table 1.3 of the impact of each nomination method on incumbent success during the twenty-first century shows no real pattern. Incumbents have lost across every nomination format. Ten incumbents lost in open primaries—those primary contests where voters can choose to vote in the either party's primary. The number of partisan incumbents defeated in open primaries since 2000 includes five Republicans and five Democrats. Nine incumbents lost in closed primaries—five Republicans, four Democrats. A closed primary is a primary contest in which voters may vote only in the primary election for the party with which they are registered. Four incumbents have lost "modified open" primaries in which the parties open up their primaries to nonpartisans (e.g., those voters claiming to be independents)—three Democrats, one Republican. One incumbent lost in a party-nominating convention. And one was shut out of the runoff in Louisiana's nonpartisan blanket primary system in which all candidates for office regardless of party were placed on the same ballot, which all voters received. Although the format of the nomination process undoubtedly contributes to campaign strategies and election outcomes, it is clear that the type of nominating contest itself is not a sufficient predictor of incumbent success.

Scandal

Where there is politics, there is money and power. And near money and power one can often find scandal, real or invented. Of the incumbents bested in primaries, eight were involved in a scandal or controversy. Earl Hilliard (D-AL) and Cynthia McKinney (D-GA) were both bested in 2002 in part due to controversial statements made about September 11, 2001, and the Israel lobby. McKinney later returned to Congress in 2006 and was again defeated after a series of high-profile

TABLE 1.3
The circumstances of successful primary challengers to incumbents, 2002–2014

Year	State	District	Incumbent	Challenger	Seniority (years)	Nomination system	Incumbent age	Challenger age	Minority incumbent?
2002	AL	7	Hilliard (D)	Davis	10	Open	60	35	African American
2002	CA	18	Condit (D)	Cardoza	13	Modified	54	43	
2002	GA	4	McKinney (D)	Majette	10	Open	47	47	African American
2004	TX	9	Bell (D)	Green	2	Open	45	57	
2004	TX	28	Rodriguez (D)	Cuellar	8	Open	58	49	Hispanic
2006	GA	4	McKinney (D)	Johnson	2	Open	51	52	African American
2006	MI	7	Schwarz (R)	Walberg	2	Closed	69	55	
2008	TN	1	Davis (R)	Roe	2	Open	49	63	
2008	UT	3	Cannon (R)	Chaffetz	12	Convention	58	41	
2008	MD	1	Gilchrist (R)	Harris	18	Modified	62	51	
2008	MD	4	Wynn (D)	Edwards	16	Modified	57	50	African American
2010	MI	13	Kilpatrick (D)	Clark	14	Closed	65	53	African American

Year	State	District	Incumbent	Challenger		Primary			
2010	WV	3	Mollohan (D)	Oliverio	28	Closed	67	47	
2010	AL	5	Griffith (R)	Brooks	2	Open	68	54	
2010	SC	4	Inglis(R)	Gowdy	18	Open	51	46	
2012	PA	17	Holden (D)	Cartwright	10	Closed	55	51	
2012	TX	16	Reyes (D)	O'Rourke	4	Open	68	40	Hispanic
2012	OH	2	Schmidt (R)	Wenstrup	8	Closed	61	54	
2012	OK	1	Sullivan (R)	Bridenstine	11	Closed	48	37	
2012	FL	3	Stearns (R)	Yoho	24	Closed	71	57	
2014	MA	6	Tierney (D)	Moulton	8	Modified	63	36	
2014	VA	7	Cantor (R)	Brat	14	Open	51	50	
2014	TX	4	Hall (R)	Ratcliffe	34	Open	91	49	
2014	MI	11	Bentivolio (R)	Trott	2	Closed	63	54	
2014	LA	5	McAllister (R)	Abraham	2	Blanket	41	60	

Source: Compiled by authors.

events, including a run-in with Capitol Police when she attempted to pass into a House office building without going through security and without displaying her member pin. Gary Condit (D-CA) lost a primary after a sex scandal emerged that Condit had been involved with an office intern who was found dead in Rock Creek Park. Rep. Albert Wynn (D-MD) had a series of controversies and at one point faced an opponent whose campaign was managed by his estranged wife. Alan Mollohan (D-WV) lost renomination after a series of investigations over alleged ethics violations, including one breach that was investigated by the U.S. Department of Justice. Rep. Carolyn Kilpatrick (D-MI) ran into ethics concerns, brought into sharper review by the criminal conduct of her son, former Detroit mayor Kwame Kilpatrick. Rep. Jean Schmidt (R-OH) was embroiled in various ethics investigations prior to her defeat in 2012.

But Eric Cantor was untainted by scandal in 2014. Earlier in his career, opponents had tried to link Cantor to House Majority Leader Tom DeLay, who was indicted in fall 2005 for crimes related to campaign finance activities. But there was little to tie Cantor to DeLay, and efforts to link Cantor to DeLay's illegal activities were ancient history by 2014. Unlike so many other incumbents who have lost their seats, Cantor's loss cannot be blamed on scandal.

Targeted for Defeat

Incumbents may lose when their votes or activities in Washington raise the hackles of politically important and well-funded groups. For example, Reps. Joe Schwarz (R-MI) in 2006 and Wayne Gilchrist (R-MD) in 2008 were defeated in high-cost primaries when they were targeted by the economically conservative group Club for Growth. In 2012 on the Democratic side, Rep. Tim Holden was defeated by Matt Cartwright when the League of Conservation Voters (LCV) and pro-health care reform groups targeted Holden in a redrawn district in western Pennsylvania. Holden had an anti-environmental voting record that landed him on the LCV "Dirty Dozen" list and had also voted against the Obama administration's health care reform law, the PPACA (Patient Protection and Affordable Care Act).

In *The Partisan Divide: Crisis in Congress*, former congressmen Tom Davis (R-VA) and Martin Frost (D-TX) and their coauthor Richard Cohen make the argument that Eric Cantor lost as a result of national factors, not local ones. They write, "It was the changing dynamics of leadership decisions that separated him from his Republican primary voters."[13] This is a very different proposition from being targeted for not being heterodox to the party's prevailing ideology. Eric Cantor was not a RINO (Republican in Name Only).

But as we will show, there is little evidence that Cantor's work in Washington was top of mind for Seventh District voters. Although Cantor's work with

President Obama on immigration reform was widely reported as explaining his loss, almost no one—including Brat's own campaign manager—thought immigration policy made a significant difference in the election results. Moreover, national political groups shied away from supporting Brat in tangible ways because they did not expect him to win and therefore did not wish to antagonize the likely next Speaker of the House of Representatives. Eric Cantor was better funded than David Brat by 50 to one, with the national organizations supporting Cantor, not targeting him.

Sophomores and Seniors

Conventional wisdom suggests that there are two opportunities to bump off an incumbent during his or her career. The first comes at the very beginning, when the incumbent is initially seeking reelection and getting established in the job. The other is deep in the career, often when an incumbent has become tired and aged and has lost the ability to mount a campaign against a determined challenger. Of the defeated incumbents, twenty (80 percent) were over the age of 50. A dozen were over the age of 60. In 20 of the 25 cases where the incumbent lost, the incumbent was older than the challenger. This is not necessarily surprising. The window of opportunity where most people initially get elected to Congress is between the ages of 35 and 55—campaigning is a demanding, taxing activity that is difficult for older people, and it is an activity that requires networks, resources, and a perception of maturity and gravitas that are often difficult for people younger than 35 to convey.

Many of the first termers who lose do so in general elections. They were elected in either a midterm wave or on presidential coattails. They often won in competitive districts. And with the change in electoral context, they find themselves disadvantaged for reelection. David Canon finds those who most often lose are the amateurs, who have more difficulty establishing themselves in the institution or who make visible mistakes that set themselves at odds with the electorate.[14]

Of the incumbents bested in the primary since 2002, seven were seeking initial reelection and one other was seeking a second term. Three had been in office for over 20 years. But the vast majority of the incumbents unseated in the primary (14) had been in office for eight to 18 years. Eric Cantor had served nearly 14 years in office when he was defeated. He was neither new to the job nor so advanced in age that he seemed a likely candidate to be ousted. On the contrary, his ascendance through the leadership ranks in Congress suggested that right up until the moment he lost, he was seen by his colleagues and constituents as being in the prime of his career. He was squarely in the broad middle of congressional tenure.

Tea Party Challenges

Recently, scholarship on incumbent losses has suggested that the tea party has changed electoral dynamics, contributing both to increased Republican Party success in congressional midterm elections and, potentially, to establishment-backed incumbent losses within the Republican Party.[15] High-profile upsets such as those of Sen. Bob Bennett of Utah in 2010 or the open-primary win by Ted Cruz over establishment lieutenant governor David Dewhurst in Texas in 2012 feed the folk belief about tea party challenges. But the tea party movement inside the GOP is either a great success or a dubious failure, depending on one's perspective.

At the outset, we need to be clear that there is no single tea party. While there are tea party groups that are national in their scope, such as Sarah Palin's Tea Party Express and the Tea Party Patriots, these umbrella organizations generally encourage the public to get involved in local affiliates or unaffiliated grassroots efforts. Thus, the tea party is best understood as a collection of local, autonomous groups loosely committed to patriotism, small government, and low taxes.[♀] Because each local group operates independently from the others, it is difficult to make claims about the tea party as a national phenomenon. Extant studies that have examined the impact of the tea party suggest that the tea party can affect candidate emergence and success, especially for Republican congressional candidates, but that this impact is primarily local in scope. When a tea party organization is relevant within a congressional district, Republican candidates, including incumbents, are more likely both to be challenged in a primary and to be challenged from the Right. This may affect all candidates' perceptions of their "primary election constituency"— Richard Fenno's term for the group of people they can count on to support them in a contested primary election—and may make it more challenging for non–tea party-supported candidates to prevail in a contested Republican primary election (although whether that is the case or not will depend upon the district's demographics and the mechanics of the candidate selection process). A tea party endorsement may be useful in certain circumstances and may allow a candidate to win a contested primary, but the endorsement may also hurt the candidate's chances to win over the broader reelection constituency—the group of voters needed to win the general election, especially in two-party competitive districts.

The impact of local tea party groups has primarily come as a result of their grassroots efforts to get out the vote in support of candidates they prefer. The vast network of grassroots conservative activists that have embraced the tea party

---

[♀]Throughout this text, when we refer to the tea party's role in the Cantor-Brat race, we are nearly always referring to the local conservative grassroots activists that were active in the Seventh Congressional District and not to any of the national tea party groups, which sat out the 2014 primary race.

label can engage other constituents that might otherwise never have been inspired to participate in congressional elections.[16] The tea party thus has succeeded in scaring some incumbent Republican caucus members into hardening their conservative stances on certain issues; it forces some Republicans further right in order to avoid challenge or court favor with the Populist political movement in their ranks. When tea party–backed candidates have entered the U.S. House of Representatives, it has likewise constrained the Republican leadership, forcing the party in Congress rightward.

Even so, the tea party's influence is likely due to perception of its power rather than a substantial threat to the status quo in the GOP. The tea party has very few electoral victories to claim in terms of knocking off incumbents since it emerged as a backlash movement to re-legitimate the Republican brand after the party's disastrous 2008 elections. In 2012, according to the popular blog *RedState*, tea party-backed candidates won 41 of 86 U.S. House primary races they contested.[17] But those wins have not upset the status quo inside the GOP's election apparatus. Tea party organizations in 2012 backed 19 incumbents, all of whom won their primaries. In open-seat and challenger-only primaries, tea party-backed candidates won 22 of 40 contests. But in 27 challenges to GOP incumbents, no tea party-backed candidate defeated an incumbent. So tea partiers backed high-win-probability candidates who likely would have won without their support. The tea party broke even in open-seat and challenger-only primaries and was completely wiped out across its primary challenges to incumbents.

In 2014, tea party-backed candidates won 41 of 59 GOP primary contests. These were again disproportionately either open-seat and challenger-only contests or contests where the incumbent was tea party endorsed. Among GOP primary election defeats, only one is a documented instance of a House Republican losing to a challenger who was actively backed and endorsed by the tea party throughout his campaign—93-year-old Ralph Hall of Texas, who lost to former U.S. attorney John Ratcliffe in a runoff. If we count the Brat challenge to Eric Cantor, there are two. But as we will demonstrate, any tea party claim to being responsible for Brat's victory is dubious—at least relative to the tea party's efforts to influence the election outcome specifically. Brat was not backed by any of the national tea party organizations, and he repeatedly claimed not to be a tea party candidate.

"Git 'Em Alone"

Lastly, some election scholars have suggested that two-candidate primary contests are more likely to spell disaster for an incumbent because multiple challengers can fragment the anti-incumbent sentiment and result in the incumbent sneaking through with plurality support. For example, political scientist Louis Sandy Maisel, writing of his own failed effort to unseat an incumbent in a

Democratic primary in Maine in the 1970s, has observed that the best chance of beating an incumbent is to get him or her alone in primary, head-to-head. But recent data suggests otherwise. Of the 25 incumbent defeats in primaries since 2002, 16 were multiple challenger primaries; only nine were head-to-head challenges.[18] Cantor was challenged head-to-head, which fits the folk science of how to beat an incumbent in a primary, but it is not typical of recent incumbent defeats.

SUMMARY

There is extensive literature on congressional elections generally and primary elections more specifically. Yet as the foregoing discussion has demonstrated, Cantor's loss defies explanation by most of the extant literature. He did not face a quality challenger. The nomination system within which he competed was not exceptional in hosting incumbent defeats. He did not have a great political scandal or even a small one. He was not targeted for defeat by national groups. He was not a party switcher, nor was he African American or Hispanic. He did not confront a fractured primary field of multiple challengers. He was neither new to Congress nor especially long serving, and he was in the prime age (50) of service in the U.S. House. He was not defeated in a redistricting year. And to the extent that 2014 was a wave election year, the wave broke in favor of Republicans, which should have helped Cantor, not hurt him.

It is said that nature abhors a vacuum; so too does the pundit class. In the absence of a clear explanation for why Cantor lost in a primary election to a political neophyte, dozens of armchair politicians and analysts weighed in with their own theories: Cantor was too close to President Obama; Cantor neglected his district; Democrats colluded to oust him; immigration reform doomed his candidacy. In truth, none of these is quite correct. Of all the possible explanations offered, that of GOP consultant Craig Shirley comes closest when he termed it "a perfect storm." We contend that Eric Cantor created a set of circumstances that placed his ambitions to lead his party in Congress and in Virginia in conflict with his reelection constituency and his primary constituency. Then his reliance on large money media campaigning proved inadequate to overcome the intense depth of opposition he had cultivated within Virginia's Seventh Congressional District. It can be argued that his campaign harmed him more than it helped him.

THE CAST OF CHARACTERS

Political science is more than the study of data and hypotheses. It is the study of people—political people—in a constructed system of popular control and popular sovereignty. In these systems, we undertake campaigns, run by people and populated by them. All campaigns are affected by the personalities of those running and working to elect their preferred candidats, so it is impossible to understand Cantor's loss without understanding the major players in the Seventh District during spring 2014. These players included the following:

- David Brat, the challenger with a chip on his shoulder
- Zachary Werrell, Brat's 23-year-old campaign manager
- the Seventh District Republican Committee, which was stacked with Cantor supporters but whose actions alienated rank-and-file Republicans in the district
- Jamie Radtke, the cofounder of the Virginia Tea Party Patriot Foundation and the founder of the *Bull Elephant* blog, one of the most important grassroots conservative forums in the Seventh District (some in the district credit Radtke with convincing Brat to run)
- the grassroots tea party supporters whose active network mobilized on Brat's behalf even as the national tea party organizations made the decision to stay out of the race
- Cantor himself, whose growing distance from his constituents—both geographical and political—worked against his ability to connect with the voters and secure reelection

The Challenger: David Brat

When he entered the race for the Seventh District Republican nomination, David Brat was considered to have virtually no chance to defeat Eric Cantor. He had never run for public office, nor did he come from a professional background that would have groomed him for a successful political career. Most of Brat's professional career had been spent as an economist at Randolph-Macon College in Ashland, Virginia. His educational background includes a bachelor of arts degree in business administration from Hope College, a master's degree in divinity from Princeton Theological Seminary, and a doctorate in economics from American University. He worked for the Arthur Anderson consulting firm and consulted for the World Bank before joining the faculty at Randolph-Macon College in 1996. Brat's first work experience in Virginia government took place in 2005 when then Virginia State Senate Finance Committee chairman Walter Stosch hired him to serve as a special assistant for economic and higher education policy. Brat and Stosch lived in the same West Henrico County neighborhood; Stosch was impressed by Brat's academic credentials and his interests in economic and educational policy. In 2006, Democratic governor Tim Kaine named Brat to the Virginia Governor's Advisory Board of Economists, and Brat served on other economic advisory boards for Virginia and the city of Richmond in the decade leading up to his election bid.

In August 2011, Brat made his first foray into elective politics when he sought the Republican Party's nomination to a midterm vacancy in the Fifty-Sixth District seat in Virginia's House of Delegates.[33] After a closed-door session, the selection committee ultimately chose a different candidate who was backed by Eric Cantor—Peter Farrell, son of Thomas Farrell, the CEO of Virginia's Dominion Resources, a power and energy company headquartered in Richmond. Farrell went on to run unopposed in the 2011 general election and assumed office in January 2012. He still holds the position. As local political analyst Bob Holsworth explained to the *Chesterfield Observer*, "[Brat] wanted a fair chance to run" for the Fifty-Sixth Virginia House District seat, but the local party establishment "didn't give Brat a chance."[34] The 2011 snub is widely considered to have been a major contributor to Brat's decision to take on Cantor in 2014.

Brat formally announced his candidacy on January 9, 2014, although word of the impending announcement was reported two days earlier by the *National Review Online,* which noted, "Brat can expect backing from much of the Virginia grass roots, especially the Libertarian and tea party activists who have long been frustrated with the state party's leaders."[35] Indeed, while the campaign took pains to portray him as a traditional Republican, the multiple tea party groups throughout the district as well as national conservatives such as Glenn Beck, Ann Coulter, Mark Levin, and Laura Ingraham embraced Brat's campaign. However, Brat was not backed by any of the national tea party groups, who presumably decided to sit out the election rather than risk the ire of the likely next Speaker of the House.

Throughout the campaign, Brat touted the Virginia Republican Creed as the best explanation of his beliefs. This creed endorses a free market system, equal rights for all citizens, the observation of constitutional limitations, a strong national defense, and faith in God. Brat's attacks on Cantor were focused on Cantor's leadership position in Washington; as the challenger, he hammered the notion that Cantor was a "career politician" who was "out of touch" with his constituents and later extended this criticism to invoke the concept of "crony corruption" to explain Cantor's unsuitability to stand in Congress.[36]

The Manager: Zachary Werrell

By his own account, when 23-year-old Zachary Werrell accepted the job working as Brat's campaign manager, no one else would take the job. Managing Dave Brat's campaign was widely perceived to be a losing proposition, and no established politicos were willing to take the career risk.[37] At the time of his hiring, Werrell was one of just two paid staff members for the Brat campaign.

Similar to many amateur challenges to incumbents, the campaign had few resources, a circumstance that changed only a few weeks prior to the June 10 primary. Young Werrell was a full-service campaign manager: coordinating strategy; sending out press releases (including an early one that somehow managed to misspell his own candidate's name); and working feverishly to find and coordinate campaign volunteers, who became known as "the Brat Pack." In his victory speech on election night, Brat referred to Werrell as "the man that worked 18-hour days, when I was passed out, exhausted from giving talks to people."[38]

There was little sweetness to relish with his victory as a rookie manager. As is often the case when insurgents post unexpected primary wins, the money people and the pros showed up, and change soon followed. Within days of Brat's June 10 victory, Werrell was replaced as campaign manager by former Cantor political director Amanda Chase. In the media accounts that followed the announcement that he had been replaced, Werrell claimed he "simply needed a break,"[39] although there was speculation that the Brat campaign replaced him in the aftermath of unflattering media portrayals of his social media activities. On the day after the primary election, *Yahoo News* reported that Werrell's Facebook posts compared the death of Trayvon Martin to abortion and advocated for localities to be permitted to secede from a state.[40] Just over a week later, Werrell was replaced by Chase. The move surprised many local political observers, who credited Werrell with Brat's stunning upset and viewed Brat's decision to hire Chase as evidence that he would move toward more establishment positions. Others applauded Brat for recognizing that Werrell had become a liability.

Linwood Cobb, Fred Gruber, and the Seventh District Republican Committee

One indicator of coming trouble was within the district's Republican Party organization—in particular the battle for control of the district committee chairmanship. These local party meetings are important in Virginia because Section 24.2-509 of the Virginia Code makes party leaders responsible for determining how to select their nominees for office.[41] This is different from most states, where there is a consistent process for selecting nominees to run for office. In Virginia, there is no state-mandated nominating process for party candidates. As a result, the parties have extraordinary control over candidate selection; often, the results of local party meetings have significant impact on the outcome of the party nominating process.

The relevant party committees may choose their candidates through whatever means they see fit—a primary election, a nominating convention, or in some cases, a vote of the relevant party leadership. Moderates within the party typically prefer to nominate candidates using a primary election, since primaries typically involve a larger swath of rank-and-file voters and as a result have a tendency to lead to more moderate nominees. By comparison, more ideological party leaders tend to prefer conventions in order to nominate candidates. Since conventions require a greater commitment from partisans, they typically are attended disproportionately by highly energized, dogmatic partisans and tend to lead to more ideologically extreme candidates. Since in Virginia the choice of nomination method is made by the relevant party committee a few months prior to the date that the nomination must be made, the process to select leaders of these local party committees has also become contentious in recent years. That was certainly the case for the Seventh District Republican Committee in 2014.

A month before the Seventh District primary election, on May 10, the Seventh District Republican Committee planned to meet at Deep Run High School in Glen Allen, Virginia, for the purpose of electing a chairman. This meeting came toward the end of a series of divisive Republican meetings in the state. In previous years, such meetings had been essentially pro forma, with the established party leaders generally being reelected without any significant opposition. But the meeting in 2014 had to be moved a few miles away to the Hilton hotel in Short Pump when it became clear that longtime incumbent chairman Linwood Cobb would face a challenge from local tea party-backed conservative Fred Gruber.

Gruber's candidacy reflected the tensions that had emerged in central Virginia between grassroots conservatives and establishment party elites. Conservatives felt excluded from nominating processes and marginalized by the party elite. This led them to mobilize supporters, who were successful at electing conservatives to the steering committees of local party organizations. In response to the growing success of the right-wing element within the state party, establishment Republican Party leaders began using "slating" during local meetings to select delegates to the statewide party convention. *Slating* is a technique whereby a slate of a small number of party-approved delegates takes the place of the entire contingent of party members eligible to participate in the party's statewide convention. Local party leaders preferred slating to selecting hundreds or thousands of party members to attend the convention because they would be more likely to be able to pack the slate with mainstream party loyalists to the exclusion of right-wing, tea party-backed members.

On March 10, 2014, Virginia Beach's local Republican committee approved a slate of 32 "mainstream partisans" to attend the state convention in lieu of the 552 partisans to which the local group was entitled.[42] A week after the Virginia Beach slating vote, the *Richmond Times-Dispatch* reported on the efforts of local activists to derail the more mainstream elements of Virginia's Republican Party by taking control of local committee meetings. These activists, according to the *Times-Dispatch*, were motivated largely out of hostility toward the practice of slating.

On March 24, 2014, the effects of slating elsewhere in the state were borne out at the Henrico County mass meeting, where in Eric Cantor's home county just north of Richmond, Right-leaning activists rejected a Cantor supporter, Don Boswell, who had been vying to lead the county party's mass meeting. Still, Cantor's allies were unconcerned. They saw the Seventh District Committee as less vulnerable to the effects of the tea party activists since their choice to head the committee, longtime Cantor ally Linwood Cobb, already enjoyed a substantial advantage over Gruber, his likely challenger.[43]

The day of the Seventh District meeting, Cantor supporters were sure they had nothing to worry about. The *Washington Post* reported the following details:

> Cantor's associates churned out mailers to support Cobb, a friend since he and Cantor met at a local Rotary Club meeting in 1992. Cantor's camp paid $3 apiece in postage to send personalized trinkets to party loyalists. On convention day, the committee bought up all the Short Pump Hilton's conference rooms to stymie Brat and provided day care for the kids of Cobb supporters.[44]

But when Cantor got up to speak during the meeting, he was met with boos and jeers. His criticism of his opponent was met with particularly loud heckling, forcing Cantor several times to have to clarify his meaning to quiet the protests. His remarks sounded defensive and frustrated; he complained about Brat that "[i]t's easy to sit here and throw stones in an environment where there are no consequences" as he chronicled his recent efforts to thwart President Barack Obama's agenda.[45] In the end, Cantor's handpicked district chairman, Linwood Cobb, lost to the tea party candidate, Fred Gruber, who managed 52 percent of the vote.

In response to the results of the committee elections, the former Virginia lieutenant governor Bill Bolling released a statement expressing his disappointment that Cobb had been ousted. In his statement, he voiced concern about the rightward direction the state party was taking and his belief that the conservative wing of the party was damaging the party's ability to win future elections. Bolling's press release called for "aggressive efforts" at moving the party back to the center, as he noted the following:

If we cannot accomplish this, we will drive away more and more traditional Republicans and it will become almost impossible for us to reach out to the broader cross section of Virginians whose support we need to win elections and earn the right to lead. [46]

Bolling had himself been a victim of right-wing control of the party's nominating apparatus back in 2013 when he planned to run for governor. Instead, however, State Attorney Ken Cuccinelli and his conservative supporters forced a nominating convention that selected Cuccinelli over the much more moderate Bolling. Cuccinelli went on to lose the 2013 gubernatorial election. Bolling's comments reflect the position that many establishment Republicans in Virginia, including Cantor, had come to embrace as the only viable long-term strategy for winning statewide elections. Local tea party activists do not embrace that strategy, however.

Jamie Radtke

Indeed, where mainstream Virginia Republicans were disappointed with the Seventh District Committee's vote, local conservative activists were ecstatic. Jamie Radtke, one of the early leaders of the tea party movement in Virginia, was quoted by the *Washington Post* as saying, "There's been an ongoing battle for years between conservatives and establishment, and it's a sweet victory when you win but you also win on the front porch of Eric Cantor."[47]

Radtke, a 40-year-old conservative activist, was one of the founders of the tea party movement in central Virginia, and she helped to start tea party organizations throughout the state between 2010 and 2012. (Like many states, Virginia has multiple tea party organizations battling for primacy and purity in leading the movement; there are over two dozen tea groups in the commonwealth.) In 2012, Radtke ran against former U.S. senator George Allen in his effort to be reelected to the U.S. Senate seat he lost in 2006 to Jim Webb. She lost but continued her local activism on behalf of Libertarian and conservative causes throughout central Virginia. Radtke is one of the founders of the *Bull Elephant* blog (thebullelephant.com), which emphasizes "those issues and concerns important to conservative and libertarian grassroots Republicans."[48]

As an early tea party supporter, Radtke had long felt that the mainstream GOP in central Virginia was marginalizing conservative voices. This view was reinforced throughout 2014, as the slating efforts in the local committees reduced the impact of the tea party within the party. Radtke was one of the principal architects of the effort to remove Linwood Cobb from his position as chair of the Seventh District Republican Committee and gave the nominating speech on behalf of Fred Gruber when the committee met on May 10:

The recent slating maneuvers that brazenly kicked to the curb almost 2,000 conservatives who wanted to participate in the Republican Party is not the right direction for our party either and certainly does not help us win elections. These tactics have been engineered and supported by Cantor, Linwood Cobb and others in leadership.[49]

Radtke's work, primarily behind the scenes through the *Bull Elephant*, has continued to provide resources, especially information resources, to local tea party groups and activists. Her blog has become one of the most important forums for local conservatives, and in the lead-up to the 2014 Republican primary, the blog provided a running narrative that catalogued the Republican establishment's slating efforts and kept the pressure on local activists to work to unseat Cantor.

Local Tea Party Activists

Radtke operated from a position of strength. The Central Virginia Tea Party, which she helped to found, played a tremendous role in the primary election outcome, opposing Cantor and activating its local network of grassroots, conservative operatives in support of David Brat. Virginia's Seventh District experienced a 226 percent increase in individuals claiming tea party affiliation between 2010 and 2012.[50] The rapid expansion of tea party support within the district in the years leading up to the Brat-Cantor primary was a key factor in Brat's successful campaign. It is important to distinguish here between local groups of tea party-affiliated activists and the national tea party organizations. The latter did not endorse Brat, and Brat himself eschewed the tea party label throughout the duration of his campaign, even as the campaign recognized the importance of the local activists.

There were 11 local tea party groups in the district during the 2014 midterm election. Five of them—Louisa VA Tea Party, Constitutional Tea Party (Culpeper), Patrick Henry Patriots (Hanover), Richmond Tea Party, and the West Chester Patriots—are organized under the Virginia Tea Party Patriots Federation (VTPPF), which is a statewide federation of tea party chapters.[51] The other 6 operate in West Henrico, Goochland, New Kent, Chesterfield, Mechanicsville, and Powhatan. Most of these tea party organizations meet independently from one another, but their leaders work together to coordinate grassroots strategy. Throughout central Virginia, these groups' bright yellow plywood billboards stand prominently on private property adjacent along well-traveled roads such as U.S. 1 through Henrico and Hanover Counties and U.S. 33 through Henrico County. The billboards highlight the tea party's disillusionment with local leaders ("Hanover County pays 83 employees over $100,000. Where to cut?"); offer commentary on local, state, and federal issues ("The federal deficit grows $36,000 per second"); and during the 2014 primary election, offered support to Brat ("Cantor: socialist—Brat: economist"). The groups shared slogan ideas and strategies through their website the *Virginia Committee of Correspondence*,[52] a reference to the pre-Revolutionary War colonial activists.

The extensive grassroots tea party network within the district rallied behind David Brat's campaign and contributed to his victory, even as Brat took pains to distance himself from the tea party label. In a phone call with *Fox News*'s Sean Hannity, Brat said, "Although I had tremendous tea party support and just wonderful people in the tea party grass roots helping me out, and they're clearly responsible for the win, I ran on the Republican principles."[53]

PLAN OF THE BOOK

The remainder of this book unpacks the Cantor loss carefully and with attention to the ways in which the circumstances that precipitated it both defy and support extant theories of incumbency and congressional elections and fit within them. We use the Cantor case to address several important questions about the state of congressional elections and governance, exploring what Cantor's loss tells us about the changing political environment, the public's orientation to its government, about the role of money in politics, and about the impact of the tea party on the Republican Party and in politics more generally. The Cantor case also allows us to engage questions relating to representation and to consider the limits of representatives' ability to control the news in an era where any citizen with a smartphone can be an opinion leader.

The next chapter opens with the local and national reactions to Cantor's loss before moving on to provide the background necessary to understand the Cantor case study. It includes an overview of Virginia's Seventh District and a discussion of the ways in which the district has been affected by political factors such as redistricting and the changing politics of the South. Lastly, it provides a brief introduction to the major players in this David-versus-Goliath story.

Chapter 3 provides a detailed look at the backgrounds of both Eric Cantor and David Brat. We begin by describing Eric Cantor's personal and pre-political career history before moving on to discuss his early career in politics. We also focus in detail on his electoral history, placing it in the broader context of state and regional politics. We then turn our focus to David Brat, discussing his pre-political career and candidacy in the context of the literature on challenger quality, political ambition, and also the small but useful literature on political "amateurs." We begin by discussing his personal and nonpolitical career history and then move on to a discussion of his political career, from his first forays into local politics on his neighborhood homeowners' association board to his volunteer and appointed positions in Virginia's legislative and executive branches. Finally, we discuss the ways in which Cantor's and Brat's paths intersected, albeit briefly, along the road to the 2014 primary.

Chapter 4 puts the Cantor–Brat race into the broader context of Cantor's tenure in Congress and his concomitant attention to his own power. As Cantor ascended to the leadership, he began to neglect his congressional district. Cantor's increased focus on Washington distanced him from his constituents. When coupled with a strong conservative grassroots presence and growing resentment over Cantor's role in debt ceiling negotiations in 2011 and 2012, his ambition began to imperil his electoral security. In Chapter 4, we discuss Cantor's rise through the House leadership, with particular emphasis on his role as a "Young Gun" and his efforts at candidate recruitment aimed at shoring up a Republican majority in the House of Representatives. We then segue to a discussion of Cantor's election to the position of majority leader and the rumblings of his plans to ascend to the Speakership. Finally, we discuss the ways in which the House leadership began to distance itself from the tea party-backed faction of the party during the 113th Congress. Back home in the district, Cantor's popularity plummeted. This created opportunities for challengers; in 2012, Cantor was challenged in a primary election for the first time in the 12 years since his first congressional election in 2000. In late 2013, Brat began to lay the groundwork for his 2014 primary challenge.

Chapter 5 focuses on the primary election campaign itself. In this chapter, we turn to a detailed analysis of Brat's campaign, from its initiation in November 2013 to its successful completion in June 2014. We also discuss Cantor's series of politically fatal miscalculations. At the outset, the chapter discusses Brat's campaign organization and his fund-raising challenges. It then moves on to a discussion of the traction that Brat gained when big-name conservatives such as Glenn Beck, Laura Ingraham, and Ann Coulter took up his cause. We also address Brat's candidacy as a reflection of an increasing factionalism within the Republican Party, particularly in the South, but specifically in central Virginia. Contrary to the narrative that emerged on election night—that Brat had waged a skillful campaign that tapped into voter concern about immigration reform—we demonstrate that there was a strong anti-Cantor sentiment within the district that almost certainly had a more significant effect on the election outcome than Brat's message on immigration. In addition, we discuss the Cantor campaign's significant missteps, including increasing Brat's name recognition districtwide, his reliance on polling data that he should have known was bad, and his lack of active campaigning for his seat. Cantor's missteps, Virginia's open primary system, and Brat's visibility in the district increased Brat's appeal while undercutting support for Cantor even in areas that previously had supported him at high rates. Finally, we discuss the impact of crossover voting by Democrats and independents in Virginia's open primary and the implications of the open primary on this election. While the literature on open primaries and crossover voting has suggested that strategic voting is unusual and not likely to affect election outcomes when it occurs, evidence from exit polls and election returns demonstrates that Brat garnered an unusually high level of support from parts of the Seventh District that remain Democratic strongholds.

Chapter 6 provides a discussion of the media coverage that emerged following the Brat victory. We discuss the message of the election—that a representative who fails to attend to his or her district will face challenges for reelection—and how the media misunderstood this message. In fact, the media, campaign consultants, and political observers relied on outdated campaigning and polling techniques, and as a consequence, they missed the signs that Cantor was in trouble. We then move to the immediate aftermath of the primary on Capitol Hill, discussing Cantor's decision to step down as House majority leader and the scramble that ensued among House Republicans, which further exposed the deep rifts in ideology within the party.

In our concluding chapter, Chapter 7, we summarize the main themes of the book and offer perspectives on the House leadership shake-up and the consequences for Congress and public policy moving forward. We present our conclusions as a series of lessons that can be drawn from the Cantor loss. Cantor's loss reinforces long-standing theories of representation and congressional elections and offers powerful lessons for journalists and political scientists about the need to be more attentive to congressional elections and to dig deeper into the races they analyze. His loss also demonstrates that campaigns still matter and that despite recent claims that congressional elections have become national referenda on the two major parties, all politics really does remain local politics.

We end with an epilogue that summarizes the general election campaign between Brat and his Randolph-Macon College colleague Trammell and offers a first look at the 2016 congressional elections.

CHAPTER 2

Eric Cantor and the Giant Slayer

*"The notion that Cantor himself would be knifed before he could knife
Boehner occurred to absolutely nobody."*

—Jonathan Chait[1]

JUNE 10, 2014—PRIMARY ELECTION NIGHT IN VIRGINIA

No one thought he could win. Yet just an hour after Virginia closed its primary
polls on June 10, 2014, David Brat, an economics professor who had never contested or won a single election before, was declared the winner of the Seventh
Congressional District Republican primary. Brat was a first-time candidate with
few resources, and it was a remarkable enough achievement to claim victory in
any primary, let alone against a seven-term incumbent. That the incumbent was
none other than the sitting U.S. House of Representatives majority leader Eric
Cantor was simply stunning. No sitting House majority leader had been defeated
for renomination or reelection since the post was created in 1899. Yet here was
Mr. Cantor, an architect of the Republican House majority and the presumptive
successor to John Boehner as Speaker of the House of Representatives, felled in
his own party primary by an amateur challenger.

Most incumbents spend Election Day in the district, making last rounds,
being seen voting, and otherwise attending to the constituency. Cantor had spent
most of Election Day 100 miles to the north in Washington, DC.[2] Late in the day,
he traveled south to Richmond for what was expected to be a victory party at a
hotel on the west side of town. But at Cantor's watch party, several hundred supporters grew silent as the day's results were announced. After Cantor conceded,
saying, "Obviously, we came up short," a hush hung over the assembled crowd.
The vanquished incumbent continued, "I know there's a lot of long faces here
tonight, and it's a disappointment, sure." What followed was a lackluster speech
that encapsulated a lackluster campaign. Local journalist Peter Galuszka, sum-
marizing Cantor's concession speech and the events that led up to it, noted that
it was a "nightcap for one of the greatest David vs. Goliath stories in American
political history."[3] Other news outlets—local and global—picked up on the theme.

Cantor's loss shocked the Republican establishment and made international
news. To those outside the Seventh District, Cantor's defeat was puzzling. *USA
Today* had previewed the race on Tuesday morning and noted, "Cantor is expected

to win renomination easily as he seeks an eighth House term."[4] *Slate* magazine had termed holding Cantor to under 60 percent a "moral victory" for the anti-immigration and tea party crowds. No journalistic outlet had rated Cantor as vulnerable, and in the 10 days leading up to the primary, not a single article had appeared in major news outlets featuring the race in any fashion. A June 2, 2014, article in the *Washington Post* on the retirements of veteran Virginia lawmakers Frank Wolf and Jim Moran accepted as a foregone conclusion that Cantor would remain in the House, offsetting the loss of clout.[5]

As far as the media and the political chattering class went, there was no reason to think that Cantor was in peril. In the weeks and months leading up to the June primary, Cantor was seemingly invincible, the brightest rising star in a party full of rising stars in their 30s and 40s. He was, after all, one of the original "Young Guns"—a group of generation-X politicians in the House Republican conference that included Cantor, Paul Ryan, and Kevin McCarthy. Together, they had developed a recruitment program to expand the number of Republicans in the House of Representatives, and their efforts led to the historic 63-seat gain and recapture of the chamber in the 2010 midterms. Cantor was the leader of that pack, widely expected to be the successor to Speaker of the House John Boehner, possibly as early as the 114th Congress in 2015. Cantor's internal polling, which had been widely publicized, suggested he would decisively win the June 2014 primary over his challenger, David Brat. Headlines following the June 10 primary screamed: "Eric Cantor's Loss: A Stunning Upset" (the *Atlantic* from Washington, DC); "Eric Cantor Loses GOP Primary: Wait, What?!" (San Francisco's *Mother Jones*); "Shocking Upset: House Majority Leader Eric Cantor Loses Primary" (National Public Radio's *Morning Edition*); "Eric Cantor Loses in Shocking Upset" (*ABC News*).

Back home in the Seventh District, however, Cantor's defeat was not wholly surprising. The lantern-jawed incumbent was rarely seen in and around Richmond and the surrounding counties; at home, people felt that he had lost touch with his constituents. His ascendance to House majority leader in 2011 coincided with the decennial redistricting, which resulted in some changes to the configuration of the district. Although the boundaries had largely been drawn to insulate Cantor from a challenge from the Left, the new district lines—lines that were drawn mostly by Cantor's people—resulted in a more conservative district than the one he had grown used to. In the 2012 congressional election, the first in the newly drawn district, Cantor was returned to the House with 58 percent of the vote—his smallest margin of victory in any general election he had contested. Some observers chalked this up to the changes in district boundaries; incumbent lawmakers often have more trouble running in new parts of the district. For example, Richard Fenno's "Congressman A" in the book *Home Style* confronted significant problems relating to new constituents after years of not having to campaign. And incumbents generally run less well in new parts of the district compared with electorally and demographically similar parts of the district where they had appeared on the ballot before.

Still, incumbents are not supposed to lose, and primary election losses affecting party leaders are virtually unheard of. Incumbency rates for the U.S. House of Representatives routinely exceed 90 percent, largely as a result of the significant advantages that incumbency confers.[6] Popular, well-liked members of Congress tend to draw fewer challenges in reelection efforts, and the challengers who do emerge tend to be less credible.[7] This ability to forestall future challenges results in part from the benefits of incumbency, including access to and contact with constituents, funds to travel to and from the district, and a staff apparatus that assists members with staying connected to their districts when they are away in Washington.[8] On the other hand, "candidate saliency," as Thomas Mann describes it, is a "double-edged sword for incumbents; while it can mean an enormous advantage in visibility over challengers, it can also spell disaster if the voters come to believe that their representative has some personal failings."[9] Thus, once elected, members of Congress work hard to protect and preserve a positive image with their constituencies.

WHEN LEADERS LOSE

In the modern era, no congressional party leader had ever lost in a primary election. However, two leaders, both Democrats, had lost their seats in general elections. Senate Minority Leader Tom Daschle (D-SD) was the only one of the 24 senators up for reelection in 2004 to lose his seat and the first Senate leader to lose a reelection bid since 1952.[10] His narrow defeat at the hands of John Thune, a former Republican member of the U.S. House of Representatives, was likely the result of the convergence of his 2004 Senate reelection bid with the 2004 presidential election. President George W. Bush defeated challenger John Kerry by more than 83,000 votes; Daschle lost by just 4,000 votes to Thune.[11] During the race, Thune ran ads that depicted Daschle stating, "I'm a DC resident," and he painted the Senate leader as out of touch with South Dakotans. Daschle countered by flooding the airwaves with ads touting the benefits to the state of being represented by a member of the Senate leadership. As the *New York Times* reported, "His message to voters was simple: Don't replace a leader with a freshman."[12]

That same message had comprised the appeal made 10 years prior to Daschle's loss in 1994 by Speaker of the House Tom Foley. Foley lost to George Nethercutt in an election year that sent a bumper crop of Republicans to Congress and allowed the Republican Party to recapture the House of Representatives for the first time since 1954. That Foley lost the Speakership was not altogether surprising—with the Republicans' return to power, he would have had to surrender it. But the loss of Washington State's Fifth District seat, which he had held for 30 years, shocked political observers. Like Daschle, when Foley saw signs that his constituents were becoming restless, he took steps in the year prior to his 1994 reelection bid to shore up support at home, primarily by running ads that reminded voters of the significant funds, facilities, and jobs he had been able to keep in the district by virtue of the power the Speakership conferred. This deliberate and strategic approach, which he employed in the months leading up to the November 1994 election, led many political observers to conclude he would win reelection, despite other signs the race would be close.[13]

Foley had managed to capture only 35 percent of the vote in Washington's September 1994 blanket primary. In a blanket primary, all candidates for office appear together on the ballot regardless of political party, and all voters regardless of their preferred party participate in choosing two candidates to compete in the general election. In Washington State's 1994 blanket primary, Foley received more votes than any other candidate, but only 6 percent more than the top Republican challenger, George Nethercutt.[14] In the general election, Nethercutt defeated Foley by a razor-thin margin. Reflecting on the loss, Kenton Bird, a longtime Washington State journalist noted, "No single miscalculation on Foley's part caused his defeat. The cumulative effect of a half-dozen issues toppled the Speaker."[15] These issues included changing public sentiment toward Congress, a rightward turn in Washington's Fifth Congressional District; the difficulty of balancing Washington, DC, work and constituency service; and the need to toe the party line even at the expense of voter support at home.

In many respects, Cantor's difficulties in 2014 mirrored the difficulties experienced by Daschle and Foley. Both Daschle and Foley struggled to connect with voters at home, and both, like Cantor, were painted by their challengers as being Washington, DC, insiders whose work on Capitol Hill was more important than representing their constituents. Moreover, all three legislative leaders lost in the second election following redistricting. Of course, this may be coincidental (most incumbents who lose due to redistricting do so in the first election after district boundaries change),[16] but it is also possible that legislative leaders are given more time by their new districts to prove themselves before being ousted for perceived lack of performance. Still, incumbents generally have significantly more name recognition, financial resources, and access to voters than do their challengers. When these incumbents are also chamber leaders, the advantages conferred upon them by virtue of their leadership positions include significant media attention, both at home and in the national press; broad access to donors and fund raisers within the party; and, for Foley and Cantor, a significant role in choosing who their constituents would be during the most proximate redistricting effort. In other words, legislative leaders would appear to have every advantage over their challengers. Paradoxically, however, leaders' access to these perquisites comes with the burden of staying connected to constituents.

But Cantor's defeat is also quite different. Foley was bested in a general election amidst a political wave that swept the Democrats out of congressional power after 40 years. And he had carried two controversial policies of the Clinton administration—the assault gun weapons ban and the Clinton revenue enhancement stimulus package—to victory by two and one votes, respectively. Daschle had sought reelection in a generally Republican state, running in a divisive political environment polarized by war and policy disputes with the Bush administration. His was the most expensive contest per vote of any election in the Senate in 2004. For both leaders, broader contextual factors and a singular national wave contributed to their losses. For Eric Cantor, running in a low-turnout primary, context was clearly different. Other explanations are required to disentangle this historic loss.

The day after Cantor's primary loss, the *Atlantic* published on its website a list of six explanations for his defeat. These included the following: (1) the issue of immigration reform, (2) Cantor's personality, (3) "trouble in the district" (a post hoc catchall that should have been noticeable before), (4) his challenger's anti-crony capitalism campaign, (5) Cantor's religion (which had not been a problem in his previous bids), and (6) crossover voting by Democrats and independents.[17] Each of these six explanations became part of the narrative about the Cantor loss, with national pundits seizing primarily on Cantor's tepid support for accommodating children brought illegally to the United States as part of comprehensive immigration reform to explain the district's turn against him.

Some of these either individually or in combination likely affected Cantor's reelection chances. But we contend that the roots of Cantor's loss were sown years before and include the following factors: (1) Cantor's relatively easy electoral circumstances throughout most of his career left him unprepared for a serious challenge—he had been lulled into a false sense of invincibility and missed the signs of an emerging challenge; (2) his desire to forestall a future, credible Democratic challenger by packing conservative Republicans into his district had made him vulnerable to a challenge from the Right; (3) his ascendance through the ranks of the party leadership required an increasing commitment to Washington activities and led him to neglect his district just 90 miles away; and (4) his role as standard-bearer for the party required votes that were in direct conflict with district interests. These conditions made Cantor's seat ripe for challenge and in many respects were endogenous to the *Atlantic*'s catchall "trouble in the district" category.

But the emergence of a challenger, even in these circumstances, also does not adequately explain Cantor's loss. There are larger historic and contextual factors that must be accounted for in explaining the felling of one of Washington's most powerful figures. He had faced challengers before, and, as we will see, many were more qualified than the man who ultimately bested him. He had also faced challengers in elections that did not favor his party. Other contextual forces also contributed to what happened to this leader at this time and in this place, including (1) the changing nature of politics in the South and (2) Virginia's ongoing use of an open-primary system, which permits voters to participate in either the Democratic or Republican primary, regardless of their own party affinity. Then, finally, there are idiosyncratic campaign elements to consider, such as (3) the Cantor campaign's significant missteps and (4) the shifting public perceptions and expectations of political leaders. All of these factors were also part of the perfect storm that resulted in Cantor's primary loss.

Unpacking Eric Cantor's loss requires an understanding of changes to politics in the South, and Virginia more broadly, as well as an understanding of the ways in which the Seventh Congressional District has changed.

VIRGINIA AND THE SOUTH

Changes to Virginia's political landscape contributed to Cantor's loss but also must be understood in the broader context of changing regional politics in the South. Once upon a time, the Commonwealth of Virginia was a one-party Democratic state where a powerful political machine, the Byrd/Flood Machine, organized politics from the local level all the way up to the vote for president. From the beginning of the twentieth century until the 1960s, in order to advance in politics in Virginia, one generally needed to be in the good graces of the machine and its operators. Political hopefuls started out in county or independent city politics, organizing a precinct or community in support of machine candidates. Then some of them would stand for county commissioner or other county office, backed by the organization. Virginia made use of a poll tax and also a literacy test, and together these devices served to keep the electorate small and therefore more easily manipulated. After some time in county politics, an individual might move on to the House of Delegates or the Virginia Senate and have the chance to participate in the one-party legislature that was dominated by the machine. A few hopefuls might go on to the U.S. House of Representatives, the U.S. Senate, or to serve in one of Virginia's three statewide elected offices (governor, lieutenant governor, and attorney general).[18]

After World War II, the head of this machine, Sen. Harry Flood Byrd Sr., stood as an opponent to progressive politics and especially integration. His "splendid silence" of not endorsing increasingly progressive, integrationist Democratic candidates for president led to Virginia's early exit toward Republican presidential voting in the 1950s. Other Virginia politicians such as Byrd's fellow senator Willis G. Robertson (father of the televangelist Pat Robertson) and powerful Rules Committee Chairman "Judge" Howard W. Smith worked to bottle up civil rights legislation in Washington while bringing defense and infrastructure dollars to Virginia.[19]

In the 1960s, the Byrd Machine's ability to dominate state politics through a small electorate and the management of Jim Crow policies collapsed. Senator Byrd died, and his son and successor, Harry Jr., proved less capable of holding together the machine. The Civil Rights Act; the Voting Rights Act; the Twenty-Fourth Amendment; and the one-person, one-vote decisions knocked the legs out from under the Jim Crow/rural-dominated electoral system, allowing African Americans into the Democratic nominating process and also shifting political power toward the cities and emerging DC suburbs. Old Byrd Machine conservatives responded by taking refuge in the Republican Party, joining with a small but growing core of previous Republicans who had been competitive in the western part of the state and some urban areas for many years. By 1969, Republicans were electing half of the congressmen from Virginia; that same year they also won the first of three straight governorships behind moderate Linwood Holton. Holton had opposed allowing conservative Democrats into the state party, but he was succeeded in office by a former Byrd Machine Democrat, Mills Godwin.[20]

Throughout the 1970s and 1980s, the Virginia GOP grew. Republicans dominated congressional delegation politics and also fell into a cycle of swapping the governorship back and forth with the Democrats every eight to 12 years. Republicans were increasingly successful at winning the other two statewide offices of lieutenant governor and attorney general and also continued to grow their state legislative numbers. Republican identifiers grew in the state electorate, but Democrats—now far more moderate—held on to control of the General Assembly and also most county offices.[21]

The 1990s witnessed a realignment of southern and Virginia politics. Across the South, GOP operatives drew from a playbook developed by evangelical Virginians who had moved into the state GOP. The model was pioneered by the Christian Coalition, an evangelical sociopolitical group that grew out of Pat Robertson's failed 1988 GOP presidential primary challenge. Virginia evangelicals had been increasingly organizing to challenge for control of party caucuses and conventions in the Old Dominion and had taken that organizing and contacting model to the Iowa caucuses in 1988. Republicans recognized the organizational value of Christian evangelicals—both the organization of evangelical churches and the evangelical theology married well to grassroots politics.

Republicans and Christian conservatives recruited attractive candidates who spoke to social issues and then worked to target and mobilize evangelical Christian voters. The culture of faith was the ideal wedge to separate moderate-to-conservative, pro-life, Democratic, white voters from the party of Jefferson and Jackson.[22]

The 1994 elections represented the culmination of this effort. The Contract with America election represented a transition from localized to nationalized congressional elections. Republicans went from holding 40 percent of southern House seats to a solid majority behind an anti-tax, pro-gun, pro-Christian campaign; captured a majority of southern U.S. Senate seats; and also made significant gains in state legislative seats across the regions.[23] The realignment continued over the next two decades. White Democratic lawmakers in particular started to disappear from the state houses and southern congressional delegations, especially in the Deep South states.[24]

Since the Civil War, Virginia had been a leading Republican state in the South. Along with Tennessee, it had offered the most organized Republican Party opposition throughout the post-Reconstruction era. Because of the level of organization in both parties, and in no small part due to factionalism within the GOP between mainstream Republicans and evangelicals, Democrats had resisted the overwhelming and swift GOP takeover witnessed in other southern states during the middle part of the twentieth century. Republicans eventually managed to pull off a state senate tie in 1995, held a majority from 1999 to 2007, then gave back the majority before again tying in the chamber before regaining it in late 2014. In the Virginia House of Delegates, Republicans finally took a majority in 1999 and continued to gain seats until they attained supermajority status by 2013.[25] Within the Virginia electorate, Republicans are now the single largest identifier group at 39 percent, and the Republican Party is almost certainly the preferred party of a majority of white partisans, although Virginia's lack of voter registration by party makes it difficult to know with certainty.

Eric Cantor was first elected in 2000, just 11 months after Republicans took back control of Virginia's General Assembly, giving them complete control of the state's governmental apparatus. The year 2000 represents, in many ways, the absolute end of the Byrd era. After decades of prohibiting the inclusion of candidates' party affiliations on the ballot—a nod to the Byrd Machine's bipartisan dominance—Republicans moved to add party identifiers to the ballot once they gained statewide control in that year. In that regard, Cantor's election to Congress was much more reflective of trends away from party- or machine-centered elections and toward candidate-centered elections.

Despite the Republican Party's recent dominance throughout Virginia, like many southern states, Virginia includes pockets of Democratic strength. Unlike other states in the region, however, most of Virginia's Democratic party strength is concentrated in the Virginia suburbs of Washington, DC. The Eighth and Eleventh Congressional Districts, which surround Washington, DC, and include Fairfax and Arlington Counties, have elected Democrats in the last several congressional elections. This makes them demographically much more similar to the DC suburbs in Maryland and to the District of Columbia itself and puts them squarely at odds with the rest of the state. The exception is the Third Congressional District, which was created as a majority-minority district pursuant to the Voting Rights Act of 1965. Since 1993, the Third District has consistently elected Democrat Bobby Scott. As is common elsewhere, the major urban areas in Virginia—Richmond and Virginia Beach, especially—tend to be more heavily populated by Democrats, although the significant military presence in Virginia Beach does temper that trend somewhat.

Regardless, Virginia Democrats have enjoyed significant success statewide over the last several election cycles. In the 2008 and 2012 presidential elections, Virginia was tallied for Barack Obama, and Democrats have controlled both of the state's seats in the U.S. Senate since 2006. In 2013, Democrat Terry McAuliffe was elected to the governorship. But at the substate level, partisan gerrymandering has ensured that Democrats are confined largely to the DC suburbs and the Third Congressional District. As our review of Virginia's election results over the last two decades demonstrates, today in Virginia, Republicans enjoy nearly complete electoral dominance in local elections, even though there are sufficient Democratic partisans throughout the commonwealth to make statewide elections much more competitive. This is a complete reversal from the Byrd era.

The consequence of this realignment and recent efforts at partisan gerrymandering within the commonwealth and the region is a return to modified one-party competition. Across the South and in Virginia, most legislative districts are safe for one party or the other. In the predominantly minority constituencies, Democrats prevail, while districts with over two-thirds white voters are dominated by Republicans. Strong candidates do not emerge from the "out" party. As a consequence, the majority of political debate and decision-making takes place in the party nominating process.

The party nominating process, particularly for Republicans, has also become the arena for the articulation of and competition between partisan sects. Over the last decade, the Republican Party in the South has been the forum for the emergence of a highly factionalized, southern white electorate. As the party grew in strength in the South, it became increasingly attractive to white conservatives. These voters came to the GOP because the philosophy and issue distance between them and the Republican candidates that emerged was less than the distance to most Democrats. Conservative voters also came to the Republican Party because, in an effort to grow the party, Republican candidates appealed to the issues conservatives cared about. Repeatedly since 1980, GOP candidates have used appeals to low-tax conservatives, American nationalists, evangelical protestants, Libertarians, and limited-government advocates. They have also targeted voters that yearn for the past and have encouraged them to enter the Republican Party. Republicans leaders have both fomented and responded to discontent within the public and have made efforts to harness the energy of the movement to win. The problem for GOP elites, including Eric Cantor, is that these movement voters do not just want to vote for someone who speaks to their issues. They want to actually effect change. They want to govern.

THE VIRGINIA SEVENTH AND REDISTRICTING

It is said that in elections, voters select their representatives, but in redistricting, representatives select their voters. Similar congressional districts can have very different election results. Inputs such as candidates, spending, campaigns, and issues can cause a particular result to differ in two constituencies with similar partisan makeup. In redistricting, political scientists and mapmaking consultants will use collections of election results from statewide elections to generate a common metric for political competition across all districts. This allows them (and the public) to compare the relative strength or weakness of parties across different constituencies absent the effects of particular, local campaigns. Political parties also use indices like these to assess the political potential of different districts in order to target campaign assets or recruit potential challengers for seats.[26] This approach is called a "reconstituted election" approach to measuring party competition.[27]

One variant on the reconstituted election approach is the ORVIS measure—the Optimal Republican Voting Index Score. Samples of elections are chosen, averaged, weighted, and then fitted to districts to determine which ones are more or less competitive. ORVIS was developed by GOP consultants in Texas in the 1980s as a mechanism to identify constituencies likely to support Republican Party challengers in California and the South. Precinct-level voting data from previous statewide elections is used to generate predictions about the extent to which Republican candidates are likely to win elections. Statisticians experiment with the weighting of the various races included in the model until they approximate actual election results in legislative districts. The model is then used to identify Democratically controlled districts that are ripe for a Republican takeover. The higher a precinct's ORVIS score, the more likely the Republican candidate is to win.[28]

In order to describe the competitive balance of the Virginia congressional map, to weigh the impact of redistricting on that balance, and to place Cantor's Seventh District into context, we generated an ORVIS for Virginia. It is an unweighted average of the 2008 presidential election result, the 2008 U.S. Senate election result, and the results of the 2009 statewide elections in Virginia for governor, lieutenant governor, and attorney general. Data were provided by the Commonwealth of Virginia's Board of Elections and were applied to the old and new district map boundaries. The distribution of ORVIS for both maps appears in Figure 2.1.

The 2011 boundary changes of the Virginia congressional map did not significantly alter the partisan balance or competitiveness of the 11 districts. The majority African American Third Congressional district continued as the most Democratic

FIGURE 2.1
ORVIS for Virginia's congressional districts

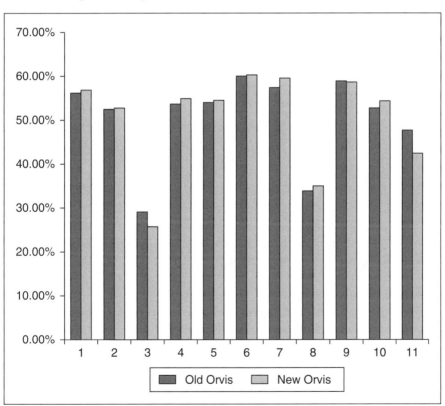

Source: Created by the authors using data available from the Virginia State Board of Elections. The larger the value of the bar, the greater likelihood that a Republican will be successful in contesting an election. The dark-shaded bars represent Virginia's congressional districts as they were drawn from 2001 to 2010; the light-shaded bars represent Virginia's congressional districts as they were drawn in the 2011–2012 redistricting process.

district in the state with an ORVIS under 30, suggesting that it is very unlikely that a Republican could successfully compete for the seat. The score shifted even more Democratic than in the previous map, as more Democratic voters were packed into the constituency. Only two other districts—the historically Democratic Eighth in suburban northern Virginia and the Eleventh District—had an ORVIS under 50, with the Eleventh shifting nearly five points more Democratic.

The Second, Fourth, Fifth, and Tenth Districts were competitive districts that leaned Republican under the old map. The new map shifted these seats slightly more into the Republican column, though they all continued to be what David Mayhew would term "marginal" seats and therefore potentially competitive under the right circumstances. And three districts remained safely Republican—the Eighth, the Ninth, and the safest of them all, Eric Cantor's Seventh, which had an ORVIS of over 60. This means that the Seventh District is considered the most favorable to Republican candidates of any of the state's congressional districts.

In its current form, the Seventh District extends from the northwest Richmond suburbs in the center of the state to the north and west to include Louisa, Orange, Spotsylvania, and Culpeper Counties, to the south and east to include parts of New Kent County, and to the south and west to include parts of Chesterfield County. The district includes parts of the city of Richmond and its surrounding suburbs as well as more rural areas extending into Louisa, Culpeper, and Orange Counties. There is no specific industry that employs a large proportion of district residents. Residents of the Seventh District commute to jobs in state and local government, health care, and banking in Richmond and are active in agribusiness in the more rural parts of the county. Connecting with the people in the Seventh District is not easy; in the absence of a specific industry, the Seventh lacks the agricultural and industrial focus of Virginia's Third and Fourth Congressional Districts; the military and U.S. Department of Defense presence of the Second Congressional District; and the population of government contractors and federal workers that call the Eighth, Tenth, and Eleventh Districts home.

In 2014, the U.S. Census Bureau reported that the Seventh had a population of approximately 761,000, 76 percent of whom were white, non-Hispanic. This is just under the national average of approximately 78 percent. Data from the Census Bureau's American Community Survey further projected the unemployment rate for the district at 6.3 percent, below the Bureau of Labor Statistics' national unemployment rate of 6.7 percent but significantly above the state rate of 5.2 percent in December 2013, with the largest census category of employment in the district being education, health care, and social work. This category employed approximately 88,992 Seventh District residents in 2014—just over 23 percent of the 383,549 residents employed. The median household income in the county in 2014 was reported to be just under $69,000; this is significantly above the

U.S. Census Bureau's estimated national median figure of $53,046 for 2014. The average household income amount in the Seventh District was reported as just over $90,000 annually. Ninety-one percent of district residents over the age of 25 have a high school diploma, and nearly 39 percent have a bachelor's degree or greater.[29] This compares with 86 percent of all Americans who have a high school diploma and 28.8 percent of Americans with a bachelor's degree or higher. In short, the electorate Cantor faced in the Seventh District in 2014 looked much like the rest of Virginia, but it was wealthier and better educated than the rest of the country. Virginia does not register voters by party, but the *Cook Political Report's* "Partisan Voting Index for the 113th Congress" rated the district R+10, suggesting that Republicans enjoy a 10-point advantage in the district.[30] The application of an open-seat congressional election model of the district gives the chances of a Democratic win at one in 19.

The district's boundaries changed in 2011 with the decennial census and redistricting. The district shed three counties—Madison, Page, and Rappahannock—and added portions of conservative New Kent County. As that ORVIS measure shows, the changes to district boundaries following the 2010 Census should have had little impact on Cantor's electoral security, except to strengthen it. In the areas added, the GOP advantage was +42.1 percent, compared with +34.1 percent in the core parts of the district. Precincts in Caroline County (-3.5 percent), Madison County (+25 percent), and Rappahannock County (+14 percent) were excised from the district entirely in the 2011 redistricting. Combined with efforts to maintain the safety for African American voters of Bobby Scott's Third District, it was relatively easy for Republicans to shore up Cantor's reelection constituency. This strategy is not unusual; sometimes during redistricting, electorally safe senior incumbents will actually spread their support around a bit to accommodate potential party gains. Tom DeLay, the longtime Republican House leader from Texas, was cautioned in 2003 during the controversial Texas redistricting not to trim his own security too much in order to accommodate GOP gains in other districts. Ultimately, DeLay "[gave] away enough R's" that he made himself vulnerable in 2006.[31] Cantor played a significant role in Virginia's 2011 redistricting process. *Politico* reported that Cantor's political director, Ray Allen, took a leading role in the process of redrawing the lines. According to *Politico*, "A Cantor spokesman would not comment on the congressman's redistricting role, but his national clout—and his local influence in helping to elect the GOP newcomers last year—gave him leverage in controlling the map drawing."[32] The plan arrived at by the members of Congress, who took the lead in drafting the redistricting plan for seats in the U.S. House of Representatives, was very specifically designed to protect incumbents, with members of Congress dividing boundary line precincts amongst themselves in an effort to maximize their chances for reelection in 2012 and beyond.

MAP 2.1
2010 Map—Seventh Congressional District

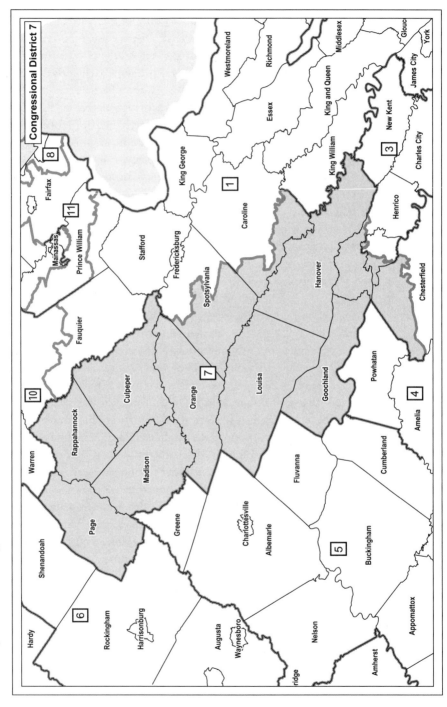

MAP 2.2
2012 Map–Seventh Congressional District

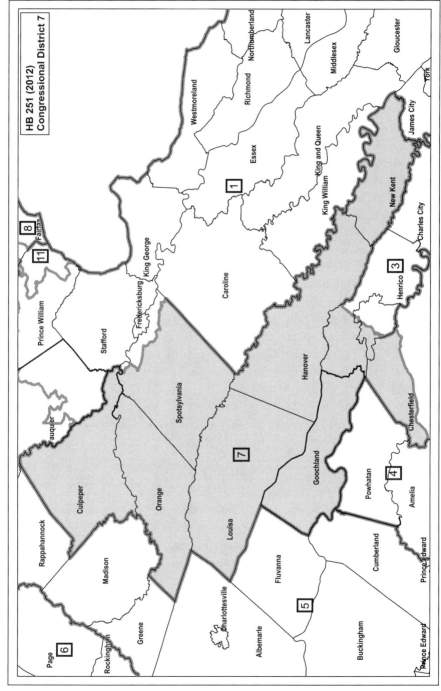

HB 251 (2012)
Congressional District 7

Source: Commonwealth of Virginia Division of Legislative Services: Redistricting 2010. http://redistricting.dls.virginia.gov/2010/DistrictMaps.aspx

SUMMARY

The Brat–Cantor story is one of an underdog defeating an opponent that was supposed to be unbeatable. Incumbent members of Congress rarely lose; those who have distinguished themselves as party leaders and important policy voices lose even less frequently. And yet, as our discussion of Tom Foley and Tom Daschle indicates, sitting congressional leaders are vulnerable to being removed from office by their constituents when their constituents perceive them to have lost touch with the district. But Cantor's drift away from his district is in many respects more surprising than that of Foley's or Daschle's. Foley's district was more than 3,000 miles from Washington, DC, on the country's West Coast; South Dakota is likewise a long way from Washington, both geographically and politically. Virginia's Seventh Congressional District is literally in Washington's backyard. So understanding the distance between Cantor and his constituents requires a fuller inquiry. We engage such an inquiry in subsequent chapters.

Here it is important to note that in addition to moving away from his constituents, Cantor seems to have been insufficiently attentive to the broader changes to the political landscape in Virginia and the South, particularly as tea party groups have sought and gained more influence over politics and policy since 2010. The steps that Cantor took to insulate himself from a future Democratic Party challenge following the 2010 decennial census left him without a sizable enough moderate coalition within the district to successfully fend off a challenge from the Right.

As we will see in the next chapter, Cantor was a lifelong resident of the Seventh District and established himself early on as a serious legislator and constituency servant. He was known for his shrewd understanding of legislative rules of procedure and, consequently, his ability to accomplish his goals. He rarely faced a challenger, either in his early political career as a state legislator or in his later electoral efforts to be elected and reelected to the U.S. House of Representatives. He was expected to be the next Speaker of the U.S. House of Representatives. But in 2014, the combination of the political environment, fissures within the Republican Party in Virginia, the appearance of a charismatic challenger, and Cantor's own miscalculations about his electoral security simply overwhelmed him.

CHAPTER 3

David and Goliath

"We have before us a choice: who we want to be as a country."

—Eric Cantor[1]

During the 2014 Virginia Seventh District congressional primary, Congress-man Eric Cantor refused to appear on the same stage as his opponent, Randolph-Macon College Professor David Brat. Incumbents often avoid appearing with challengers. They do not want to elevate them, as too many things can go wrong. The two men had shared the stage before, years earlier, when Brat moderated a question-and-answer session following Cantor's lecture as part of Randolph-Macon College's "Legislative Leaders" series in March 2011. That series, which brought congressional leaders such as Cantor, former Speaker of the House Newt Gingrich, Sen. Tim Kaine, and Sen. Mark Warner to campus, included a speech by the invited guest followed by the moderated question-and-answer session. Less than six months later, Cantor would support Brat's challenger during Brat's effort to obtain the Republican nomination for the Fifty-Sixth District's seat in the Virginia House of Delegates. But on the stage at Randolph-Macon College in March 2011, the two men were all smiles.

That event three years before the primary was the only time the two men shared a stage, and it might well be the only instance in which they ever shared a room. But beyond this momentary public link, an examination of Cantor's and Brat's backgrounds demonstrate that they are similar in many ways: both grew up as one of three sons in upper-middle-class households with professional parents; both grew up in families in which religion was important, and both continue to be guided by their religion as adults; both are Republicans; both were influenced by their fathers' political leanings; and both worked for Virginia State Senator Walter Stosch before beginning their own political careers. They also lived only a few miles apart from each other on the west side of Richmond throughout much of decade preceding their meeting in the 2014 Republican primary election.

But the two men are also quite different. Cantor is Jewish and married a Jewish woman; Brat was raised Presbyterian and married a Catholic. Although both men are highly educated, Cantor pursued a career in law and real estate, while Brat pursued a career in higher education. Brat is a gregarious, outgoing man who is known for his tendency to speak in staccato sentences and mixed metaphors, sometimes expressing ideas before he has fully considered them. Cantor is more reserved and careful when he speaks, presenting as part of the establishment wing of the Virginia Republican Party. He assumed the role of standard-bearer for the party after Republicans were swept from statewide office in 2013, leaving him as the top office-holding Republican in the commonwealth. Brat signed on to the tea party-backed wing of the Republican Party in Virginia, whose message of fiscal responsibility aligned closely with his own view of the need for the federal government to dramatically reduce budget deficits and the national debt.

In this chapter, we provide a biographical overview of each man, with a focus on their pre-political and career histories prior to their first election's to Congress. Much has been written about Eric Cantor's congressional career. Cantor was essentially a lifelong resident of the district he would ultimately serve for nearly seven terms. Brat—like many academics—was a more recent transplant to the suburban Richmond district. Their paths crossed only fleetingly, but as we will show, Cantor loomed large in Brat's consciousness in the two years prior to Brat's decision to challenge the incumbent congressman in the 2014 Republican primary election.

ERIC CANTOR

Eric Cantor was born June 6, 1963, in Richmond, Virginia, the middle of three sons of Eddie and Mary Lee Cantor (the other sons are Stuart and Paul). Eddie Cantor was a first generation Richmonder, as his father (Eric's grandfather) had relocated to Richmond from New York in the 1930s to open a grocery store that primarily served the Church Hill and Jackson Ward neighborhoods—working-class enclaves housing Richmond's Jewish and African American communities. The Cantor clan—Eddie, his brothers, and Eric Cantor's grandmother—continued to live above the store even after Eric's grandfather's death when Eddie was just two years old.[2] Eddie was schooled in Richmond City before attending college at Virginia Tech and then pursuing a law degree at the University of Richmond. He then went into business as a real estate lawyer and developer. Mary Lee Cantor, Eric's mother, was a graduate of the University of Maryland and had pursued a teaching career. After marrying Eddie, she opened and ran a maternity shop with her mother-in-law.[3]

Although Eddie had grown up in Richmond proper, he and Mary Lee raised their three sons in the West End area just outside of Richmond's city limits. The West End, where Eric and his wife Diana still reside, is considered the more upscale part of the Richmond area. Eric and his brothers were sent to the private Collegiate School, which is set on a large wooded property near the University of Richmond in one of the wealthiest parts of the city. After graduating from

Collegiate in 1981, Eric enrolled at George Washington University in Washington, DC, where he earned a bachelor of arts degree in political science in 1985. During his years at George Washington, Cantor had the opportunity to engage with several different aspects of politics; the connections he made during his college years would continue to be important to him throughout his career in politics.

Civic participation was an important value in the Cantor family. Cantor's parents were active in a range of state and local political and civic causes. Eddie espoused a range of conservative viewpoints and was a prominent Republican in Richmond who held many leadership positions in the Republican Party. He was the Third Congressional District Republican Chairman in the 1970s and served as the statewide treasurer for Ronald Reagan's presidential campaign in 1980.[4] It was Eddie Cantor who recruited Tom Bliley, a Democrat and the former mayor of Richmond, to run as a Republican for Congress in Virginia's Seventh District. The Bliley family ran a successful local chain of funeral homes, and it was through that business that Bliley became known to the Cantors. As Bliley recounted to *Tablet Magazine* in 2011, "We buried most of the Jews in Richmond, almost all of them, so I was well known in the Jewish community. Eddie and Mary Lee welcomed me with open arms and supported me in my bid for the nomination." Eric, who was entering his senior year in high school, volunteered for the campaign.[5]

It was his parents' political activism that led to Eric Cantor's earliest forays into the field: canvassing alongside his father for a Republican Senate hopeful, Dick Obenshein, in the late 1970s and handing out literature in support of Republican candidates at the polling places with his mother, for example.[6] But during his first year in college, Cantor got a taste of what it is like to work in Congress when he went to work as an intern for Bliley. In 1982, a year that included Bliley's first congressional reelection, Cantor served as Bliley's driver.[7] Cantor and Bliley became close—Cantor has been called Bliley's protégé—but his initial work for Bliley did not lead Cantor immediately into a political career. He went on to the College of William and Mary for law school, graduating in 1988, and then he pursued a master's degree in real estate development at Columbia University in New York City. After Cantor finished his master's degree in 1989, he returned to Richmond and joined his family's real estate business.[8] When he returned from New York, he brought his fiancée, Diana Fine. The couple, who met on a blind date, married in 1989 and have three children.[9]

The Jewish Question

One of the factors that has been proposed in explanation of Cantor's loss in 2014 is that Cantor's Jewish religion activated latent anti-Semitic sentiment in his district. This possibility is unsatisfying as an explanation for his loss. For one thing, since 1991 Cantor had won 12 consecutive general elections, both to a seat in the Virginia General Assembly and to the U.S. House of Representatives, prior to losing in the 2014 primary. It would be strange if local voters had only just realized his Jewishness. For another thing, the Jewish community in Richmond also abandoned Cantor in 2014; at the Weinstein Jewish Community Center (JCC), where Cantor's mother continues to be an active participant in the women's club, members lament Cantor's disappearance from their events and activities. According to a staff member who was for many years involved with the JCC's legislative reception for local, state, and federal elected officials, it had been years since Cantor had attended.[10]

Furthermore, the history of the Jewish community in Richmond both explains why Cantor was so successful for so long and demonstrates that anti-Semitism was not responsible for Cantor's ouster. Richmond, Virginia, has been home to Jewish men and women since the middle part of the eighteenth century. As historians Herbert Tobias Ezekiel and Gaston Lichtenstein note in *The History of the Jews of Richmond from 1769 to 1917,* "The history of the Jews of Richmond is the history of Richmond."[11] Jews were well integrated into the Richmond community from the very beginning of its existence, serving in important roles in local governance beginning in the early nineteenth century.

Even during the Civil War, there was an active and well-accepted Jewish community in Richmond—and this reflected the South's general acceptance of Jews. That Jews were accepted in the South is surprising to many people, given the South's less-than-robust record of tolerating diversity. But as Robert N. Rosen notes in *The Jewish Confederates,* "The acceptance of the Jews in the Old South was a simple matter of a small, law-abiding, educated, and productive minority who brought diversity to Southern life, together with much-needed mercantile skills and loyalty to the existing order."[12] Perhaps no member of Richmond's Civil War-era Jewish community was more prominent than Judah Benjamin, a Jewish lawyer and former U.S. senator from Louisiana who was appointed to multiple positions in the Confederate president Jefferson Davis's cabinet, including attorney general, secretary of war, and

Photo 3.1: Memorial to Jewish Confederate soldiers at at Hollywood Cemetery in Richmond, Virginia

The Jewish community in Richmond is one of the oldest in the country, and its members have played a significant role in local, state, and southern history.

Photo credit: Lauren Cohen Bell

secretary of state.[13] In addition to Benjamin, thousands of Jews fought for the Confederacy during the Civil War, although estimates as to the precise number vary widely.

Richmond Jews were also important to the movement to oppose violence against Jews worldwide at the turn of the twentieth century. According to the Institute for Southern Jewish Life (ISJL), the following took place:

> After the brutal Kishinev pogrom in Russia in 1903, Jews in Richmond held a mass protest and relief meeting at the Bijou Theater which drew over 1,000 people, including the governor, the mayor, and several Christian ministers. After another wave of anti-Jewish violence in Russia in 1905, a similar mass meeting was held, chaired by Rabbi Calisch.[14]

Richmond's Jewish community was also active in the resettlement of refugees affected by the Holocaust during the 1930s and 1940s. Grandsons of William Thalhimer, the founder of Thalhimers department stores, one of the most successful retail businesses in the South, were active in the effort to rescue and resettle German refugees displaced by Adolph Hitler's regime in Nazi Germany.[15] After the war, there were approximately 7,500 Jews living in Richmond, including many who had joined relatives to escape persecution in Europe.[16]

Richmond became a safe haven for many Jews who relocated during and after the Second World War. Still, the history of the Jewish community in Richmond has not been free of anti-Semitism. The ISJL notes that there have been moments of anti-Semitism that have affected Richmond Jews, notably during the civil rights movement of the twentieth century:

> During the turmoil of the civil rights era, Richmond Jews sometimes found themselves in the crossfire. When the Richmond office of the Anti-Defamation League provided information to an NAACP workshop in Charlottesville in 1958, local newspaper editor James J. Kilpatrick wrote an editorial blaming Jewish support for civil rights as the cause of recent anti-Semitism. Richmond Jews were deeply unsettled by the editorial, although no local synagogues or other Jewish institutions suffered any physical attack during this era.[17]

While anti-Semitism is never acceptable, the antipathy of segregationists toward the local Jewish community was not entirely surprising, given the latter's support of civil rights. The Thalhimers, for example, were among the leading forces for integration and civil rights in Richmond. As early as 1960, African American and white employees of the Thalhimers department store shared dining facilities, and Thalhimers is considered "the first retail establishment in Richmond to fully integrate."[18] Where the Jewish community—including such pillars as Thalhimers—had been considered a full partner in supporting the Confederacy, the Jewish community in the 1960s was more firmly on the side of civil rights. This put the members of this community at odds with civic leaders in the city during that era. Nevertheless, despite this tense period, the Jewish community in Richmond continued to expand in the years following the civil rights movement.

The point of this brief foray into Richmond's Jewish history is to demonstrate the extent to which the Jews in Richmond were well accepted and integrated into civic affairs. Jewish residents of Richmond have served in important civic roles for more than two centuries, and the Jewish community in Richmond never suffered anti-Semitism at significant enough levels to prevent Jews from thriving. Richmond's Jewish community has not only survived but thrived in Richmond. The sixth-oldest synagogue in the United States was founded in Richmond; its successor congregation, Beth Ahabah, continues to operate.[19] Richmonders still nostalgically recall Thalhimers, which closed locally in 1992 after being acquired two years earlier by the May Company.[20]

The city's openness to Jewish civic and political leaders is an outgrowth of the positive relationship between Jewish and non-Jewish Richmond. Nearly two decades prior to Cantor's first run for the U.S. Congress in 1982, Democrat Norman Sisisky, himself Jewish, had been elected to represent the Fourth Congressional District. Prior to being elected to Congress from Virginia's Fourth, Sisisky had served for nine years as a member of the Virginia House of Delegates, representing the city of Petersburg. Virginia's Fourth borders the Seventh Congressional District; depending upon redistricting results, the Fourth has from time to time shared parts of suburban Richmond neighborhoods with the Seventh.[21] Sisisky served as the Fourth District representative for almost two decades—from January 1983 to March 2001—when he died suddenly. But for two brief months in early 2001, the 11-member Virginia delegation included 2 Jewish representatives, significantly overrepresenting Virginia's Jewish population, which was estimated at 0.9 percent in 2000–2001.[22]

Cantor made no secret of his religion at any point in his political career—and, as we have shown, there is no reason that his electoral fortunes would have been different had he done so. He won every election he contested right up until he was bested in the 2014 Seventh District primary.

Richmond's vibrant Jewish community has for more than two centuries given rise to business and political leaders who garnered the utmost respect from their fellow citizens. And the Jewish community is equally a vital part of Richmond's history. Cantor was very much a part of both of these communities, having been born into them and having lived virtually all of his life within them. As we will see, evidence of Cantor's upbringing in Jewish Richmond found its way into his legislative work in the early parts of his career as a member of the Virginia General Assembly. During these early years, Cantor deepened his ties to his Jewish and Richmond communities through his work, which made him the clear heir apparent to the Seventh District's congressional seat when it became available in 2000.

In the Virginia General Assembly

Virginia boasts the longest continuously meeting state legislative assembly in the United States. While this might suggest that it should lead the nation in legislative professionalism, Virginia also has a long-standing tradition of the "citizen legislator" that dates back to the colonial era. The idea of the citizen legislator is that those who serve in government will not make careers of it; instead, they will have full-fledged careers in other things—banking, the law, medicine, business, education—from which they will take brief leaves of absence to serve their fellow citizens. The very design of Virginia's government promotes this model of public service. Under the Virginia Constitution, "long" sessions of the General Assembly, held in even-numbered years, are 60 days long, and short sessions, held in odd-numbered years, are just 30 days long.[23] Legislators generally have other full-time careers and have very limited staff resources to support their work. In the most recent update of his legislative professionalism index, well-known political scientist Peverill Squire ranked Virginia 32nd in the nation, putting the state nearly in the fourth quintile of all states with regard to how professionalized it is.[24] Virginia remains the only state where governors are limited to a single term.

As a result of the limited amount of time that state legislators spend in the state capital, Richmond has a less fully developed interest group and lobbyist community than many other state capitals. A recent study of democratic policy congruence within the states found that on 39 different public policy issues, the General Assembly acted in accordance with public opinion 46 percent of the time.[25] This lack of policy congruence and public opinion has not resulted in significant antipathy toward the General Assembly, however. This is partly because there is a strong tradition of members of the General Assembly introducing legislation upon the request of their constituents, but it is also partly because it can be difficult for constituents to access information independently about the disposition of legislation about which they have an interest. Unlike the U.S. Congress, which records its debates in written form and makes these documents widely available, the Virginia General Assembly does not publish records of its proceedings. The only records of floor debate are videotapes held in the House and Senate clerks' offices, and these may only be viewed in person and by appointment at the General Assembly Building following a request to view a specific date's tapes. The commonwealth's lack of publicly available information not only creates challenges for citizens wishing to keep track of legislative activity, but it also makes it very challenging to reconstruct the full range of representational activities Cantor engaged in while a member of the House of Delegates. Nevertheless, there are sufficient records of Cantor's work as a candidate for the House of Delegates and as a state legislator to allow us to explore his early political experiences in some detail.

As we previously described, the Cantor family was well known in Richmond by the time Cantor was in high school. They were active in the legal and retail communities as supporters of Republican candidates and conservative politics, and they were deeply engaged in their faith community. In short, when Cantor returned to Richmond from college and graduate study, he came back to a city that had embraced his family for decades. By that time, Cantor's father and uncle owned a commercial real estate firm, Cantor and Cantor, and his brother ran a mortgage company nearby.[26] With his law degree and real estate development master's degree in hand, it is unsurprising that Cantor went to work in the family business—real estate.

Within three years, however, Cantor decided to make a move into politics and run for the Seventy-Third District House of Delegates seat in the Virginia General Assembly when incumbent Walter Stosch made the decision to seek higher office in the Virginia State Senate. Cantor worked briefly for Stosch as a legislative assistant in the mid-1980s.[27] The Seventy-Third House District is located northwest of Richmond City in an area known as Richmond's "near West End." The district straddles Interstate 64 headed west toward Charlottesville and is largely suburban, although there is a significant retail and professional presence ranging from small businesses to large employers such as Altria (formerly Phillip Morris, the tobacco giant), as well as the headquarters of Anthem health insurance and Comcast.

Cantor's first election to the delegates was the Republican nominating contest in September 1991. That year the local Republicans held a nominating convention, and Cantor competed against two other Republicans hoping to be the local party's choice to replace Stosch. The 27-year-old Cantor won, despite the fact that his opponents were older and had more experience. Recounting his successful effort in the nominating meeting, *Richmond Magazine* noted that Cantor's mother brought club sandwiches, a memorable gesture that, combined with the assistance Cantor received from his father's political friends, likely helped her son to win the nomination.[28] In the 1991 general election, which followed soon after, Cantor ran unopposed. His victory made him the youngest member of the Virginia General Assembly.[29] In fact, with only one exception—Cantor's first reelection effort in 1993—Cantor never faced a Democratic party opponent in a general election.

Table 3.1 presents the general election results for each of Cantor's reelection efforts. Even when he was challenged in 1993, Cantor's share of the vote reached nearly 80 percent. This is reflective of a larger pattern in Virginia, where General Assembly incumbents frequently run unopposed or face only nominal opposition from independents and write-ins.[30] In the 2009 and 2007 Virginia House of Delegates races, 57 percent and 32 percent of races, respectively, involved candidates who were running unopposed.[31] In 1987 and 2003, the proportion of races featuring a single candidate reached 64 percent or nearly two-thirds of all incumbent members of the General Assembly.[32] Beyond the number of seats that go uncontested in each General Assembly election, many of the races in which there are two or more candidates are considered to be uncompetitive, with the incumbent having the overwhelming probability of winning the race. This lack of competitive elections in Virginia means that once elected, members of the General Assembly tend to stay in office for decades unless they voluntarily retire or seek higher office, as Cantor would eventually go on to do.

At the time of Cantor's first election, his nonpolitical résumé was quite brief. As Table 3.2 reveals, Cantor's first House of Delegates biography listed him as a member of local Rotary, Freemason, and Kiwanis Clubs and indicated that he sat on the board of directors of Congregation Or Atid, a relatively young Conservative synagogue in Richmond's West End.[33] Upon his election, Cantor was placed on three committees: Claims; Counties, Cities, and Towns; and General Laws. Over the course of his career in the House of Delegates, Cantor also served on the Virginia House of Delegates Committee on Courts of Justice, whose

TABLE 3.1

Cantor's early electoral history—Virginia House of Delegates, District 73

Election year	Opponent	Number of votes (%)
1991	Unopposed	11,735 (96.5%)
1993	Reed Halsted (I)	19,513 (79.3%)
1995	Unopposed	15,509 (99.5%)
1997	Unopposed	22,519 (98.9%)
1999	Unopposed	10,030 (98.5%)

Source: Compiled by the authors from Virginia State Board of Elections data.

TABLE 3.2

Eric Cantor's social capital connections as a delegate

Term	Outside memberships
1992–1993	Western Henrico Rotary
	Lodge No. 53, AF & AM
	Kanawha Kiwanis
	Congregation Or Atid (board of directors)
1994–1995	Congregation Or Atid (board of directors)
	Western Henrico Rotary
	Lodge No. 53, AF & AM
	Henrico Education Foundation
	Jewish Community Center of Richmond (board of directors)
1996–1997	Congregation Or Atid (board of directors)
	Western Henrico Rotary
	Lodge No. 53, AF & AM
	Henrico Education Foundation
	Jewish Community Center of Richmond (board of directors)
	Virginia-Israel Foundation (co-chairman)
	Virginia Commission on Youth
	Elk Hill Farm (board of trustees)
	Knesset Beth Israel
	Virginia Holocaust Museum (board of trustees)
1998–1999	Western Henrico Rotary
	Lodge No. 53, AF & AM
	Henrico Education Foundation
	Jewish Community Center of Richmond (board of directors)
	Virginia-Israel Foundation (chairman)
	Virginia Commission on Youth
	Elk Hill Farm (board of trustees)
2000	Knesset Beth Israel
	Western Henrico Rotary
	Lodge No. 53, AF & AM
	Henrico Education Foundation
	Jewish Community Center of Richmond (board of directors)
	Virginia-Israel Foundation (chairman)
	Virginia Commission on Youth
	Elk Hill Farm (board of trustees)
	Virginia Holocaust Museum (board of trustees)

Source: Compiled by authors from the Virginia General Assembly's Legislative Information System (http://lis.virginia.gov).

responsibility it is to identify and process prospective state court judges (Virginia uses a legislative appointment process exclusively); on the Committee on Corporations, Insurance, and Banking; and, in his last term in office, on the House Science and Technology Committee. Each of these committees' agenda is set largely by the Speaker of the House of Delegates, whose job it is to refer legislation generally related to the topics identified in each committee's name.

During Cantor's first term in office, 1992–1993, the freshman neither sponsored nor had enacted by the General Assembly a single bill. But with his reelection and the start of his second term in 1994, Cantor established himself as a prolific legislator. His legislative activities focused on issues with which he had professional experience—for example, with aspects of real estate and property ownership—or issues of personal importance to him, such as education, animal welfare, and support for Israel. Table 3.3 lists Cantor's successful legislative efforts during each year of his service in the House of Delegates. His successful legislation is substantially similar to the measures he introduced that were not passed. Several of his proposals were incorporated into other legislative proposals, and several others failed. Still, as Table 3.3 demonstrates, Cantor was the lead sponsor of a number of successful measures during his years in the Virginia House of Delegates.

(text continues on page 62)

TABLE 3.3
Eric Cantor's Virginia House of Delegates career

Committee assignments	Successful legislative proposals
	1992–1993
Claims Counties, Cities, and Towns General Laws	None
	1994–1995
Claims Courts of Justice General Laws	• *HB 218 Special license plates for Special Olympics supporters* • *HB 626 Air emission credits* • *HB 630 Fire protection—Statewide Fire Prevention Code* • *HB 631 Virginia Health Services Cost Review Council* • *HB 655 Criminal solicitation of juveniles* • *HB 1140 Certain uncompensated transfers of assets and Medicaid eligibility*

(Continued)

TABLE 3.3
(Continued)

Committee assignments	Successful legislative proposals
	• *HJ 49 Commending Hermitage Vocational and Technical Center in Henrico County* • *HJ 264 Study—Virginia Retirement System* • *HJ 337 Commending Tuckahoe Little League* • *HJ 350 Commending George "Bucky" Wise* • *HJ 393 Commending Douglas Southall Freeman High School* • *HB 1851 Duties of attorney general in criminal cases* • *HB 1872 Property Owners' Association Act—condemnation of common areas* • *HB 1883 Garnishments* • *HB 1884 Duties of real estate brokers and salespersons* • *HB 2293 Economic development partnership* • *HB 2294 Health Services Cost Review Council* • *HB 2297 Comprehensive Services Act* • *HB 2567 Medical records copy fees*
	1996–1997
Claims Courts of Justice General Laws	• *HB 375 Truancy* • *HB 412 Public Procurement Act—minimum purchases before sealed bids* • *HB 416 Public Procurement Act—negotiations for professional services* • *HB 417 Extended Service Contract Act* • *HB 603 Alcoholic beverage control—use of false identification* • *HB 621 Professional regulation—Board of Psychology* • *HB 789 Professional regulation—nursing home administrators* • *HB 791 Medicaid—fraudulently issued benefits, civil action to recover costs* • *HB 793 Support payment provisions—how paid, payroll deduction order* • *HB 1324 Virginia Board for Architects, Professional Engineers, Land Surveyors, & Landscape Architects* • *HB 1325 Virginia-Israel Advisory Board created* • *HB 1327 Commercial Real Estate Broker's Lien Act* • *HB 1328 Certificates of public need—moratorium, exception* • *HB 1448 Economic Development Partnership created* • *HB 1449 Department of Business Assistance created* • *HJ 38 Study—youth services* • *HJ 207 Study—alternative investments in retirement system* • *HJ 208 Study—capital access and business financing* • *HJ 227 Issuance of tax-exempt industrial development bonds to promote economic development* • *HB 1766 Virginia Museum of Fine Arts—designated an educational institution*

TABLE 3.3
(Continued)

Committee assignments	Successful legislative proposals
	• *HB 1889 Arson of a church—penalty*
	• *HB 2011 Alcoholic beverage control—licenses generally*
	• *HB 2041 Charitable gaming*
	• *HB 2460 Unemployment compensation—newspaper carriers*
	• *HB 2867 Public Procurement Act—applicability*
	• *HB 2868 Public Procurement Act—state-aid projects*
	• *HB 2869 Place for bringing an action under a contract for construction*
	• *HB 2870 Health maintenance organizations—continuing care facilities*
	• *HB 2873 Duties of real estate brokers and salespersons*
	• *HJ 490 Study—status offenders and children in need of services*

1998–1999

Claims (co-chair) Corporations, Insurance, and Banking	• *HB 265 Major business facility job tax credit*
	• *HB 591 Persons entitled to vote absentee and absentee ballot applications*
	• *HB 592 Securities—registration of investment advisor representatives*
Courts of Justice General Laws	• *HB 594 Warning lights on certain vehicles*
	• *HB 595 Litter Control and Recycling Fund Advisory Board membership*
	• *HB 596 Fees for professionals at adult involuntary commitment proceedings*
	• *HB 642 Residential Landlord and Tenant Act—rent, appeals*
	• *HB 834 Property Owners' Association Act—special assessments*
	• *HB 835 Escheators' bonding requirements*
	• *HB 836 Jurisdiction of corporate authorities*
	• *HB 837 Assignment of lottery proceeds*
	• *HB 838 Purchase of handguns by fire marshal*
	• *HB 1236 Procurement Act—contracts*
	• *HB 1237 Telecommunications tower—acquisition of property*
	• *HB 1240 Contract rental vehicles for state use*
	• *HB 1242 Brokers' liens*
	• *HB 1426 Speed limits in residence districts*
	• *HJ 93 Study—truants and runaways*
	• *HJ 182 Study—Medicaid and mental retardation waivers*
	• *HJ 238 Study—adult care residences*
	• *HB 721 Credit insurance*
	• *HB 1631 Alcoholic beverage control—applications for licenses*

(Continued)

TABLE 3.3
(Continued)

Committee assignments	Successful legislative proposals
	• HB 1632 Condominium and Property Owners' Associations—access to books and records • HB 1633 Guardians and wards • HB 1805 VRS early retirement options (50/30) • HB 1818 Corporate income tax—apportionment • HB 1935 Public Procurement Act—exemptions • HB 2008 Definition of child in need of supervision • HB 2097 Automatic external defibrillators • HB 2148 Professional solicitors • HB 2391 Public Procurement Act—withdrawal of bid • HB 2392 Solicitation of contributions—enforcement and penalties • HB 2393 Public Procurement Act—decisions of public bodies and review • HB 2441 Corporations—shareholder action without meeting/prior notice • HB 2442 Professional counselors • HB 2500 Contractor Transaction Recovery Fund—definition of claimant • HB 2501 Contractor Transaction Recovery Fund—amount recoverable • HB 2708 Medical savings accounts • HB 2719 Corporations—proxies (electronic and other authorizations) • HB 2721 Corporations—electronic notification of shareholders' meetings • HJ 557 Study—annual leave for state employees • HJ 563 Commending Tuckahoe American Little League Major All Stars • HJ 564 Commending Tuckahoe American Little League All Stars • HJ 576 Commending Glen Allen Youth Athletic Association • HJ 685 Study—cost of legislative studies • HR 35 Commending Peggy Ann Ladd Winchester
	2000
Courts of Justice Corporations, Insurance, and Banking Science and Technology General Laws	• HB 123 Motor fuels tax—exemption for recreational pleasure boats and ships • HB 126 Special license plates—Virginia Federation of Women's Clubs • HB 275 Power of circuit court over juvenile offender • HB 453 Insurance—notice of exclusion of coverage for flood damage • HB 454 Fair Housing Law—housing for older persons

TABLE 3.3
(Continued)

Committee assignments	Successful legislative proposals
	• *HB 455 Insurance agents—continuing education requirements*
	• *HB 456 State treasurer—appointment*
	• *HB 457 Security for Public Deposits Act—exemption for certain deposits*
	• *HB 744 Functions of a multijurisdictional grand jury—animal cruelty*
	• *HB 745 Building code violations*
	• *HB 746 Utility consumer services cooperatives*
	• *HB 747 ABC—payment of taxes and fees by credit or debit cards*
	• *HB 763 Uniform Disposition of Unclaimed Property Act*
	• *HB 1046 Procurement Act—thresholds for small purchases and contracts*
	• *HB 1047 Procurement Act—architectural or professional engineering services*
	• *HB 1048 Small Business Growth Fund*
	• *HB 1049 Registration of automated external defibrillators— immunity*
	• *HB 1051 Adult care residences*
	• *HB 1205 Eviction notices—service by sheriff*
	• *HB 1206 Juveniles—fingerprints and photographs*
	• *HB 1207 Priority of certain refinance mortgages over subordinate mortgages*
	• *HB 1209 Procurement Act—protest of awards*
	• *HB 1211 Health maintenance organizations—exception to license requirement*
	• *HB 1212 School property—schools may permit use thereof*
	• *HB 1213 Summonses issued by attorneys—Bar Association to study effectiveness*
	• *HB 1214 Solicitation of Contributions Act—enforcement*
	• *HB 1216 Sale of real estate for delinquent taxes—process*
	• *HB 1547 Civil remedies—appeal bond*
	• *HB 1548 University of Virginia—endowment funds*
	• *HJ 142 Commending Barbara E. Childress*
	• *HJ 143 Commending Glen Allen Youth Athletic Association*
	• *HJ 187 Study—State Corporation Commission*
	• *HJ 298 Armenian genocide*
	• *HJ 378 Study—allocation of funds to Governor's School Programs*

Source: Compiled by authors from the Virginia General Assembly's Legislative Information System (http://lis.virginia.gov).

But the House of Delegates, by design, is a part-time position. In 2014–2015, the salary for a delegate was $17,640—not nearly enough to live on. Members must have their own careers outside the General Assembly. Cantor continued to work in real estate law throughout his General Assembly career until his election to Congress in 2000.

From the House of Delegates to Capitol Hill

When Tom Bliley decided to retire from Congress in 2000, he chose Cantor to run for the seat. Cantor had remained close with Bliley throughout the early years of his career, and as Bliley contemplated retirement, he turned to Cantor as a young Republican candidate with a track record of legislative ability. Cantor was just 38, at the lower end of the age opportunity window for state lawmakers looking to move to Congress.[34] Reflecting on his decision to encourage Cantor's candidacy, Bliley told *Tablet Magazine* the following:

> I have advised all my former colleagues, when you get ready to retire, you pick the person you think is best to succeed you. You go right in and get the best person elected—you don't do this "good government" thing and stay out of it.[35]

By the time Cantor ran for the U.S. Congress in 2000, he had established himself as a reliable conservative voice within the Virginia Republican Party. Although as we note in Chapter 3, Cantor easily won the 2000 general election to replace Bliley, he had a difficult time of it in the Republican primary. Cantor drew an endorsement from then governor Jim Gilmore and spent nearly $750,000 during the primary but only narrowly defeated his opponent, Republican state senator Steve Martin.[36] During the race, Martin's campaign raised allegations that Cantor's business, Cantor and Cantor, had failed to pay taxes and publicized a lawsuit pending against the business by a minority partner.[37] Martin had the backing of several Christian organizations and ran advertisements portraying himself as the only real Christian in the race. To the extent that Cantor ever had to confront anti-Semitism during one of his campaigns, that was the moment. But Cantor's religious background also aided his bid; Richard November, president of the Jewish Federation of Richmond, sent a letter to the Federation's mailing list regarding the following:

> [He] urg[ed] Jews to vote for Cantor over Steve Martin, the Chesterfield senator, in the 2000 GOP primary. The letter, in effect, said that Jews— Democratic proclivity notwithstanding—should back one of their own, a reflex strengthened when Martin allies described their man as the only Christian in the race.[38]

Ultimately, the *Richmond Times-Dispatch* endorsed Cantor over Martin, noting Cantor's legislative prowess and that "[he] puts the citizens first. That's the spirit Washington needs."[39] Once Cantor won the primary election, it was smooth sailing through the 2000 November general election; he was sworn in at the outset of the 107th Congress in January 2001.

Cantor's political upbringing, his strong sense of Jewish identity, and his early career in Virginia's General Assembly all were shaped by the broader Richmond community in which he grew up. Cantor reflected on this to *Tablet Magazine* in 2011:

> I can only say that I grew up in a very active and vibrant Jewish community, and then a larger civic community in Richmond that didn't happen to be Jewish also contributed to who I am and what kind of officeholder I hopefully am.[40]

DAVID BRAT

David Alan Brat was born in Detroit, Michigan, in July 1964, just 13 months after Eric Cantor. He was raised in Alma, Michigan, where his father, Paul, practiced medicine and his mother, Nancy, worked as a social worker. Like Cantor, Brat has two brothers, although—also like Cantor—neither brother has pursued a career in politics. Brat's family moved to Minnesota when he was in middle school; he ultimately graduated from high school in Brooklyn, Minnesota, before attending college at Hope College in Holland, Michigan.[41] Brat's high school yearbook notes that he was involved in band, the National Honor Society, the debate team, and the tennis team.[42]

Media accounts suggest that Brat came from a politically diverse family. His father was a Republican, while his mother reportedly was much more liberal.[43] Brat was active in student government in high school, but his father claims that Brat did not develop a serious interest in politics until he was a graduate student. Following his graduation from Hope College in 1986, Brat worked briefly as a management information consultant at Arthur Anderson & Company in the company's Detroit and Chicago offices. Brat attended Princeton Theological Seminary in Princeton, New Jersey, where he earned a master's of divinity degree in 1990. He went on to attend American University, earning his doctorate in economics in 1995.[44] While there, Brat worked as a research assistant for a faculty member in the Agency for International Development's (AID) Development Studies Program and served as a consultant and research assistant regarding primary education in the Philippines at the World Bank in Washington, DC.[45] He taught tennis lessons on the side to earn extra money. After he completed his degree, Brat served as a research fellow at the Army Institute for the Behavioral and Social Sciences in Washington, DC, and taught mathematics at Mount Vernon College, also in the District of Columbia.[46]

Randolph-Macon College

Brat's first full-time professional job out of graduate school was also the position he held when he decided to run for Congress: faculty member at Randolph-Macon College. Founded in 1833, Randolph-Macon College is a selective, private liberal arts college in Ashland, Virginia, approximately 15 miles north of Richmond. The college is named for two nineteenth-century legislative leaders, John Randolph and Nathanial Macon, although neither attended the college. Randolph, a native Virginian, served for a total of 24 years in the U.S. House of Representatives and briefly in the U.S. Senate. Macon, who hailed from North Carolina, served nearly 40 years in Congress, including 24 years in the House and 13 additional years in the Senate. He was Speaker of the House from 1801 to 1807.[47] Several other important political leaders did attend Randolph-Macon over the course of its history: Claude Swanson (Randolph-Macon Class of 1885), who served in both the U.S. House and U.S. Senate and as governor of Virginia; Hugh Scott (Class of 1919), a Pennsylvania Republican who served in the U.S. House and U.S. Senate; Porter Hardy Jr. (Class of 1922), a Virginia Democrat who served in Congress for 22 years during the middle part of the twentieth century; and J. Randy Forbes (Class of 1974), who was elected to Virginia's Fourth Congressional District seat in the U.S. House of Representatives in 2001 after Congressman Norm Sisisky's sudden death.[48] Randolph-Macon College's 15th president, Robert R. Lindgren, took to calling the college "the cradle of congressmen" during the 2014 congressional midterm election.

In addition to the legislators among the distinguished alumni, there are several former diplomats and E. Barrett Prettyman (Class of 1910). Prettyman served as the chief judge of the U.S. Court of Appeals for the District of Columbia circuit, which is considered to be just one step below a prestigious appointment to the U.S. Supreme Court. The federal courthouse in Washington, DC, carries Prettyman's name.

Throughout its history, Randolph-Macon has been a politically engaged institution, and its faculty and staff have been active citizens within the local community. Randolph-Macon's campus sits astride the railroad tracks that connect Washington, DC, and Richmond. The railroad provides the Randolph-Macon College community with quick access both to the national capital and the Virginia state capital, which has given its students, faculty, and staff the ability to engage with a number of important political events and activities. In many respects, then, it is not surprising that Brat entered political life directly from his position as a faculty member. One of the perks of private college teaching is that faculty are able to take a more active role in partisan politics and direct governance without the conflict of interest that can result from working for a taxpayer-supported institution. Indeed, in more recent history, the faculty and staff have boasted several members of the town council of Ashland. Faculty members at Randolph-Macon are encouraged to be actively engaged in their communities, and "community service" is considered to be a plus factor in reappointment, tenure, and promotion decisions.

Brat joined the faculty of Randolph-Macon College as assistant professor of economics in 1996, and he and his wife Laura (née Sonderman) moved to Glen Allen, Virginia. By late 1998, they had a son, Jonathan, and four years later, they added daughter Sophia to their family. Brat remained employed at Randolph-Macon until his election to the U.S. House of Representatives in November 2014; he had worked his way up through the faculty ranks, earning tenure and promotion to associate professor in 2002 and promotion to the rank of full professor in 2008. At Randolph-Macon, Brat's teaching portfolio included introductory courses in microeconomics and macroeconomics and upper-level courses on microeconomics, public finance, international trade and finance, and economic development, among others.[49]

As a professor, Brat was well liked by students and generally well liked by his colleagues, although some bristled at his unabashedly conservative perspective and found his tendency to speak his mind a bit off-putting. But Brat was generally affable and enthusiastic, and he had a way of filling a room with his presence. One colleague noted that Brat has a good sense of humor. To many of his students, he was larger-than-life. After he defeated Cantor in the primary, *CNN* interviewed several of Brat's former students and reported the following:

> Students described Brat as a friendly, approachable, and extremely intelligent professor. They always felt comfortable engaging him during class, office hours, or around their tight-knit campus. He ate with students every day in the dining hall and frequently attended sporting events.[50]

During his tenure at the college, Brat was also known for his high expectations of students. He imposed and enforced a dress code in his classes that included no baseball caps or flip-flops; violations of these rules were met with the requirement of completing "ethics papers," short writing assignments that asked students to address the ethics of their behavior. A former student, Samuel Ahonen, explained further to *Mashable* in June 2014:

> The first day of class [Brat] would let everyone know that you must show up to class in business attire or do not bother coming at all. The first week of

class we had a student show up in sweatpants, and he told him to go change or write a one-page ethics paper on the topic of his choosing. The student chose to write the paper, and Brat read it to the class the next class period.[51]

Brat himself explained this policy in a syllabus provided to a summer class in 2009:

> You are preparing to be professionals and you need practice. We dress for important activities and this class is important. Summer is over. I wear flip-flops at the beach. They are not evil. Students slouching in their desks, half-way asleep with flip-flops and hats is just too much to take. This school needs character. You will have to think before coming to class. That is good. Ten years from now, you can all have a good story about Brat's class. When you come back to visit at Homecoming games, we can laugh.[52]

Brat's dress code and penchant for meeting conduct violations with ethics papers both were well known amongst the students. Nevertheless, students who had Brat for class—even those that disagreed with his political views—tended to espouse respect and admiration for him as a teacher.

At Randolph-Macon, Brat served on a number of college committees and boards. He was a member of the Academic Integrity Council from 1999 to 2001 and served as an elected faculty representative on several faculty committees that were related to his academic expertise, including the Benefits Committee and the Committee on Resources and Plans (in consultation with the college's provost and board of trustees, the latter committee is responsible for allocating funds to the academic program).

Brat also served as the coach of the college's "ethics bowl" program. The ethics bowl is an annual program sponsored by the Virginia Foundation for Independent Colleges (VFIC), which for almost two decades has hosted the event that brings students from the 15-member VFIC colleges together to debate issues of applied ethics and is organized each year around a central theme.[53] Brat's work with the ethics bowl team from Randolph-Macon made good sense. He had been part of the group of faculty who had designed and implemented the college's minor program in ethics, which he would go on to direct from 2005 to 2012.[54] During that same time period, Brat was also named the chair of the college's Department of Economics and Business. The combination of Brat's background in theology and his training as an economist prepared him to take on these two somewhat disparate leadership positions.

Shades of each of these principal faculty leadership roles found their way into the 2014 Seventh District congressional primary, where Brat emphasized his credentials as an economist as well as his study of ethics. He said the following to the *Culpeper Star-Exponent* in October 2014:

> I think for right now where the United States sits on the world scene, the most profound issues we face are economic. . . . Having an economist going up to DC with an ethics background, I think people think that is an attractive option.[55]

But Brat's dual academic interests in economics and ethics also came to the attention of John Allison, the former CEO of the Branch Banking & Trust (BB&T) Corporation, which through its foundation had begun to offer sizable grants to colleges and universities to promote the teaching of Ayn Rand's books and political philosophy. In 2005 in his new role as chair of the Department of Economics and Business, Brat successfully wrote for a $500,000 grant through BB&T's "Moral Foundations of Capitalism" grant program. A National Public Radio report on grants to colleges from conservative foundations noted that "foundation agreements often include the expectation that Ayn Rand's *Atlas Shrugged* will be taught," but that "the BB&T Foundation never has a say in hiring decisions."[56]

Although the BB&T program has drawn criticism in recent years, when Brat's successful effort to secure the grant was announced, there was little concern on campus. Over time, as grants to other institutions generated controversy, however, some of Brat's faculty colleagues expressed concerns about whether corporate interests were affecting the college's course offerings or impinging upon students' academic freedom. John Allison's visit to Randolph-Macon in November 2009 also raised some faculty members' concerns about the BB&T program, but those concerns had largely dissipated by the time Brat announced his candidacy.[57]

Senator Walter Stosch

As Brat was transitioning into leading Randolph-Macon College's economics and business and ethics programs and managing the half-million-dollar BB&T grant, he was also pursuing opportunities to engage more fully with state politics. One of the most influential circumstances contributing to Brat's path to the U.S. House of Representatives was his relationship with Walter Stosch, who had successfully been elected to the Virginia Senate in 1991, the year Eric Cantor was elected to replace him in the House of Delegates. Stosch and Brat lived in the same West End neighborhood, Twin Hickory, and the two of them met while Brat was serving on the board of directors of the Twin Hickory Homeowners Association. Stosch and Brat became friends, and Brat impressed Stosch with his higher education credentials. In 2005, Stosch invited Brat to join his state senate staff in an unpaid capacity as special assistant for higher education. Because, as we have noted, Virginia's state legislature is not a full-time job, Brat was busiest with this responsibility from January through March each year. Brat continued to teach a full course load and to direct two departments at Randolph-Macon College, but his presence on campus was reduced by his responsibilities in Stosch's office. According to one of his colleagues, "He generally spoke up on most of the issues that were happening, although that kind of tapered off once he became involved in state politics." In 2011, Stosch became chair of the Senate Finance Committee, and Brat became a special assistant to the committee.[58]

Stosch's influence on Brat's career trajectory was enormous. Through Brat's work in Stosch's office, he made several important political connections. Brat's work with Stosch, and in turn, Stosch's leadership role in the Virginia Senate gave Brat access to a number of opportunities to serve in state government. In 2006, Brat was appointed to the Governor's Advisory Board of Economists (GABE), which is charged by the Code of Virginia with reviewing the governor's general fund revenue estimates "with respect to economic assumptions and technical econometric methodology."[59] In addition to his service on the GABE, in 2007 Brat was appointed as a member of the Governor's Advisory Committee on Mega Projects (also known as major employment and investment projects); they are defined by the Code of Virginia as the following:

> [Mega projects are] high-impact regional economic development project[s] in which a private entity is expected to make a capital investment in real and personal property exceeding $250 million and create more than 400 new full-time jobs, and is expected to have a substantial direct and indirect economic impact on surrounding communities.[60]

Contrary to the claim that Cantor would make during the 2014 Republican primary, neither of these appointments was political, nor did Brat have any direct gubernatorial advisory authority. The positions were unpaid and essentially recognized Brat's expertise in economic and financial policy. And while Brat was originally appointed to the GABE by the then governor Tim Kaine, a Democrat, he was reappointed to the board by former Republican governor Bob McDonnell, who took office in January 2010.

Brat's First Foray

Because of his role as chairman of the Department of Economics and Business at Randolph-Macon College and his outspoken conservative opinions, Brat had been a frequent guest at local tea party meetings beginning in 2010, and at approximately the same time, he began making radio appearances on the *Doc*

Thompson Show on Glenn Beck's conservative The Blaze Radio Network. Local conservative leaders began to encourage Brat to consider running for office.[61] According to the *Chesterfield Monthly*, Brat took time to make his decision:

> [Local activist Gerry] Baugh brought in Dave Brat to speak with members of the Mechanicsville Tea Party for the first time in 2010. Baugh also continued to lobby Brat to challenge Cantor, but Brat was on the fence and didn't decide to run for the Seventh District seat until four years later.[62]

In August 2011, Brat made his first foray into elective politics when he sought the Republican Party's nomination to a midterm vacancy in the Fifty-Sixth District seat in Virginia's House of Delegates.[63] After a closed-door session, the selection committee ultimately chose a different candidate, Peter Farrell, son of Thomas Farrell, the chief executive officer of Virginia's Dominion Power; Farrell was backed by Eric Cantor. He went on to run unopposed in the 2011 general election and assumed office in the House of Delegates in January 2012. Farrell still holds the position. As local political analyst Bob Holsworth explained to the *Chesterfield Observer*, "[Brat] wanted a fair chance to run" for the Fifty-Sixth Virginia House District seat, but the local party establishment "didn't give Brat a chance."[64]

That 2011 snub is widely considered to have been a major contributor to Brat's decision to take on Cantor in 2014.

SUMMARY

A September 2007 *Richmond Magazine* profile described the extent to which Eric Cantor was considered by most political observers to be untouchable: "The common wisdom is that he can keep his seat as long as he wants it."[65] A *New York Times* front-page story a few days after the June 2014 Republican primary election noted that "[Brat's] bid to unseat Mr. Cantor, the second most powerful Republican in the House of Representatives, was akin to a youth soccer league taking on Brazil."[66]

To be sure, these assessments sum up the perceptions of those on the outside with regard to Cantor's political career. But as we will see in Chapters 4 and 5, Cantor was weaker than anyone realized. His weakness was not, as some have suggested, the result of his Jewishness or his district's latent anti-Semitic feeling. Rather, Cantor was weak because over time, he moved away from his roles as legislator and representative, which were readily apparent during his early career, and moved toward more political concerns, such as his own legacy. Over time, this depleted the storehouse of goodwill he had built with his constituents during his early career, both as a state legislator and as a member of Congress.

Dave Brat was in the right place at the right time. His activities as a college professor and volunteer legislative aide in the Virginia General Assembly brought him into contact with a number of important Republican politicians and leaders in the years leading up to his decision to challenge Cantor. His unsuccessful effort to be nominated for the 2011 vacancy in the Fifty-Sixth District for the Virginia House of Delegates is widely believed to have left him with something of a grudge against Cantor, who supported one of Brat's opponents in the contest.

Cantor and Brat come from distinct factions of the Republican Party of Virginia that currently are vying to lead the party into the future. They are, as one political operative put it, "from different parts of the political jungle." Cantor very clearly reflects the establishment perspective. Cantor's political mentor, Tom Bliley, was a former Democratic mayor who ran for and served in Congress as a Republican. Brat, for his part, was courted over the years by the conservative, tea party-backed wing of the Republican Party and was the obvious choice when that wing of the party decided to mount a challenge against Cantor. In many ways, the tea party movement has supplanted the evangelicals in the establishment-versus-activist fight that has typified Virginia politics since the 1980s. As we will show in the next few chapters, Cantor initially embraced the tea party movement until he realized that the movement's expectations could not be reconciled with political reality—another characteristic shared with the predecessor evangelical political movement in the state.

The next two chapters focus on Cantor's career in Congress and the 2014 primary contest between Cantor and Brat.

CHAPTER 4

Lost between DC and Richmond

"[T]he bottom line is that Cantor would have lost to SpongeBob SquarePants. . . . Period."

—Barry Wolk, Daily Kos[1]

Incumbents who wish to have long careers in Congress must continually expand and protect their constituency. In *Congress at the Grassroots,* Fenno explains that statement:

> When constituents vote, they are taking stock of and passing judgment on a whole set of activities that have been taking place for at least two years. . . . If an incumbent wins reelection, that outcome is only a punctuation point in that member's continuous, long-running efforts at representation.[2]

A member of Congress's ability to respond to local issues rather than national conditions is central to this process; as former Speaker Tip O'Neill famously noted, "All politics is local politics."[3] When district demographics change or when incumbent members of Congress fail to adequately protect their constituency bases, opportunities for strong challengers emerge. In addition, major national events can affect the dynamics of candidate emergence and success in congressional elections.

In this chapter, we turn to an examination of Eric Cantor's career as a member of Congress. After a brief overview of the scholarship on how members of Congress allocate their time and of what ultimately makes a successful congressperson, we review Cantor's career in national politics and demonstrate that the seeds of his stunning 2014 primary loss were sown much earlier than anyone realized. We discuss each phase of his congressional career and reveal that despite his efforts to control his electoral fate through redistricting, Cantor's loss resulted from his failure to maintain the support of the electorate through even the most basic representational activity. This lack of attention to the voters at home, coupled with Cantor's failure to identify and react to changes in the American political landscape—including the tea party's grassroots activism, the elimination of earmarks and targeted spending by the U.S. Congress, and the public's growing distrust of political leaders—created the conditions that led to his defeat in the 2014 primary. In hindsight, Cantor's primary election loss seems almost predictable, but no one took the time to see the signs until after it happened.

LIFE ON CAPITOL HILL

Members of Congress have many goals, including reelection, making good public policy, and gaining prestige within the Congress.[4] New members of Congress also face a myriad of responsibilities upon entering the House of Representatives. They must select a staff, allocate their time, select and serve on committees, and begin planning for their next election. They must also make the shift from campaigning for votes to representing their constituents. This is increasingly difficult, as campaigning has become a permanent part of the lawmaker's life. Almost every day is consumed with contacting, credit-claiming, promoting, fund-raising, and other efforts to maintain a seat where lawmaking and the exercise of political power might take place.

Serving in Congress has both a national and a local dimension. Elected members of Congress owe their positions in Washington to their constituents at home and are dependent upon their constituents in biennial elections to return them to their posts. Constituents expect members to act in their stead on matters of national policy and to protect local interests as they do so. Over time as members of Congress continue to serve, their activities and behaviors settle into clear patterns, both with regard to their work on Capitol Hill and with regard to their relationships with their constituents. Members who have served multiple terms generally have more freedom to pursue their policy goals, have opportunities to enter the chamber leadership, and may make fewer trips home to the district.[5] They build up a bank of goodwill that presumably gives the lawmaker discretion to act based on his or her own judgment or preferences instead of following the district.[6]

Having built trust with their constituents, longer-serving members are freed to pursue their own goals and, from time to time, they may even be able to cast votes that are unpopular at home. These are not one-time activities in the representative's career. Members of Congress must constantly monitor and adapt their representational and legislative styles to meet the needs of the district and to shore up their reelection chances, especially as redistricting occurs or natural patterns of movement in or out of the district change the makeup of the constituency they initially won. Those members who do not adapt to changes in their constituencies—or to changes in their constituents' expectations—eventually lose.

It is well understood that members of Congress must first be reelected in order to accomplish any of their goals. The pioneering work of political scientist Richard Fenno Jr., who during the 1970s provided congressional scholars with important insights into the member–constituent relationship, makes one thing clear: Members must be attentive to their districts if they wish to be reelected. He explained in the following way:

> Representatives, and prospective representatives, think about their constituencies because they seek support there. They want to get nominated and elected, then re-nominated and re-elected. For most members of Congress most of the time, this electoral goal is primary. It is the prerequisite for a congressional career and, hence, for the pursuit of other goals. And the electoral goal is achieved—first and last—not in Washington, but at home.[7]

Once elected, members of Congress must focus on shoring up the support of the constituents who elected them and hedging their bets for reelection by capturing the favor of new constituents as well. Donald Matthews, in his 1960 study of the U.S. Senate, noted that many members of Congress use their early years in the institution to enlarge their "circle of friends."[8]

In his 1977 and 1978 analyses of House members in their districts, Fenno noted that members view their constituents in distinct bands: The geographic constituency is defined by the legally prescribed borders of the district and contains all of those adult individuals who live within the district's boundaries. This is the entire pool of eligible voters that *could* vote for the member in his or her reelection bid, but as a practical matter, members know that many of these constituents will never vote for them. Still, when it comes to constituency service, each person in the geographic constituency is entitled to the member's assistance. Most members, however, focus on two smaller bands of constituents: the reelection band and the primary band. The reelection constituency includes all those individuals in the district that can be expected to vote for the representative in a contested general election, and the primary constituency includes those constituents most committed to the member, who would vote for him or her in a contested primary.[9]

A common practice among congressional staff across the political spectrum is to find out if a constituent request comes from a resident of the district—a potential voter—or whether the request comes from a friend or supporter, which would merit the highest level of attention. Most staff members will not respond to requests or inquiries from individuals who are not constituents. For example,

Congressman Dave Brat's House of Representatives website notes, "All feedback is of value and welcome. However, as an elected representative of the 7th District of Virginia my priority is to the district from which I was elected and its residents."[10]

After a candidate wins office for the first time, he or she works to enhance the base of support throughout the district, making the local rounds at different businesses, schools, unions, churches, and clubs.[11] The focus is on the reelection and primary constituencies, since these groups of people are essential to ensuring reelection. Fenno refers to members' efforts to grow their constituencies as the "expansionist" phase of a member's constituency career. Once a member of Congress maximizes his or her support base within the district (generally signaled by a peak in electoral-vote share), he or she then moves into what Fenno calls the "protectionist phase" of the relationship with his or her constituents. In this phase, a representative's goal is to "maintain the existing primary-plus-reelection constituencies" by reinforcing and stabilizing existing patterns of support.[12] Fenno is careful to note that the expansionist and protectionist phases of the constituency career are fluid. If an established member begins to lose the support of his or her constituents—as measured by internal polling or by slipping numbers at the ballot box—he or she is likely to move back to expansionist activities in an effort to shore up support and forestall the possibility that the constituency will abandon him or her. In addition, if district demographics shift either because of organic patterns of migration or because of a deliberate change in the district's political boundaries, a representative will work to appeal to his or her reelection constituency and expand outreach to new voters.

In this way, a member of the U.S. House of Representatives is always preparing for the next election. The representative–constituent relationship for House members requires constant communication with the attentive public.[13] Even a representative elected above 55 percent of the popular vote (what many congressional scholars consider a "safe" margin of victory) must continuously concern him- or herself with reelection. As Fenno notes in *Congress at the Grassroots,* "Representing a constituency takes a lot of hard work *in* the constituency."[14]

But if members of Congress are "single-minded seekers of reelection," to use David Mayhew's words, they are so because reelection permits them to pursue other goals, chiefly making public policy and securing influence in Washington. Junior members of Congress once found it difficult to pursue these goals early in their careers; the norm of apprenticeship was pervasive, which meant that new and junior members of the House had little ability to gain influence or pursue their own policy goals. The apprenticeship norm died in the 1970s as the number of interest groups exploded and electronic media began to dominate. These developments changed the incentive structure and reelection calculus for individual members of Congress, who began to seek the spotlight as soon as they were first elected.

Television's pervasiveness led to cameras in the House and Senate chambers by 1986. Coupled with the advent of the 24-hour news cycle in the 1980s and 1990s and later with the ubiquity of social media, the incentives to pursue policy and prestige goals in Congress have increased dramatically over the last several decades. Today, no member of Congress can afford to delay active engagement in the policymaking process from the outset of his or her earliest service in the institution. The disruption of the Democrats' longtime control of the House and its systematized "leadership ladder" gave way to an era of Republican majorities and leadership that was accompanied by controversy and the somewhat personalized organizational construction within the chamber. Republican leaders emerged less from climbing the leadership ladder than from using their time on the backbench to carve out expertise and intraparty influence. Newt Gingrich, Tom DeLay, and Eric Cantor illustrate variations on this theme.

This shift came first in the form of movement conservative Newt Gingrich, who led a resurgent GOP to a congressional majority in the 1994 elections. Gingrich was, for many, an unlikely congressional leader. He had spent over a decade as a backbench firebrand, passing no meaningful legislation and instead concentrating on recruiting other conservatives to run for Congress. In 1989, he had moved into the GOP leadership as minority whip, upsetting the establishment's preferred candidate by two votes. He waged war with liberals on the Democratic side and conciliatory moderates in his own party. In 1994, with minority leader Bob Michel retiring, Gingrich had recruited attractive candidates for Congress and also crafted a national campaign called the "Contract with America." It propelled Republicans to a congressional majority and Gingrich to the Speakership. However, his three-year, 10-month tenure as Speaker was controversial and not necessarily very productive. No meaningful elements of the "Contract" campaign were implemented as law, and Gingrich lost significant showdowns with President Bill Clinton over spending; Social Security; taxes; and also, ultimately, impeachment and attempted removal of the philandering president.

But Gingrich had crafted a model for the new leadership, that of the caucus entrepreneur. When Gingrich resigned in the wake of the 1998 elections after Republicans failed to gain seats and his evident successor, Bob Livingston (R-LA), was felled within 24 hours by a sex scandal, the Speakership landed with Illinois Republican Dennis Hastert. Hastert was not next in the leadership ladder; he was the deputy majority whip, fourth behind the felled Speaker-designate, majority leader Dick Armey (R-TX), and majority whip Tom "The Hammer" DeLay (R-TX). DeLay had been crafting majorities not just for Gingrich's legislation but also for his own power base. His control over the caucus, through fund-raising, recruitment, and the crafting of relationships with lobbyists on the Hill, had given him the leverage to propel his deputy into the presiding officer's chair, even as it had made him sufficiently unpopular that he himself would never be elected to the post. Hastert was the opposite of the professorial, ideological Gingrich—a conservative, to be sure, but also amiable and risk averse. He did not run legislation that he could not pass without the support of his entire caucus. But the power was The Hammer.

In 2002, Dick Armey retired from Congress, leading to DeLay's ascension as floor leader. DeLay concentrated no small effort on crafting a takeover of Texas politics through creative campaign fund-raising that landed him in federal court and also by engineering a controversial redistricting that chased all of the moderate Democrats from Texas out of Congress. He ultimately resigned from Congress while under indictment in 2006, roughly coincidental to the departure of Denny Hastert from the Speaker's chair and the loss of the GOP congressional majority to the Democrats after 12 years in power.

Behind the scenes, young entrepreneurial members had set about creating bases of support by recruiting candidates to run and expand the GOP caucus. The most potent team was the "Young Guns," a group of three generation-X lawmakers who had come into office after Gingrich's fall. They would eventually set about recruiting a new majority for the GOP—but would do so using a much more professional, corporate leadership style than that exhibited by the bombastic Gingrich or the wily DeLay.

THE THREE PHASES OF A CAREER

Figure 4.1 offers a timeline of major milestones in Eric Cantor's career. A close look at Cantor's tenure in office demonstrates that his career consists of three distinct phases: the early years of 2001–2004, his midcareer years between 2005 and 2010, and then his final years in senior leadership, 2011–2014. In the early phase of Cantor's career, he was more engaged and involved with the district, and his election results reflected this closer relationship. But as his leadership responsibilities expanded and as he felt safer electorally, Cantor's focus shifted to management of internal House procedures and the Republicans' legislative agenda at the expense of his constituents' interests and his frequent appearances in the district. By 2006, evidence began to surface that Cantor's shine was beginning to dull back home. As Table 4.1 demonstrates, after a peak in 2004, his share of the vote declined in each subsequent reelection attempt. Cantor began to be criticized in the local media for his relationships with DC insiders, and his efforts to shore up reelection seemed to shift from genuine efforts at providing constituency service to securing victory through gerrymandering. The latter phase

FIGURE 4.1
Timeline of Cantor's service in the U.S. House

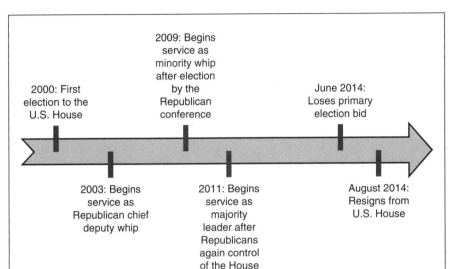

of his career coincided with the growing tea party movement within his district, which Cantor initially embraced, but which ultimately turned its back on him.

Cantor's Early Years (2001–2004)

In many respects, Eric Cantor's career trajectory and constituency relationship began much as the literature on careers in the U.S. Congress would predict. Despite only narrowly winning the 2000 Republican primary election, Cantor won a decisive victory in the 2000 general election, his first general election campaign for the U.S. House of Representatives. That year he garnered just under two-thirds of the vote in the Seventh District. This vote share turned out not to be unusual for Cantor. As Table 4.1 illustrates, throughout Cantor's career he was elected and reelected by double-digit margins across seven straight elections. This margin allowed him to pursue both his own interests as well as to secure legislation on behalf of his constituents, since "[l]arge electoral margins allow members more legislative flexibility and autonomy over their legislative agendas."[15]

In the early years of his career, Cantor engaged in a mix of local and national policymaking, focused on his constituents, and worked to generate positive media attention. He easily withstood the 2001 redistricting, which had dramatic impact on the shape of his district, although to the extent that redistricting

TABLE 4.1

Eric Cantor's electoral history (general elections), 2000–2012

Year	Principal challenger	Cantor vote total (%)	Opponent vote total (%)
2000	Warren A. Stewart	66.9	33.0
2002	Ben L. "Cooter" Jones	69.4	30.5
2004	W. Brad Blanton	75.5	24.3
2006	James Nachmann	63.8	34.4
2008	Anita Hartke	62.7	37.1
2010	Rick E. Waugh	59.2	34.1
2012	E. Wayne Powell	58.4	41.4

Source: Compiled by authors from Virginia State Board of Election Results, 2000–2012.

altered the district's partisan composition, it did so in ways most likely to favor Cantor's reelection.[16]

Just eight months into his first term, the World Trade Center and Pentagon were attacked by terrorists, and Cantor joined the Congressional Task Force on Terrorism and Unconventional Warfare. He also took on an active role in Israel–U.S. relations as one of only two Jewish Republicans in the House of Representatives. Later when New York's Ben Gilman retired, Cantor was the only Jewish Republican in the House for the remainder of his time in office, and his floor statements, legislative activity, and repeated trips to Israel during his tenure reflect the extent to which he became the party's intellectual leader on these issues.

Closer to home, Cantor reintroduced a bill that his predecessor, longtime Seventh District representative Tom Bliley, had championed, which would require the text of the U.S. Constitution to appear on all U.S. currency bills. A group of students at Ashland's Liberty Middle School, together with their teacher Randy Wright, developed this bill, the Liberty Bill Act. Cantor, like Bliley before him, introduced the bill after hearing a presentation from the middle schoolers.[17]

Reintroducing this bill helped Cantor to build some trust with his constituents; local media throughout the district reported on the bill frequently. It was a constituency-oriented bill that also held important symbolism and was noncontroversial. With a young, energetic champion, the bill picked up momentum locally as students at James Madison University in Harrisonburg also began lobbying on behalf of the bill. As is often the case for most legislation, the Liberty Bill Act made little progress in the 107th Congress and, as it had several times before, died in committee.[18] In addition to the Liberty Bill Act, during Cantor's first term in office he also authored a bill to rename a post office within the district for Bliley. The bill passed by voice vote in the House and by unanimous consent in the Senate.

All together during the 107th Congress, Cantor sponsored 10 pieces of legislation, which promoted issues such as tax credits for education (including homeschooling) expenses, a prohibition on support for the Palestinian Authority, Social Security waivers for the terminally ill, and the redesign of the nickel coin to commemorate the anniversary of the Louisiana Purchase. With the exception of the post-office renaming and the five-cent redesign, none of his proposals made it out of committee, and the nickel redesign passed the House but not the Senate (he reintroduced the commemorative coin design bill at the start of the 108th Congress in 2003, and it became law in April that same year). Still, as a new member, Cantor had wasted no time in sponsoring legislation in support of his district. And he fairly regularly went to the House floor to offer congratulations or words of remembrance for individuals and groups in his district, making use of the sometimes-politicized "one-minutes" that occasionally fill time on C-SPAN.

In addition to the bills he cosponsored, Cantor also cosponsored legislation introduced by other members of the Virginia delegation, as well as legislation that could affect Virginia and the Seventh District, including a bill in 2003 to tie driver's-license expiration dates to the dates of expiration for U.S. entry visas for foreign nationals, a 2004 financial incentives measure that provided tax breaks for NASCAR tracks, and the Freight Rail Infrastructure Capacity Expansion Act of 2009. He was instrumental during the 108th Congress in acquiring public funds to build the Library of Congress's National Audio-Visual Conservation Center in Culpeper, Virginia, in the Seventh District,[19] as well as securing funding to support Virginia Commonwealth University's Massey Cancer Center in Richmond.[20] But these activities provided primarily diffuse support to causes that affected a limited number of people in the district. As the news cycle in the district moved on after each of these successes was announced, Cantor's role was largely forgotten.

Beyond his legislative activities, Cantor worked with fellow members of the Virginia delegation to push for favorable decisions from executive agencies. Just five months after his swearing in, Cantor joined with other members of the delegation to seek a legislative remedy to a federal judge's ruling that Virginia could not limit the amount of out-of-state garbage entering the state.[21] He was also proactive in creating an antiterrorism task force in the Seventh District within weeks of the September 11, 2001, attacks; the task force subsequently identified the Richmond International Airport as a potential target, and Cantor worked with the Federal Aviation Administration to identify funds to expand baggage screening at the airport.[22]

The *Richmond Times-Dispatch* covered Cantor frequently during the first few years of his tenure, and during that time period, Cantor was by all indications an active and engaged representative of the Seventh District. Cantor also penned several guest columns that appeared in the *Times-Dispatch* that discussed his legislative activity in Washington and kept his constituents informed. His engagement with his constituents was primarily evident through Cantor's nonlegislative activity, but the literature on Congress suggests that constituents do not distinguish between legislative success and nonlegislative representational activity; by one analysis, "constituents seem more likely to be concerned with the legislator's overall productivity and level of accomplishment than with the percentage of the legislator's agenda that passed."[23]

Constituents learn about their members' activities through a variety of means; the most important of these is media coverage. The *Richmond Times-Dispatch* covered Cantor in overwhelmingly positive terms during his first several years in office—in fact, the newspaper did not publish a single critical article, editorial, or letter to the editor. A few weeks before the 2002 congressional midterm election, Cantor's first opportunity to be reelected, the newspaper endorsed Cantor, calling him "indispensable."[24] Cantor's opponent in 2002 was Ben Jones, a former Democratic member of Congress from Georgia and the actor best known for his portrayal of the mechanic "Cooter" on the 1980s hit television series the *Dukes of Hazzard.* The election itself was largely unremarkable, save for the modest star power that Jones brought to the race.

As the 108th Congress began in January 2003, Cantor was named chief deputy majority whip, a remarkable accomplishment for a legislator so young in age and in length of service. The job of the party whips is to ensure that members of the party in Congress support the party line. With approximately 200 members to keep in line, the parties' elected whips appoint dozens of deputies to assist with the task, and Cantor was then majority whip Roy Blunt's choice to be first among this cadre of junior party disciplinarians. The position was Cantor's first foray into House leadership, and he found that it suited him.

But it also added significant responsibility to his work on the Hill. Although he reintroduced the Liberty Bill Act and successfully shepherded a resolution through the House to commemorate "the firefighters, police, public servants, civilians, and private businesses who responded to the devastating fire in Richmond, Virginia, on March 26, 2004," the only one of his proposals to result in a new law was the reintroduction of the commemorative nickel coin design he had first proposed in the 107th Congress.[25]

During the 108th Congress, the local Richmond media began sharpening their focus on Cantor. As a March 2003 feature in the *Richmond Times-Dispatch* noted, "Higher visibility means greater scrutiny," and within a month, the newspaper published its first critical piece on Cantor since he had initially been elected in 2000.[26] Cantor had waded into a dispute between the city of Richmond and workers at city hall; the city had ordered an American flag removed from a wall inside the building because it offended several city workers who were opposed to the war in Iraq. The flag was not a permanent fixture installed by the city but had been hung in city hall by two city employees who wanted to show support for U.S. troops. As reported by the *Times-Dispatch*, Cantor sent a letter to the city to complain about the removal. A columnist for the newspaper subsequently took Cantor to task for using a local issue—that had ended the way Cantor preferred, with a permanent flag and flagpole display—to score political points. The column pointed out that Cantor's approach included an implied threat against the city; Cantor had written of the flag controversy, "It does highlight a possible need for legislative action that would tie federal appropriations to cities that fail to clarify and protect the right of any local, state and federal employee to fly the American flag." The author went on to note that Cantor's willingness to protect citizens' rights to display the flag was admirable, but he wondered if Cantor "ha[d] to punish the entire city in the process" of securing those rights for the city employees who had originally hung the flag in city hall by threatening to slash federal funding.[27]

But this was the only criticism Cantor received during his second term, with his hometown newspaper highlighting his support of a Habitat for Humanity "blitz build" in June 2004[28] and praising him as being "ahead of the curve" on matters relating to terrorism and the Middle East.[29] Just a few months prior to the 2004 general election, after a tropical storm caused millions of dollars in damage to areas within Cantor's district, Cantor was dogged in his efforts to obtain disaster relief funding from the federal government. As Cantor approached his third election, the *Richmond Times-Dispatch* again declared him indispensable and crowed that the Seventh District had much to be proud of in its member of Congress.[30] Cantor's share of the vote grew to more than 75 percent in the 2004 general election.

Cantor's Midcareer Years (2005–2010)

Writing in *Young Guns: A New Generation of Conservative Leaders,* Cantor describes the end of the first session of the 109th Congress as a turning point in his orientation toward his party's work in Congress in the following way:

> I remember the moment I realized my party had lost its way. It was the morning of November 6, 2005. I opened the Sunday paper and saw the cover of *Parade* magazine. It featured a full-color mock-up of the infamous "Bridge to Nowhere" in Alaska. . . . The nation was still reeling from the

scenes of devastation and corresponding government incompetence we all saw in the aftermath of Hurricane Katrina . . . and now Americans were learning that Congress was writing $223 million checks to obscure towns in Alaska with well-connected congressional representatives.[31]

· It was at that point, Cantor claims, that he realized that there was a need for the Republicans in Congress to reclaim their footing as the party of fiscal discipline. Cantor became an early champion of the elimination of earmarks—targeted spending within congressional districts. He did not distinguish between "Bridge-to-Nowhere" largesse and smaller, more-targeted projects such as the ones he had previously supported, including Virginia Commonwealth University's Massey Cancer Center.

Having decided to forgo earmarks and as a member of the party's leadership, Cantor's focus shifted toward more Washington activities beginning with the opening of the 109th Congress. Cantor claims that he realized that the public "didn't like what they were seeing" from the party in power and saw himself as an important catalyst for change.[32] Cantor subsequently threw himself into his work on behalf of the party.

After introducing two bills with decidedly local focus in each of his first two congresses in office, Cantor now reduced his locally oriented legislative activity. In the 109th Congress, Cantor reintroduced the Liberty Bill Act—by this point a purely symbolic action—but the remainder of his legislative activity consisted primarily of proposing modifications to the tax code. Not a single one of his legislative proposals was approved by the House of Representatives, although as a junior leader in the majority party, Cantor introduced and had approved the resolutions to seat members on committees, as well as a joint resolution to allow the Capitol Rotunda to be used to commemorate Holocaust victims.

Cantor's decision to focus on national issues and the tasks of party leadership makes sense in the context of his electoral results in 2004. He had been reelected in 2004 by a three-to-one margin—a margin comfortable enough to permit a focus on matters more personally interesting to him. He began to devote significant time and attention to bolstering the Republican Party's electoral fortunes. He had founded the Every Republican Is Crucial Political Action Committee (ERICPAC) during the 2004 election cycle, raising and giving away a half million dollars to Republican candidates in 2004; by 2005, fund-raising for Republican candidates consumed significant amounts of his time. During the 109th Congress, Cantor served as the fund-raising chair of the National Republican Congressional Committee (NRCC); the NRCC raised $36 million during the 2006 election cycle, nearly twice as much as its goal.[33] His own fund, ERICPAC, raised and spent $1.2 million during the 2006 election. Nearly all of the money went to support Republican candidates for the House of Representatives.[34]

Despite the fund-raising success, the Republicans lost the House of Representatives in the 2006 congressional midterm elections. The 2006 elections were not kind to Cantor, either, although he successfully retained his seat. Cantor's share of the vote began a steady decline that would continue over the next four election cycles, until 2012's November general election when he was returned to the House with just over 58 percent of the vote. In the 2006 congressional midterm, Cantor lost 12 points on the two-party vote share from his previous reelection effort. While it would be impossible for Cantor to know in November 2006 that his share of the vote would continue to decline, it is surprising that Cantor does not appear to have done more to make sure he was holding on to the support of his constituents.

The Young Guns

But if Cantor was fazed by the 2006 election results, his actions and activities on the Hill did not reveal it. Republican Whip Roy Blunt ran for the position of majority leader following the scandal-plagued Tom DeLay's resignation in January 2007. Cantor campaigned for the vacant whip position but failed to move up the leadership ladder. Blunt was instead reelected to the whip position after losing his bid to be majority leader to Ohio Republican John Boehner. Cantor was rehired by Blunt as chief deputy whip for the 110th Congress. Now in the minority, however, Cantor was not content to simply marshal his party colleagues to oppose Speaker Nancy Pelosi and the Democrats. Instead, Cantor became one of the intellectual leaders of the movement to recapture the House majority through a carefully targeted candidate recruitment program.

In *Young Guns: A New Generation of Conservative Leaders,* Rep. Kevin McCarthy explained that 2007 found both recently beaten and potential future Republican candidates depressed about their prospects for the future. McCarthy, Cantor, and their colleague Paul Ryan were seen as a "new generation of pro-market, small government leaders."[35] The *Weekly Standard*'s Fred Barnes christened the three Republicans the "Young Guns," a moniker that Cantor, Ryan, and McCarthy in turn used to describe what would become their candidate recruitment and support effort. The three congressmen "scoured the country looking for like-minded conservatives who shared their uncompromising commitment to shrinking the federal government. They showered these Young Gun recruits with money and support and exhorted them to maintain a laser-like fiscal focus."[36]

In its early form, the Young Guns program consisted of volunteer Republican House members who, like Cantor, McCarthy, and Ryan, wanted to be a part of recapturing the House of Representatives in 2008. The group held meetings to analyze demographic data and review emerging Republican leaders. Their main targets were Democrats holding seats in districts that they determined might be ripe to flip to the Republicans. Cantor, McCarthy, and Ryan personally visited many of the target districts and met with prospective candidates. As the Young Guns program took shape, Cantor almost entirely abandoned any focus on his district, at least vis-à-vis securing legislation or appropriations on its behalf.

The Young Guns' efforts did not pay off immediately. In the 2008 congressional elections, the Republicans lost 24 additional seats as Democrat Barack Obama's election as president over Republican candidate John McCain swept Democrats down the ticket into Congress. Still, Kevin McCarthy noted the following in *Young Guns:* "[O]f the five Democratic incumbents that lost their seats in 2008, four of them were beaten by Young Guns challengers, and three Young Guns candidates also won races in open seats."[37] These successes told the Young Guns that they were onto something.

As the 110th Congress began, the Young Guns and their supporters vowed to expand their efforts during the next election cycle. In addition that year, members of the Young Guns program became actively engaged in the policy process, working to promote the party's core principles in the legislative process.[38] Recruiting candidates and convincing voters to support them would require tangible evidence that there was a place for fiscal discipline in Washington, and the Republicans who were actively working to take back the House knew they would need to focus on policy, not just politics.

During 2009, the National Republican Campaign Committee adopted the Young Gun approach and worked closely with Cantor, Ryan, and McCarthy to create benchmarks tied to levels of party support for prospects. In a program that continues today, Republican candidates move from being "on the radar" to "contender" to "Young Gun" by virtue of meeting standards for campaign organization, fund-raising, and levels of public support (for a detailed explanation of the criteria to move between each of these levels, see www.gopyoungguns.com).

Cantor, Ryan, and McCarthy continued to travel the country in search of candidates that could help them to recapture the House. As they did so throughout 2009 and 2010, they became aware of the nascent tea party movement that had begun to take shape. The Young Guns' emphasis on fiscal discipline, reduced government spending, and lower taxes made the tea party an obvious strategic partner in their efforts.

The Tea Party

Originating with the Ron Paul presidential primary bid of 2008 and CNBC reporter Rick Santelli's fiery call to arms from the floor of the Chicago Board of Trade, the "taxed enough already" (tea) party movement has been influential in affecting the outcomes of elections and legislation since 2009.[39] The movement's ideology is a mixture of conservatism, Libertarianism, and materialism, with a heavy emphasis on economic values and limited government. Although the tea party is generally discussed as if it were monolithic, it is not a cohesive movement or group; it is composed of loosely affiliated conservative interest groups with no central leadership. Tea party supporters promote particular candidates whose ideologies best reflect their own.[40] Tea party groups across the country emphasize different things, depending on their geography and the political environment that surrounds them. They often conflict with one another; the decentralized nature of the movement allows each autonomous group to set its own agenda, which then reflects the specific interests and objectives of each group. Although priorities and goals may conflict, the decentralization has helped minimize external co-opting and internal corruption.[41]

That is not to suggest, however, that the tea party arose independently from the Republican Party. Although McCarthy claims that the tea party protests of 2009 simply "happened," evidence suggests that these protests were not just grass roots' activities. On the contrary, Republican luminaries such as former House majority leader Dick Armey and his FreedomWorks group and the Charles and David Koch-backed Americans for Prosperity took an active role in the earliest stages of the tea party's formation. These organizations were a part of coordinating and actively promoting tea party events and activities; in July 2010, for example, the Americans for Prosperity Foundation sponsored a summit for tea party activists in Austin, Texas. A 2010 *New Yorker* article noted the following:

> Americans for Prosperity has worked closely with the Tea Party since the movement's inception. In the weeks before the first Tax Day protests, in April 2009, Americans for Prosperity hosted a Web site offering supporters "Tea Party Talking Points." The Arizona branch urged people to send tea bags to Obama; the Missouri branch urged members to sign up for "Taxpayer Tea Party Registration," and provided directions to nine protests.[42]

Cantor must have been aware of the role that Americans for Prosperity and FreedomWorks were playing vis-à-vis the tea party movement during the 2010 election cycle. The congressman received a $10,000 campaign contribution from Koch Industries' political action committee in both the 2008 and 2010 cycles.[43] In addition, Cantor had begun to engage actively with the tea party movement at the same time; a 2013 profile of Cantor in the *New Yorker* noted that "[a]s the Tea Party movement took off, in 2009, Cantor worked to harness its energy" on behalf of his efforts to identify and elect conservative Republicans to Congress.[44]

Shifting Priorities

As the Young Guns were harnessing the tea party in support of their recruitment efforts, Cantor was actually distancing himself from the budding tea party movement in the Seventh District. On Capitol Hill, he refused to join the tea party caucus founded by House colleague Michele Bachmann, and during the 2010 general election, it was his independent challenger, Floyd Bayne, who claimed the support of local tea party groups during the campaign. Still, even without embracing the local tea party in 2010, Cantor knew his election was all but certain. Coverage of the 2010 debate over the Affordable Care Act and Cantor's work as one of the leaders of Republican opposition gained him significant attention in both the national and local press. At home, the 2010 election kept Cantor's name in the newspapers, as did speculation that if Republicans regained control of the House of Representatives, Cantor would ascend to the role of majority leader. No one from Virginia had ever served in that position before, and the prospect led to glowing commentary from the *Richmond Times-Dispatch* editorial board during the year.

Still, a review of Cantor's Hill activity demonstrates that by the end of 2010, he had completely abandoned district-specific representational activity and had come to focus nearly exclusively on national issues and party politics. Cantor's broad neglect of his district is curious, given that his leadership positions would probably have improved his chances at legislative success, likely without having to work as hard for it as would have rank-and-file members. Evidence demonstrates that "House majority leaders, committee leaders, and subcommittee leaders reaped the benefits of their privileged positions with . . . more bills reported than other House members."[45] Yet Cantor's efforts to secure benefits for his constituents through legislation were virtually nonexistent by the start of the 110th Congress. In fact, the 110th and 111th Congresses saw his lowest levels of bill sponsorship to that point in his congressional career, with nine and seven measures introduced, respectively.

Indeed, by most measures of bill sponsorship activity, Cantor's career average of 11.6 measures introduced per Congress is low. A 2003 study of the 103rd Congress found that members of the House of Representatives introduced an average of just over 15 pieces of legislation and that 12 percent of the measures introduced were "local bills," or legislation that "benefits the district directly and provides electoral benefits for the legislator."[46] Cantor's career average is particularly low considering that the data are compiled from congress.gov and include sponsorships of all types of legislative proposals, including simple resolutions and amendments to legislation. Over the course of his career, Cantor does not come close to meeting the averages identified by previous scholarship as typical for members of Congress. Furthermore, while Table 4.2 suggests that his legislative productivity increased dramatically beginning in 2011, nearly all of the proposals Cantor introduced from 2011 through 2014 were procedural and organizational activities related to his responsibilities as majority leader. Not a single legislative measure he championed between 2005 and 2010 was enacted into law.

TABLE 4.2
Eric Cantor's legislative productivity, 2001–2014*

Congress	Number of measures sponsored	Number of measures passed by the House	Number of measures enacted into law	Number of "local" measures sponsored
107th	10	2	1	2
108th	13	6	1	2
109th	16	4	0	1
110th	9	0	0	1
111th	7	0	0	1
112th	20	16	2	0
113th	6	5	0	0

*Cantor only served through August 2014.
Source: Compiled by authors from **congress.gov** data.

In fairness, Cantor was well respected by other members of the Virginia delegation, who could count on him to support efforts on behalf of their constituents. Cantor's clout as majority leader was important to members like Randy Forbes, whose Fourth District includes parts of Newport News, Virginia, where U.S. naval shipbuilding and related industries depend on federal money and support. Forbes, speaking in the wake of Cantor's primary loss, praised Cantor's consistent efforts in Washington on behalf of the military and ship-building industries in the Fourth District and noted that the loss would require the Virginia delegation to come together to try to regain the lost influence.[47] But at home in the Seventh, where there is no single industry or common interest, Cantor's efforts elsewhere in the commonwealth were of little consequence.

There are, of course, other mechanisms besides legislation for demonstrating to constituents that a member is working on their behalf. One mechanism is through targeted appropriations, or earmarks, that direct federal revenues directly to the district. Earmarks have long been scrutinized, but as political scientists Sean Kelly and Scott Frisch note in their 2011 book on the subject, *Cheese Factories on the Moon,* earmarks are another way that members of Congress can work on behalf of their constituents.

Yet during his career in Congress, Eric Cantor appears never to have sought a single earmark—even prior to the Republican leadership's moratorium (and subsequent ban) that began in 2010. According to the Office of Management and Budget's earmark tracking database, Cantor did not seek or obtain earmarks in any of the years tracked—2005, 2008, 2009, or 2010. He later championed the permanent elimination of earmarks as a conservative, fiscally responsible approach to reigning in congressional spending. In a 2010 *Politico* commentary, Cantor argued that earmarks took hard-earned dollars from his constituents and hinted that private philanthropy ought to be used to complete the projects that previously had been made possible through earmarking.[48] In fact, when considered in light of his declining electoral results during this time period, Cantor's lack of legislative efforts on behalf of the Seventh District become's even more surprising. The literature on Congress suggests that Cantor should have moved to protect his constituency following on the 2006 elections—or certainly soon afterward, as his support at the ballot box continued to decline. Yet evidence abounds that not only did Cantor not redouble his efforts on behalf of his constituents, he actually moved in the opposite direction, focusing instead at the national level. Republicans were in the minority, a situation that did not sit well with Cantor.

Cantor's Final Two Terms (2011–2014)

Although Cantor had been moving away from the district during the half decade between 2005 and 2010, his ascension to House majority leader in January 2011 seemed to be a turning point in his congressional career. Before 2011, Cantor allocated at least some of his time and energy to constituency concerns. But beginning in 2011, Cantor's exclusive focus seemed to be on national policymaking and on amassing as much personal power for himself as possible. Although Cantor had introduced the Liberty Bill in every congress between the 107th and 111th, he did not introduce it in either the 112th or 113th Congresses, abandoning even a symbolic gesture of goodwill for the district. With a stable of new members of Congress that Cantor had helped to elect in the 2010 congressional midterms and now serving in the second-most senior position in the House, Cantor not only controlled access to the House floor but also could count on the loyalty of many new members of Congress as he opposed President Obama at nearly every turn.

In a *60 Minutes* report on Eric Cantor, journalist Leslie Stahl summed up the situation in the first session of the 112th Congress:

> Driving much of the gridlock is the large Republican freshman class in the House. Eric Cantor was the one who went out in 2010 and recruited most of the freshmen, who are conservative and backed by the Tea Party. He meets with them regularly, and several of them told us that Cantor is their inspirational leader and father figure. . . . In Republican circles, he's seen as an ambitious man on the rise.[49]

Abandoning Home

As majority leader, Cantor found himself the Republican standard-bearer on the major policy issues that confronted the 112th and 113th Congresses. Perhaps no issue was more important to the Republican conference and to the country during this time as the 2011 debt-ceiling showdown.

The debt ceiling is a cap on the amount of borrowing the U.S. Treasury Department is legally able to undertake. The purpose is to constrain government borrowing and spending while providing flexibility to policymakers in the borrowing process. Prior to the Franklin Roosevelt administration, Congress would authorize the executive branch to borrow money for specific purposes—the construction of the Panama Canal, for example, or for the war efforts in the late nineteenth and early twentieth centuries.[50] Beginning in the 1930s, however, Congress began to allow more flexibility by eliminating the need for specific authorization to borrow. Instead, an aggregate limit on the amount of money that can be borrowed was put in place.

The debt ceiling is set by law—but has been raised dozens of times in order to accommodate increasing governmental spending obligations, particularly during periods when revenues lag behind expenditures. The end of the first decade of the 2000s was one such time; the 2008 recession and subsequent economic stimulus plans, combined with growing entitlement obligations and required interest payments on existing national debt, meant that government expenditures were outpacing revenues and necessitating borrowing. In February 2010, the Democrat-controlled Congress had approved a $2 billion increase in the debt increase—just months before approving the Affordable Care Act, which initially was projected to cost between $1 trillion and $2 trillion during its first decade (although there were also projected to be offsetting cost reductions as well). House Republicans were incensed. At the 2011 House Republican conference retreat, Cantor noted that there would be a need to raise the debt ceiling again that year and encouraged House Republicans to view that moment as an opportunity to extract concessions from the White House.

The battle over the debt ceiling increase lasted for several months during 2011. Emboldened by a large number of tea party-backed freshmen, the Republican House leadership held firm against the White House; the country came dangerously close to defaulting on its financial obligations. As time marched on, however, it became clear that the new crop of tea party Republicans might be willing to let the United States default on its debts. According to the *Washington Post*, the "lightning-fast feedback loop of the Internet" meant that Republicans were bombarded with messages from constituents and outside groups:

FreedomWorks and other tea party groups warned Republicans to stick to their fiscal promises. . . . The Tea Party Patriots encouraged organizers in districts across the country to keep up the pressure on their representatives. . . . Erick Erickson, editor of *RedState*, a conservative blog with a large following, attacked the House leadership's apparent willingness to compromise. He implored rank-and-file conservatives to stand strong. "Fear has no business entering into your negotiations," he wrote. "There is no fallback. There is no alternative. Hold the freaking line."[51]

By July 2011, however, the party leadership recognized that they would need to temper the new members' zealous opposition if a deal was to get done. Many of the freshmen Republicans were eventually persuaded to vote in favor of the debt limit increase after Republican leaders implored them not to "push too far."[52] But damage was already done. In the aftermath of the fight, the credit-rating agency Standard and Poor's downgraded the United States' credit rating from AAA, its highest level, to AA+ after concluding that the agreement reached by the White House and Congress did not do enough to stabilize the country's debt.[53] In addition, the House leadership now had to bring disgruntled freshmen back into the fold—as well as to help provide them cover as they worried about how their votes would play back home.

So when twin natural disasters struck Cantor's district within weeks of the debt ceiling brinksmanship, Cantor was constrained. Just days after a 5.8 magnitude earthquake struck Mineral, Virginia, in the Seventh District's Louisa County, Hurricane Irene caused flooding in parts of Richmond and Henrico County. But where the younger Representative Cantor had pushed for disaster relief funds for the district in 2004, he was cagey about federal relief to his district immediately after the earthquake, declaring that any appropriation of federal emergency disaster relief funds, including funds to help his constituents recover, would need to be offset by spending cuts elsewhere in the federal budget.[54] This was similar to the position he had taken three months earlier when tornadoes devastated the town of Joplin, Missouri.[55] Cantor later backtracked, claiming that Democrats had misrepresented his comments to make it seem as though he was withholding funds from his own constituents.[56] And by late September 2011, Cantor began pushing the Federal Emergency Management Agency (FEMA) to release funds to aid the disaster recovery in Virginia. But Cantor continued to push for offsetting spending cuts into September;[57] PolitiFact Virginia, a fact-checking organization, rated Cantor's shift on federal disaster relief between 2004 and 2011 as a "full-flop" (a major shift in position), and a narrative emerged that Cantor had abandoned his constituents in favor of Washington power.[58] To add insult to injury, FEMA ultimately rejected Virginia's request for disaster relief. One report suggested that Cantor himself was to blame for this result;

because he had previously pushed to link disaster funding to offsetting spending cuts, FEMA's relief funds were still tied up in the ongoing budget struggles.[59]

Unpopular votes and positions are not necessarily fatal to a member of Congress who has built the trust and confidence of his constituents. But Cantor's tepid support for earthquake and hurricane victims in his own district did little to stem constituents' waning confidence in their representative. The earthquake and hurricane that struck the Seventh District in August 2011 gave constituents the opportunity to evaluate the relative benefits of being represented by the House majority leader as compared with a member that might be in a better position to push hard on their behalf. Many concluded that perhaps they might be better off with someone who could be more vocal.

But once again, Cantor seemed unconcerned about his constituents' perceptions. Rather than assuring constituents' support by reinvigorating his efforts at constituency service, Cantor focused on guaranteeing his chances to win reelection through a focus on redistricting. In light of the 2010 census data, Virginia's congressional district lines would once again be redrawn. In Virginia, the congressional district lines are largely drawn by the members of Congress themselves and proposed to the Virginia General Assembly, which generally approves them as proposed. There are exceptions—in 1991, the Democrat-controlled General Assembly redistricted then representative George Allen out of his seat, but such examples are unusual. In 2010, Republicans controlled the General Assembly, so Cantor and his longtime political strategist Ray Allen faced little challenge to their proposed changes to the Seventh District's boundaries, which were largely aimed at ensuring that Cantor would not face a credible Democratic challenger in 2012 and beyond. As they drew the new lines, the Cantor camp excluded precincts with significant Democratic Party leanings, as evidenced by percentages of support for Cantor's Democratic opponent, Rick Waugh, in the 2010 congressional midterm. The excised precincts included five Richmond precincts with nearly 4,000 voters, who combined had supported Waugh by a three-to-one margin over Cantor in 2010.

Cantor won an average of 65 percent of the two-party vote in 2010 across the 181 precincts that were included in the new Seventh District when it was redrawn in 2012. Eleven of the precincts that were eliminated from the Seventh in the 2012 redistricting had voted two to one against Cantor in 2010. The changes to precincts in the Seventh Congressional District between the 2010 and 2012 elections, particularly in the Richmond and Fredericksburg areas, excised Democratic-leaning precincts and moved the district even further to the Right.

In 2012, Cantor drew a challenge both in the Republican primary and in the general election. His primary challenger was Floyd Bayne, who had challenged him as an independent in the 2010 general election. Cantor easily defeated Bayne by nearly a four-to-one margin in the primary. He then faced E. Wayne Powell, a

Photo 4.1: Handmade "Wayne Powell for Congress" signs

One of Wayne Powell's campaign themes in his 2012 effort to unseat the incumbent was that Cantor was for sale to Republican donors. His campaign team peppered the district with handmade "For Sale" signs like these. Powell's own campaign signs read: 'Wayne Powell: Not For Sale.'"

Source: Wayne Powell for Congress, https://www.facebook.com/PowellForVA.

lawyer from the south side of Richmond, who challenged Cantor during the 2012 general election.

The Powell campaign is best remembered in the Seventh District for its handmade "For Sale" signs that suggested that Eric Cantor himself was for sale. An image of two of these signs appears in Photo 4.1; the phone number on the signs dialed the Cantor campaign headquarters in downtown Richmond. As a follow-up to the "For Sale" signs, which popped up along roads throughout the district, Powell's printed campaign signs employed the slogan "Not for Sale."

For the first time since he had debated Ben "Cooter" Jones in 2002, Cantor agreed to debate his Democratic opponent a few weeks before the November election. But the campaign insisted that it was unconcerned about Powell. Cantor's longtime political strategist Ray Allen echoed this sentiment, as reported by the *Washington Post*:

> [Allen] placed Powell just a notch above a string of characters who have challenged Cantor since then [2002], including a nude group therapy practitioner who ran against him twice and an "unemployed social worker who followed us around in a chicken suit."[60]

During the debate and throughout the campaign, Powell laid the blame for gridlock in Washington squarely at Cantor's feet. Powell asked voters to hold Cantor accountable for the fiscal brinkmanship of the 2011 debt ceiling standoff.

But where Powell and the Democrats wanted Cantor to pay for what they considered to be excessive obstructionism, the growing tea party movement in the Seventh District was still angry over what it perceived as Cantor's capitulation to President Obama on the debt ceiling matter. The distance that Cantor had deliberately put between himself and the local tea party groups meant that he did not court the tea party's support in 2012. Local tea party groups likewise were skeptical of Cantor, keeping their distance as a result of his role in the compromise with the White House over the debt ceiling increase. Joshua Huffmon of the *Virginia Conservative* blog noted in a May 2012 post that at a mid-May meeting of the Mechanicsville Tea Party, just a few weeks prior to the primary election contest between Bayne and Cantor, there was a "complete lack of Cantor materials. . . ." He continued with the following description:

[A]t the Mechanicsville meeting, there were neither Cantor campaign signs nor his literature. By contrast, I could easily find brochures for his [independent] opponent, Floyd Bayne. I have to wonder, is this situation an anomaly? Do many of the grassroots organization [*sic*] in the 7th congressional district oppose majority leader Eric Cantor? Or has his campaign simply chosen to ignore tea party groups like Mechanicsville?[61]

In response, blog commenter "Trevor Ripchord" wrote the following:

Any true tea party understands that Eric Cantor is exactly the problem (on the republican side) we are fighting. I can't begin to imagine what a true patriot would see in Eric of value to our freedom, our Constitution or our future.[62]

In the 2012 general election, the first to test Cantor's new district lines, he won by his smallest margin of victory in any election, 58.4 percent to 41.4 percent.

THE IMPORTANCE OF MONEY

Part of the grass roots' objection to Cantor was the extent to which he seemed to be focused on money—money for his own campaigns, money to support the campaigns of like-minded lawmakers, and in the cynical eyes of many constituents, the money that would come from supporting industries and interests with proposals pending before the House of Representatives.

All lawmakers raise money for reelection, and they aggressively do so. From the moment freshman lawmakers enter Congress, they will need to raise approximately $3,000 a day over 18 months to prepare for a campaign. Others raise much more. Cantor was known on the Hill for being a particularly effective fund raiser, a fact that may have contributed to his rapid rise through the ranks of the House leadership. But back home, Cantor's fund-raising efforts and his links to moneyed interests would eventually come back to haunt him.

There are two main reasons that members of Congress wish to raise large sums of money. The first is that a large campaign war chest sends a signal to potential opponents that they will be in for a fight if they take on the incumbent. The more money challengers spend, the greater the likelihood of defeating the incumbent, so the scaring of opponents who have the potential to raise big money by signaling that a financial arms race will take place is one way to ensure reelection. The second reason is to prepare for a potentially vigorous challenge. Running for Congress has become more expensive with every passing year.

Eric Cantor presents the definitive example of the well-financed incumbent. From Cantor's first reelection bid in 2002 until his last effort in 2014, the average amount of money spent by an incumbent congressman increased from about $1.1 million to $1.7 million, an increase of about 55 percent. By comparison, Eric Cantor's spending increased by 500 percent, from over $1.4 million in his initial reelection to nearly $7.5 million by 2012 and $5.7 million just for the primary in 2014. He was obviously prepared to raise and spend even more money, with a general election campaign presumably in the offing (see Table 4.3). And Cantor rarely if ever left any money in the bank. Most incumbents spend heavily, even though they do not have strong opponents. But in lopsided races, they also reach a point where they cease to burn through cash and leave behind some war chest for the future. Cantor did not; he usually spent in excess of 90 percent of all the dollars he brought in. At the same time, Cantor never confronted a well-financed opponent for reelection. Only one opponent ever spent more than $200,000 in a challenge, and even then, he was outspent nine to one by the incumbent. Figure 4.2 shows Cantor's meteoric spending trend. His spending totally dwarfed his Democratic opponents' in a safe Republican district.

A common trend in campaign finance is that as lawmakers become settled in DC and build up seniority, the structure of their campaign financing changes. They become less dependent on individual donors in the district and take more money from political action committees and also individual donors from outside their states who are tied to specific industries.

This occurs for two reasons. First, whether as an open-seat candidate or as a challenger, candidates are most often raising money from their existing political networks, which largely exist in their district's and the states. Second, after getting to Washington, they are winners—they have a vote, a committee assignment, and influence in some small subsystem that will be important to certain policy domains or advocacy coalitions. Within these policy subsystems, campaign dollars flow from the advocacy community to the elected members of Congress. This in turn reinforces relationships between interest groups and lawmakers. Groups need access and influence, and lawmakers need reelection dollars. It is a symbiotic relationship.

When Eric Cantor first ran for Congress in 2000, he raised over 90 percent of his money in Virginia and took less than 10 percent from out-of-state donors (see Table 4.4). Overall, his campaign committee took in about $650,000. For each of the next four election cycles, his campaign committee receipts and the share of dollars coming from outside Virginia steadily climbed. From 2002 to 2008, he

TABLE 4.3
Fund-raising and spending by Cantor and his opponents, 2002–2014

Year	Cantor fund-raising ($)	Cantor spending ($)	Opponent spending ($)
2002	1,440,000	1,402,000	179,936
2004	2,472,000	2,147,000	0
2006	3,310,000	3,489,000	108,061
2008	3,990,000	3,823,000	63,152
2010	5,407,000	5,955,000	148,349
2012	7,632,000	7,477,000	800,647
2014	6,165,000	5,794,000	

Source: Compiled by the authors from data available at http://www.opensecrets.org.

FIGURE 4.2
Cantor's meteoric spending climb per election cycle

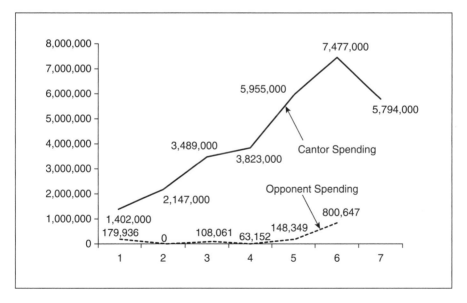

took between 33.6 percent and 45.5 percent of his campaign dollars from non-Virginians. After becoming majority whip, his campaign dollars were over 60 percent from out of state, and upon being named majority leader, almost

TABLE 4.4

The Cantor campaign committee's out-of-state receipts, 2000–2014

Year	In state	Out of state	Out of state (%)
2000	586,000	61,000	9.4
2002	463,000	234,000	33.6
2004	664,000	465,000	41.2
2006	882,000	567,000	39.1
2008	1,049,000	875,000	45.5
2010	1,195,000	1,868,000	61.0
2012	1,200,000	3,350,000	73.6
2014	731,000	2,311,000	76.0

Source: Compiled by the authors from data available at http://www.opensecrets.org.

three-quarters of his dollars were in the form of out-of-state contributions. Eric Cantor had moved from having a Virginia-dominated campaign finance constituency to a national/DC-oriented one.

Cantor also undertook a common practice of lawmakers since the 1990s and created a "leadership PAC." Leadership PACs are political action committees created by individual members to raise money and then target it into races where they might help friends and build allies inside the party caucus. One of the first of these was created back in the 1970s by California congressman Henry Waxman. Other lawmakers similarly followed suit, and leadership PACs became a vehicle not just to build legislative majorities but also to build coalitional support for particular politicians who were seeking institutional power. Cantor's ERICPAC was part of the Young Guns strategy for identifying, recruiting, and supporting potential congressional Republicans in order to recover the majority. However, it had existed for six years before the GOP takeover. As Cantor's power grew and he attracted more money to his own campaign committee, the coffers of ERICPAC also grew (see Table 4.5).

Lawmakers do not attract money in general. They attract specific money. For example, labor union money is given overwhelmingly to Democratic lawmakers, while corporate money flows disproportionately toward Republicans. Agricultural PACs mainly give money to lawmakers who sit on the agriculture committees in the House and Senate. Arthur Denzau and Michael Munger argued nearly three

TABLE 4.5

Fund-raising and spending by Every Republican Is Crucial (ERIC) PAC

Year	Raised ($)	Spent ($)
2002	1,400,000	1,300,000
2004	2,400,000	2,400,000
2006	2,500,000	2,500,000
2008	4,400,000	3,800,000
2012	5,500,000	5,400,000
2014	4,100,000	4,500,000

Source: Compiled by the authors from data available at http://www.opensecrets.org.

decades ago that there was a "purchase price" to legislation. Moneyed interests who are tied to different industries have sophisticated strategies for placing their campaign donations.

In a Denzau/Munger model, the donor strategy balances the cost of getting a lawmaker to influence the course of legislation against the likelihood that the lawmaker can deliver on an outcome. Lawmakers can influence legislation based on the committees they sit on, their seniority, their membership in the majority party, and their institutional leadership power. There is a balancing point where some members become too expensive to purchase policy influence from; for other junior members, there is a low price to pay to get them to help. Denzau and Munger contend that money from particular industries will gravitate to particular members with specific seniority or power, based on their discrete committee assignments; in other words, money from industry sectors lines up with lawmakers on the committees that oversee regulation of those sectors or with powerful leaders. Multiple studies have put the model to empirical test and repeatedly found it to be a functional model of understanding how donors direct money to congressmen.

Eric Cantor's legislative career lent itself to attracting PAC dollars, especially dollars from financial-sector actors. Upon his arrival in the House, he was placed on two committees (Financial Services and Ways and Means) that virtually guaranteed lots of campaign donations. These two committees exercise substantial oversight of the banking, insurance, and investment sectors. The Ways and Means Committee in particular is very powerful because it is where all tax legislation originates; for investors, it is a very important committee. This ensures that

PACs affiliated with firms in real estate, banking, insurance, and investment will direct money to lawmakers on those committees.

The refining of Cantor's support from these sectors is evident in the financial data from the Federal Election Commission (FEC). His most frequent donors also changed over time. Table 4.6 shows the top three industry groups that gave to Cantor's reelection bids from 2002 forward. In 2002, real-estate interests were the top-donating industry group for Cantor. His personal background in real estate created obvious connections, and they were also significant supporters of his state legislative campaigns in the 1990s. Real estate would give more and more to Cantor over time and remained among his top three donor groups through 2014. His second largest donor set in 2002 was pro-Israeli groups, followed by securities and investment groups. Securities and investment donors continued among Cantor's top three groups for every election cycle except 2006 and emerged as his top donor industry from 2010 forward. Insurance industry donors joined the top three contributing groups for Cantor in 2006 and stayed among his top donors through his last election.

Not only was Cantor able to amass a large amount of cash, he was also a profligate spender. As Figure 4.2, demonstrates, Cantor's spending in each electoral cycle, save his final one, increased at a very steep, linear rate. Despite never confronting a serious challenger in any of his first six election efforts, Cantor's spending culminated at nearly $8 million in the 2012 election cycle. Had he not lost in the 2014 primary, it is likely that his spending in the 2014 cycle would have exceeded the 2012 figure.

TABLE 4.6

Cantor's top three donor industry groups' contributions (in dollars), 2002–2014

	2002	2004	2006	2008	2010	2012	2014
Real Estate	106,000	165,000	194,000	325,000	401,000	394,000	434,000
Securities/ Investment	72,000	162,000		263,000	560,000	908,000	697,000
Insurance			187,000	261,000	312,000	362,000	255,000
Health			191,000				
Lawyers		134,000					
Pro-Israel	84,000						

Source: Compiled by the authors from data available at http://www.opensecrets.org.

As this review of Cantor's campaign finance history demonstrates, Cantor's shift away from the Seventh District occurred not only with regard to traditional measures of representative behavior but also with regard to his fundraising and spending behaviors during his time in office. By the time Wayne Powell challenged Cantor in 2012, it was not hard to see why Powell's campaign would select a theme of Cantor as being for sale. Yet despite all the fund-raising and the acquisition of power positions, Cantor was unable to forestall a challenge in 2014. And when he was challenged, his sizable fortune did little to help him.

The One Percent: Cantor's Other Cash

During his time in office, Cantor was amassing a personal fortune in addition to raising large sums of capital to support his political allies. His family was in real estate, and he had continued to run the business while in the House of Delegates. Table 4.7 presents Cantor's personal financial data to demonstrate that as his campaign and PAC coffers grew, so too did his personal fortune. In 2004, the first year for which we have net-worth data, until the year before he ascended to the House leadership (2010), his net worth increased from $3.6 million to $5.9 million.

TABLE 4.7
Eric Cantor's personal wealth

Year	Net worth (in millions)	House average (in millions)
2004	$3.6	$4.2
2005	$4.5	$4.5
2006	$4.2	$5.0
2007	$4.6	$5.7
2008	$4.3	$4.7
2009	$4.9	$5.0
2010	$5.9	$5.9
2011	$6.4	$6.4
2012	$9.3	$5.9
2013	$13.1	$7.2

Source: Compiled by the authors from data available at http://www.opensecrets.org.

This tracks roughly with the change in net worth of all members of the House (for all but two years in this time frame, Cantor ranked behind the average member in net worth). From 2011 forward, after he entered the leadership, his net worth increased substantially, from $5.9 million in 2010 to nearly $13.1 million in 2013, an increase of 120 percent in three years; the typical House member's net worth increased just 22 percent over the same time period.[63]

Cantor's personal wealth put him at a financial distance from the overwhelming majority of his constituents—as we note in Chapter 1, the median income in the Seventh District was approximately $69,000 in 2014. Cantor's financial circumstances found him 190 times as wealthy as the median family in the district; this did little to alter the image of Cantor as out of touch with his constituents and interested only in his own personal success.

A Challenger Emerges

Popular, well-liked members of Congress tend to draw fewer challenges in subsequent elections, and the challengers who do emerge tend to be less credible.[64] The ability to forestall future challenges results in part from the benefits of incumbency, including access to and contact with constituents, funds to travel to and from the district, and a staff apparatus that assists members with staying connected to their districts when they are away in Washington.[65] On the other hand, "candidate saliency," as Thomas Mann describes it, is a "double-edged sword for incumbents; while it can mean an enormous advantage in visibility over challengers, it can also spell disaster if the voters come to believe that their representative has some personal failings."[66] Thus, once elected, members of Congress work hard to protect and preserve a positive image with their constituencies.

As he had in every election before, Cantor survived the 2012 general election, but with just over 58.1 percent of voters supporting him. The newly drawn district had not stemmed the steady slide in his election results that had begun in 2006. And Cantor was headed back to work in as negative a climate for government as anyone could remember. A January 2013 poll conducted by Public Policy Polling (PPP) found that Congress had an approval rating of just 9 percent and that the public preferred root canals, lice, colonoscopies, traffic jams, used car salesmen, France, and the band Nickelback to the U.S. Congress.[67]

Cantor himself was also deeply unpopular. Letters to the editor in the *Richmond Times-Dispatch* called for his ouster and accused him of voting in his own interests rather than in the interests of the district.[68] A May 2013 survey by PPP found that just 26 percent of voters in Virginia had a favorable opinion of Eric Cantor, with 40 percent of voters expressing an unfavorable view. Even among voters who claimed to be "somewhat" or "very" conservative, Cantor's favorability ratings did not hit 50 percent statewide.[69] While the statewide survey did not look explicitly at Cantor's approval ratings in the Seventh District, the numbers were largely unchanged from a similar survey conducted by PPP in September 2012, demonstrating that Cantor's activities as House majority leader were not playing well in his home state.[70]

Moreover, Cantor's constituents were starting to realize that he was not paying much attention to them. He often substituted virtual town hall or constituency meetings for the real things. Just one month before the primary election, Cantor posted a photo on his website of him at his desk in his congressional office, engaging in a videoconference with school children in his district a mere 90 miles away. The caption on his website read: "Congressman Cantor chats with students from Glen Allen, Deep Run, and Maggie Walker High Schools." To be fair to Cantor, the demands of his position made it more difficult for him to return home during the week. During much of 2013, the Republican-led House of

Photo 4.2: In 2010, Eric Cantor would not agree to debate his opponent, Democrat Rick Waugh. Waugh's camp created "Wanted to Debate" flyers, modeled on Old West fugitive posters, which he distributed throughout the district in order to call attention to Cantor's unwillingness to engage with his opponent. The flyers neither inspired Cantor to agree to debate Waugh nor did much to bolster Waugh's electoral fortunes. Cantor defeated Waugh by a margin of 59–34 in the 2010 congressional midterm election

Source: Caroline County Democratic Committee

Representatives was engaged in a fight over the federal budget, and Cantor was on the front lines. The battle lines were similar to those that had been drawn during the 2011 debt limit crisis, with hard-line, tea party-backed members refusing to support the Republican leadership's efforts to work with President Obama to fund the government. But back in the district, Cantor was portrayed as both hyperpartisan and powerless to make the rank and file fall in line. His lack of in-person constituency relations did little to quell concern that he was overwhelmed in Washington.

As the budget fight raged, the tone of stories and editorials in the *Richmond Times-Dispatch* became more pointedly critical of Cantor. A September 18 column noted that

Cantor seemed unable to marshal the Republican conference in the House of Representatives to do the nation's business. The column pointed to his inability to hold the right wing on the Farm Bill and government appropriations, as well as expressed moderates' frustration over a pending transportation measure. The column went on to note that Cantor's leadership was imperiled by national activist groups such as the Club for Growth and "[t]he similarly minded Americans for Prosperity, [who] in an email to activists in Cantor's Henrico County-anchored 7th District, declared, 'We're not here to be friends with politicians. They're our employees!'"[71]

By the end of 2013, the climate was ripe for a serious challenger to emerge; in fact, two candidates emerged from Cantor's right to mount challenges to the leader in the upcoming primary election. Only one of these, David Brat, would mount a credible campaign. While Cantor had been engaged in the 2013 budget battle and the aftermath of the October government shutdown throughout fall 2013, Brat, a conservative professor of economics at Randolph-Macon College, had spent much of fall 2013 exploring the possibility of running for Cantor's seat. He had crunched the numbers, and in his estimation, he would need to win just 30,000 votes in the 2014 primary in order to unseat the incumbent.[72] He formally announced his candidacy on January 9, 2014, although word of his intention was circulated to the media several days prior.

The campaign launch was at the Adams Sports Mart—essentially a gas station/mini-mart—in conservative New Kent County. It drew just a handful of interested attendees. Brat was running to be "Eric Cantor's term limit," he said repeatedly throughout the campaign. In reflecting on the campaign's launch on its one-year anniversary, John Pudner, Brat's main campaign consultant, noted the following:

> We wanted to make the campaign announcement that he was running against Majority Leader Eric Cantor here in the small New Kent County in the southeast tip of the district for one simple reason: to make sure every citizen of the 7th district knew that they—not out-of-state donors—would be Dave's focus if they would elect him to represent them in Congress.[73]

SUMMARY

In his important work on congressional careers, political scientist John Hibbing notes that there is a direct relationship between the number of terms a member has served and his or her probability of losing in a primary election.[74] As members stay longer, they become more connected to the institution and less connected to their constituents. This is particularly true for members of the congressional leadership. A month prior to the 2014 primary election, Cantor's hometown newspaper, the *Richmond Times-Dispatch* had noted, "The closest people in New Kent County come these days to seeing their congressman, Eric Cantor, is his sagging 4-by-6 campaign sign on the south side of U.S. 60, just beyond a filling station."[75]

Assessments like these were common in Cantor's district during the last few years of his tenure—with good reason. Just weeks before the primary election, a large photo prominently displayed on the congressman's website depicted Cantor engaging in a video chat with high school students from his district, whose borders began only a few miles outside the metropolitan Washington, DC, area; these videoconferences were staples of Cantor's outreach to schools. A November 2013 story in the *Richmond Times-Dispatch* reported on a "Google Hangout" between Cantor and students at two local schools, noting that it was the sixth time he had engaged in such an activity.[76] Cantor's office touted the congressman's use of technology and cited the videoconferences as an example of Cantor using every available method to stay connected to his constituents. But in the absence of significant face time in the district, Cantor's use of videoconferencing technology was a reminder to many of the gulf between them and their representative.

Nearly everyone who followed politics in the Seventh District had a story that illustrated how disconnected Cantor was from the district: One local lobbyist recalled the time Cantor showed up to serve as the commencement speaker for a local high school and spent most of his time prior to the ceremony hunched over his Blackberry instead of talking to students, parents, and teachers. Residents of Cantor's West End neighborhood in Richmond complained about his security detail. Constituents complained of receiving automatically generated letters in response to complaints that did not address their concerns—if they received a response from his office at all. Writing for *Real Clear Politics* the day after Cantor's loss, Sean Trende, who had once lived in Cantor's district, noted this observation:

> I never once saw Cantor, not at county fairs, not at school board meetings, and not in the parades that would sometimes march past our house. . . . This isn't to say that Cantor never did these things, only that they weren't frequent enough to register.[77]

Four months after the June primary, an editorial on the eve of the 2014 general election that ran in the *Richmond Times-Dispatch* declared that the "likely cause" of Cantor's primary defeat "was the perception that he had spent too much time in

Washington and lost touch with his constituents back home."[78] To be sure, that was part of the reason Cantor lost. As Cantor ascended to the leadership, he began to neglect his congressional district. Cantor's increased focus on Washington distanced him from his constituents. Eventually, as his responsibilities in Washington consumed his time, Cantor began to miss scheduled appearances back home. But the *Times-Dispatch* understated the case. By his last term, constituency frustration over Cantor's apparent jockeying to become Speaker of the House of Representatives and his failure to keep promises to attend local events, such as the fall 2013 Republican Round Up, reached its apex.[79] By spring 2014, Seventh District voters were ready to replace their seven-term congressman. But even so, there were serious structural impediments to doing so—the district's partisan demography and the lack of a credible challenger chief among them. But as we will see in the next chapter, Cantor's own actions largely led to his undoing and propelled Brat to victory.

CHAPTER 5

The Primary Contest

"The prospect of a loss seemed to have gone uncontemplated in the Cantor camp."

—*Washington Post*[1]

The 2014 Seventh District Republican primary election unfolded within a political environment that, in hindsight, was almost certain to create problems for Eric Cantor. Cantor had won his previous election in 2012 with just 58 percent of the two-party vote, demonstrating that there was a sizable number of voters in the Seventh District that did not support him. Public opinion polls conducted throughout the first half of 2013 by Public Policy Polling also revealed the difficulties confronting Cantor. Statewide among Republicans, Cantor's favorability rating never got above 50 percent—it was 44 percent in January 2013 and 48 percent in July 2013.[2] Potentially as problematic for Cantor, however, was that by mid-2013, just 24 percent of independents across Virginia claimed to have a favorable opinion of Cantor, down from 31 percent just six months earlier. Cantor's statewide favorability among Democrats had dropped from 9 percent to 5 percent during the same time frame.[3]

In another state, the decrease in support particularly among Democrats and independents might be of little concern. But Cantor was running for reelection in Virginia, whose open primary rules meant that any registered voter could participate, whether a member or supporter of the Republican Party or not. Although we observed in the introduction to this volume that there was little evidence that open primaries lead to more incumbent primary defeats, that does not mean that a potential vulnerability does not exist. For example, Cynthia McKinney's 2002 primary defeat was often ascribed to crossover white Republican voting in Georgia's open primary (it was a possible contributing factor, but not the main reason why she lost).[4] In order for the vulnerability to be acted on, however, Cantor's political opponents would have to overcome substantial coordination issues involved in widespread strategic voting. As will become clear, they did undertake those efforts, and Cantor was in fact facing a concerted effort by conservatives and Democrats to unseat him.

Yet most observers—including the Cantor campaign itself—seemed to think that Cantor's reelection was assured. After all, the Seventh District had been drawn to protect Cantor; certainly there were not sufficient Democratic votes to create a problem for him, even if Democrats went to the polls. In fact, no credible Democratic challenger emerged for the Seventh District seat in Congress until the day of the Republican primary on June 10, 2014. The only Democrat to even hint at an interest in running for the seat during primary season was Mike Dickinson, who failed to file to run by the April 10, 2014, deadline and whose failure to file caused the Seventh Congressional District Democratic Committee to cancel a planned nominating convention on May 3, 2014.[5] Candidly, many local Democrats were relieved. Dickinson, a strip club owner who compared the tea party and National Rifle Association to the Ku Klux Klan, was not the type of candidate that Seventh District Democrats wanted to support.[6]

And there seemed to be little reason to worry about the emerging Republican primary challenger, David Brat. Brat had never run a campaign before. He had almost no money, little name recognition, and a small and inexperienced campaign staff. As Cantor surveyed the landscape at the time of Brat's announcement that he would seek the Republican nomination, he would almost certainly have seen nothing to be worried about.

In fact, incumbents generally have little to fear from upstart challengers or restive electorates. Granted, there have been some recent exceptions, as Robert Boatright explains in his 2013 book *Getting Primaried,* but by and large, most incumbents will not be affected in significant ways by a primary challenge. Writing a decade prior to the Cantor–Brat race, elections scholar Barry Burden described contested primary elections in the following way:

> Much of the time the dominant candidate need not worry terribly much about the policy preferences of voters. His "non-policy" advantages in skill, name recognition, campaign resources and stylistic fit with the district tend to overwhelm voters' ideological considerations. The literature on congressional elections shows that non-policy advantages like these are great enough to scare away strong opponents. In many cases the weaker candidate does not even have a large enough endowment to convey a persuasive message to the median voter. In short, lack of parity in the non-policy qualities of candidates will allow for more policy divergence, with the favored candidate having the luxury of remaining distant from the median voter.[7]

Burden might as well have been describing the Cantor campaign's approach to the 2014 primary election. Cantor had name recognition, a substantial war chest of campaign funds, significant prior campaign experience, the promise of an important leadership post, and—perhaps most importantly—had essentially selected his own voters through the 2011 redistricting process. But the Cantor team had not yet realized that Cantor had lost whatever "stylistic fit with the district" he had ever had. They did not recognize the threat that the ideological zeal of the increased tea party presence in the district posed to Cantor's reelection. The Cantor campaign saw little to worry about from local Democrats, and it perceived Brat as a nuisance, easily swatted away. Simply put, the campaign did not take him seriously.

For Brat's part, national interest groups were little engaged in his 2014 campaign. Unlike the situation that Boatright describes in *Getting Primaried*, in which extreme interest groups work to sponsor a partisan challenger to an incumbent, the national tea party organizations were not active on Brat's behalf. This is likely because the conventional wisdom held that Cantor would win his primary election and ultimately ascend to the Speakership. Moreover, without control of the House at stake—it was clear that the Republicans would hold the House and likely increase their seats in the chamber—there was little reason for national organizations to involve themselves in the Seventh District race. The national conservative interests undoubtedly weighed the costs and benefits of antagonizing the next Speaker of the House and decided against wading in. Thus, Cantor was not "primaried," at least not in the way that the term has been used by Boatright and others to describe a concerted effort on the part of national interests to unseat an incumbent. Additional evidence of this can be found in the collaboration between Democrats and conservative Republicans, who worked together in the 2014 election cycle, united by their shared interest in removing Eric Cantor from office.

Nevertheless, Brat and his campaign staff did a better job of identifying and managing the political climate in the district. But a focus exclusively on the 2014 primary election ignores the fact that the effort to unseat Eric Cantor began years before the 2014 Republican primary. The Brat campaign was able to win because it was aided by an unlikely coalition of long-frustrated Democrats and a motivated grassroots network of recently frustrated local tea party sympathizers. He was later aided by a handful of members of the national conservative pundit class, especially Laura Ingraham, who since 2011 had wanted the Republican leadership in Congress to do more to frustrate President Barack Obama's agenda.

Brat also would not have won without substantial assistance from the Cantor campaign's poorly executed strategy. Where in the end the Brat campaign managed to do everything right, the Cantor campaign seemed to do everything wrong from the very beginning of the contest. In this chapter, we unpack the stunning 2014 Republican primary election that unseated Eric Cantor. Because we have already described the unique features of Virginia's nominating process and Cantor's long shift away from his district, in this chapter we focus primarily on

Cantor's troubled campaign before moving on to discuss the development of Brat's challenger campaign. We demonstrate that the Cantor campaign's failure to identify Brat as a serious candidate, its failure to recognize the district's anti-Cantor sentiment, and its own significant campaign missteps combined with structural factors in Virginia's political environment to bring down a sitting House majority leader for the first time in history.

CANTOR'S MISSTEPS

In the entirety of his political career from 1991 to 2014, Eric Cantor faced a challenger in a primary election just twice before being challenged by David Brat in the 2014 primary. In 2000, Cantor narrowly defeated the Virginia state senator Stephen Martin by just 263 votes to become the Republican nominee for Congress. In 2012, Cantor was challenged by Floyd Bayne for renomination; he won by a much larger margin in that contest. Despite his significant electoral success over more than two decades of campaigning, Cantor and his team had little experience running primary campaigns. What the Cantor team lacked in experience, it made up for in money and confidence. At the end of 2013, Cantor had $1.9 million on hand.[8] Brat had $0. By the end of the first quarter of 2014, Cantor's cash advantage had grown to $2.5 million, compared with $90,765 raised by the Brat campaign.[9]

Cantor felt secure in the district, and he felt secure with his sizable fund-raising advantage. When Brat announced his candidacy on January 9, 2014, the Cantor campaign responded immediately with an e-mail to its mailing list that, remarkably, did not solicit funds, although it did encourage signing up to volunteer. It also included Cantor's first use of what would become his main critique of Brat—the statement that Brat was a liberal college professor. The e-mail read, in part, "Today a liberal economics professor announced he will challenge Congressman Cantor in the Republican primary. Professor David Brat has kicked off his campaign pretending to be a conservative, but don't be fooled."[10]

Calling Brat a "liberal economics professor" was Cantor's first mistake of the election campaign, and it came within hours of Brat's announcement. Those who knew Brat knew that he was conservative to the core; to them, Cantor's response to Brat's campaign was trite and lazy, suggesting that the Cantor campaign had not done any research about his new opponent. Within a few weeks, as word of Cantor's claims spread among Seventh District conservatives, the conservative base was incensed by what it viewed as yet another of Cantor's distortions. A post on the *Virginia Right!* blog called Cantor a "desperate, despicable liar."[11] Cantor doubled down on his claim, however. By April, he was running a television advertisement in the Richmond media market that made the same claim. He also sent correspondence, including anti-Brat mailings, into homes throughout the district during the first quarter of 2014, spending a total of $11,500 on postage to do so.[12]

By late April, media outlets, local blogs, and campaign fact-checking organizations weighed in: Brat was no liberal. Factcheck.org quoted three of Brat's colleagues in the Economics and Business Department at Randolph-Macon who assured the watchdog group that Brat was not a liberal. The *Hanover Conservative Caucus* blog posted images of the Cantor flyers—glossy, multipage "exposés"—and stated, "There isn't a shred of truth in these flyers."[13] Brat himself responded to the claims, telling the following to supporters at an April rally:

> If you don't have a record to run on, and if you don't have a record that you're proud of, then you have to stoop to that level. And that's what's going on with the U.S. majority leader. And that's a low level.[14]

The anti-Brat mail, combined with the April television ad, bought Brat more name recognition than he was capable of buying for himself. As the *National Journal* noted, Cantor "used much of his huge cash advantage . . . to launch a negative ad campaign that increased Brat's name recognition rather than hurting him."[15]

In addition to increasing Brat's name recognition, the Cantor attack ads alienated voters, many of whom had voted for him in previous elections. A *Richmond Times-Dispatch* article noted that Brat supporters were "outraged by Cantor's attempt to reduce Brat to a punch line." The article continued by quoting a New Kent County voter as saying, "Where [Cantor] has really upset me is with the untruths he's mailed out about Dave."[16] This echoed voter sentiment at Brat rallies and campaign events throughout the primary season. Cantor's mailings made Brat, a virtual unknown when he announced his candidacy, into a household name within a matter of weeks. But more than that, they raised doubts about Cantor's honesty. As one post concerning Cantor's misleading flyers noted, "If he lies about Dave Brat he's lying to you about everything else as well."[17] A volunteer at the Brat campaign headquarters noted that she had voted for Cantor in every previous election, but when she received the mailing from Cantor inviting her to look into Brat's background, she did and discovered, "Oh my God, Cantor is lying."[18]

Had the anti-Brat attack ads been just part of the Cantor strategy, they might not have been as important to the campaign dynamics as they ultimately were. But because Cantor had not anticipated a serious challenge, his campaign lacked a clear messaging strategy. Moreover, the antileadership and anti-incumbency sentiment that was prevalent throughout the district and throughout the country during the 2014 election cycle meant that Cantor was further constrained in his campaign communication. Anything that might have been touted as an accomplishment would be perceived by a large swath of the constituency as evidence that Cantor was a Washington insider too willing to compromise with Democrats and moderate Republicans. Cantor's lack of attentiveness to the district as he had ascended through the leadership ranks meant that he had little connection with or record of direct service to the district to run on.

As a result, Cantor had difficulty making his pitch to Seventh District voters, and he was on the defensive throughout most of the campaign. When Brat charged that Cantor refused to investigate the Obama administration's handling of the Benghazi incident, writing, "Eric Cantor's failure as House Majority Leader to support Congressman Frank Wolf's (R-VA) bill to establish a full investigation into this crucial matter shows a clear lack of leadership,"[19] Cantor responded with a mailing that claimed he was "fighting for the truth about Benghazi."[20] When Brat hit him as being soft on amnesty for undocumented immigrants, Cantor fired back with mailers that read, "Conservative Republican Eric Cantor is Stopping the Obama Reid Plan to Give Illegal Aliens Amnesty."[21] Throughout April 2014 as Brat hit Cantor on a range of issues—Obamacare, Benghazi, taxes, and the targeting of conservatives by the IRS—Cantor's mailings increasingly focused on Cantor's efforts in these areas. By mid-May and early June as the election crept closer, Cantor's mailings almost exclusively focused on issues that Brat had been talking about during his upstart campaign. There was no effort by the Cantor campaign to discuss Cantor's legislative accomplishments or to otherwise define Cantor relative to his constituents in the Seventh District.

"Don't Piss Off the Grassroots"

In Congress and in previous elections, Cantor was viewed as a tactician. Never quite comfortable with constituency relations, Cantor's history of political and electoral success resulted in part from his extraordinary ability to make and keep important political allies, especially within the House of Representatives. On Capitol Hill, he was known for his keen grasp of House procedure and an ability to get things accomplished. These qualities did not necessarily translate into admiration from his constituents, but Cantor benefitted from a lack of quality challengers during his 14 years in office—which in turn was likely the result of the perception for most of his career that his standing in Washington would make him unbeatable.

Cantor's prowess at gerrymandering allowed him to cherry-pick his constituents, particularly following the 2010 decennial census. This should have forestalled a serious challenge for the next several election cycles. But in 2012, he won by his smallest margin since winning election to the House in 2000.

Following that relatively narrow victory, Cantor, along with his campaign team, should have been looking for ways to strengthen support for his 2014 reelection campaign. His own professional circumstances made doing so difficult. His position as majority leader meant that he had less time to spend in the district, so personal efforts to reacquaint himself with his constituents and make a case for himself were not feasible. And with Tim Kaine's victory over George Allen in the 2012 U.S. Senate election and Terry McAuliffe's victory over Ken Cuccinelli in the 2013 Virginia gubernatorial race, Cantor also became the most senior Republican elected official in Virginia. State and local Republican officeholders were expecting him to assist them to win elections, but he was not in a position to stump for them any more than he was in a position to spend significantly more time in his own district. Instead, ever the tactician, Cantor and his team turned to more strategic means of influencing election outcomes: slating.

Ordinarily, the Republican party in Virginia allocates delegates or votes to its conventions on a proportional basis, relative to what it calls "Republican voting strength" in a particular jurisdiction.[22] "Slating" is a parliamentary maneuver in which a majority of rank-and-file partisans in attendance at a mass meeting can elect a "slate" of like-minded partisans to cast all of a jurisdiction's votes for the purpose of selecting a party leader or nominee for elective office at a subsequent convention. This is not a spontaneous move but instead a well-orchestrated effort by a party faction to use the party's rules to its advantage. If enough of a single faction's supporters attend, such that the faction holds a majority in the room, the faction's leaders can propose to substitute a predrafted list of candidates to cast votes at the upcoming convention in lieu of the sometimes hundreds of votes to which the local party might be entitled. In essence, slating eliminates proportional representation for delegate selection and replaces it with a winner-take-all system.

The impetus for the Cantor-backed slating efforts was the 2013 Virginia Republican gubernatorial nominating process, during which supporters of conservative candidate Ken Cuccinelli successfully took control of the commonwealth's Republican Central Committee and forced the gubernatorial nominating process to take place at a convention rather than through a state-run primary election.[23] Cuccinelli lost the general election, in large part because he was perceived to be too conservative even for many Republicans in Virginia.[24]

Following on Cuccinelli's loss, Cantor worked through his Young Guns (YG) organization to mobilize loyal Republican partisans in the mainstream. The goal was to ensure that moderate Republicans would be able to control the congressional district conventions, which ultimately would control the selection processes for state conventions. Ultimately, Cantor and his supporters were seeking to control the statewide nominating processes that would be essential to securing electoral victories for Republican general election candidates. One account explained it in the following way:

> "Slating" was a procedural move by [Cantor political adviser Ray] Allen and YG operatives to push out grassroots delegates to congressional district conventions that vote on seats to the state central committee. The central committee is the body that decides whether statewide candidates are elected by a convention or primary. Cantor wanted to restore primaries and get rid of conventions to protect his allies in the state, as well as his own seat.[25]

The *Richmond Times-Dispatch* concurred, noting, "The current infighting, in which Cantor loyalists figure prominently, is a preliminary to the main event in 2016: the battle for the GOP's governing body, the central committee. It will be concurrent with the presidential race in purple Virginia."[26]

The slating efforts took place primarily in March 2014. As the *Richmond Times-Dispatch* noted, the infighting got "vicious" at times during the monthlong series of party mass meetings. In Virginia Beach, which is not part of the Seventh Congressional District, the slating effort successfully led to 552 prospective delegates being replaced by 32 handpicked partisans. Opponents of the slating procedure claimed that the slate's supporters had tried to "steal" the election; tea party supporters were especially angry.[27] In Henrico County, which is part of the Seventh District, proponents of the slating technique were thwarted. At that county's Republican mass meeting on March 24, establishment party member and county GOP chairman Don Boswell was defeated for election to chair the mass meeting by a vote of 164–170. Upon his defeat, conservative Russ Moulton from the First Congressional District was nominated and elected to the meeting chairmanship by a vote of 178–173.[28]

The outcry over slating by the press and conservative blogosphere in Virginia was enormous. In a post on the conservative *Bearing Drift* blog titled "Don't Piss Off the Grassroots," writer D. J. Spiker declared the following:

> [W]hile there were mild rumblings and grumblings about Cantor prior to the Virginia Beach slating fiasco, this was an [*sic*] the first shot in the "war on grassroots" by YG, and so far as the grassroots were concerned, this was a declaration of war by Cantor. Whether or not Cantor had anything to do with it is a point of debate, yet by extension of the actions of his consultants, Eric Cantor was now even more of a target.[29]

And yet as the conservative grass roots were becoming increasingly infuriated with Cantor, the campaign seemed little concerned, even when confronted with growing evidence of the electorate's discontent. Their rage boiled over at the Seventh District's convention on May 10, 2014, when the delegates narrowly elected a tea party-backed district chairman over Cantor's longtime friend and preferred candidate, Linwood Cobb. The Cobb and Cantor supporters reportedly booked all the meeting rooms in the Short Pump Hilton, where the convention was held, forcing Brat to rally his supporters at the HoneyBaked Ham store down the street.[30]

Throughout the primary, the Cantor campaign could not escape charges that it was manipulating voters and the electoral system by spreading falsehoods about the primary challenger and by meddling with the rules of the game to make it more difficult for Brat to win. Even the minor nuisance of booking all the hotel rooms in the convention hotel contributed to the narrative that Cantor was more concerned with his own power than with representing his constituents or with promoting a fair election. Remarkably, however, the campaign seemed unfazed by the negative publicity that the slating scandal and Cantor's absence from the district seemed to be generating. The Cantor campaign continued to rely on its own internal polling that put Cantor ahead of Brat by 34 points as late into the contest as mid-May, even as public polls showed the race narrowing.[31] When confronted with polling data just two weeks prior to the primary, Cantor's campaign adviser Ray Allen told the media, "We're going to win by a much stronger margin . . . our internal polling shows that."[32]

Until the very end, the Cantor campaign seemed to be going through the motions, disconnected from the reality of what was happening at home in the district and from the looming impact of its own actions. Cantor himself spent nearly all his time during this crucial period in Washington, DC.

THE BRAT CAMPAIGN

Brat's announcement that he was running for Congress was not entirely surprising. He had wanted to run for a General Assembly seat in 2012 but was not selected by local party leaders widely perceived as Cantor faithful, who instead chose the son of Tom Farrell, the CEO of local energy giant Dominion Resources. Dominion, through its political action committee, was the top contributor to Eric Cantor's campaigns between 1999 and 2014, and Cantor's backing of Peter Farrell was widely considered to have tipped the scale toward him and away from Brat in 2012's closed-door contest to be nominated to replace state delegate Bill Janis. By many accounts, Brat's decision to run for Congress in 2014 was fueled by his anger at local party elites.[33]

But not only was Brat looking to redeem himself from the nominating process in 2012; he was also hearing from conservatives throughout the district that they wanted him to run. Because of his role as chairman of the Department of

Economics and Business at Randolph-Macon College and his outspoken conservative opinions, Brat had been a guest at local tea party meetings, and conservative leaders began to encourage him to consider running for office.[34] One, Gerry Baugh, had been encouraging Brat to run for office from as early as 2010, according to the *Chesterfield Monthly*:

> Baugh observed during his two-year term as leader of the Mechanicsville Tea Party that local conservatives had grown restless with Cantor over his inability to de-fund Obamacare, his unwillingness to put the brakes on government spending and his support for a Republican version of the DREAM Act. Baugh believed Cantor could be beaten and thought a little-known economics professor from Randolph-Macon College was just the man to do it. Baugh brought in Dave Brat to speak with members of the Mechanicsville Tea Party for the first time in 2010. Baugh also continued to lobby Brat to challenge Cantor, but Brat was on the fence and didn't decide to run for the 7th District seat until four years later.[35]

Brat did, in fact, feel victimized by what he experienced as a lack of openness to outsiders in the Republican Party in Virginia when he sought elective office for the first time in 2012. He used this anger to fuel his 2014 congressional primary supporters' antipathy toward Cantor. In an April 2014 speech to supporters at the Bass Pro Shop in Ashland, Brat used his own experience to criticize Cantor and his supporters as being unwilling to consider new ideas and as hostile to new people entering public office. Using the Virginia Republican Creed's plank of supporting equal opportunities to highlight Cantor's role in slating, Brat noted the following:

> I am not going around the state slating people and kicking people out of the democratic process. I ran for office two years ago, and the machine had something to say to me then, the machine kicked me out of the process.[36]

For good measure, he alleged that Cantor was too busy pandering to wealthy liberals to agree to debate Brat during the primary season:

> You want to know where he was [when he refused]? He was on Amelia Island at the Ritz-Carlton in Florida, meeting with Soros-backed liberal folks who want to moderate the Republican Party and slate and kick off Republicans and conservatives.[37]

The crowd booed. Like Brat, they were good and angry with Cantor for closing ranks and pushing conservatives out of the party.

But if Brat had been thinking about running and quietly amassing support for his candidacy for years, it did not show—at least outwardly. His early campaign appearances brought only a few curious Seventh District constituents. He had no financial resources, which required his campaign to deploy a "low economic over-head" model for spending. Brat's campaign was headquartered in a small office; the décor consisted primarily of a large American flag tacked behind the front desk. The campaign recycled handmade signs at rallies and events, and these were stacked on the floor, reminding visitors that "Dishonest ads = Dishonest politi-cians," that Cantor was "1 of 28 republicans who gave Obama a blank check," and that "Eric wants to be your speaker, Dave wants to be your Congressman."[38] Brat's campaign manager, Zachary Werrell, had graduated from college just eight months earlier. In an interview with his college alumni magazine, Werrell tried to explain his hiring:

> I am not sure whether my hiring had more to do with my credentials and personal characteristics or with the fact that no Republican political opera-tive in their right mind would take on who many considered to be the most powerful Republican in the Congress.[39]

Although Brat did not make a formal announcement of his candidacy until January 2014, Werrell began working for Brat in November 2013.[40]

The Bipartisan Effort

What Brat lacked in the way of formal experience he made up for with the support of both conservatives on the right and Democrats on the left who shared an interest in ousting Eric Cantor. Democrats saw in Brat a challenger they could vote for in order to oust a member of Congress that they despised. If Brat won, their thinking went, his lack of experience might pave the way for a Democrat to prevail in the general election. (That there was no viable Democrat in the race until June 10 did not seem to be a deterrent to this line of thinking.) For tea party supporters, Brat represented an ideal candidate—a conservative economist with a background in theology. He, too, had been burned by the backroom political deals cut among Republican Party leaders; he was one of them.

As conservative tea partiers pushed Brat to run, Democrats were also closing ranks and uniting behind their desire to oust Cantor from office—and they had convinced themselves that they could do it. In a November 25, 2012, post on the Democrats' *Blue Virginia* blog, columnist Eric Steigleder celebrated the reelec-tion of President Barack Obama and the election of Democrat Tim Kaine to the U.S. Senate. But he noted the presence of a "problem named Eric Cantor," writing, "Eric Cantor makes headlines more for his anti-woman, anti-gay, anti-compromise cry-baby antics than for any significant legislative accomplishment. Lucky for us, while Mr. Cantor is a significant impediment to progress, he's also exceedingly beatable."[41]

Behind the scenes, some Democrats were already working with conservative allies to orchestrate a Cantor loss. In a *Washington Post* op-ed just three days following the 2014 primary election, Brian Umana, who had managed Democrat Rick Waugh's 2010 general election campaign against Eric Cantor, described a series of meetings between Republican and Democratic activists, who met in various locations in Richmond for the purpose of discussing their mutual interest in removing Cantor from office. "At first, we were suspicious that one side was trying manipulate the other, but soon we developed a sense of trust over our shared frustrations with Cantor," Umana wrote. He then went on to describe the range of strategies the activists discussed, including capitalizing on the local tea party groups' grassroots mobilization efforts. The meetings of this bipartisan group of anti-Cantor activists solidified the alliance between Seventh District conservatives and Democrats for the purpose of defeating Cantor. According to Umana, "We shared data-science techniques for voter targeting and for evaluating the relative cost of earning the votes of different types of voters." Among those present at these meetings, according to Umana, was Republican Tammy Parada, who would go on to work for the Brat campaign.[42]

Running from Behind

As ready to support a new face as Seventh District voters were, Brat had a lot of ground to make up. Zachary Werrell, Brat's campaign manager, acknowledged that Brat could not have won were it not for Cantor's blunders, which played into the Brat campaign strategy. That strategy was to capitalize on voter anger at Cantor by reinforcing the image of him as being out of touch and at a distance from the district. When Cantor immediately launched his "liberal college professor" ads on *Fox News* and in e-mails to Seventh District voters, the Brat campaign used Cantor's words against him. They were careful never to call him a liar; instead, the strategy was to "amplify Cantor's attack ads as false and misleading," which would encourage people to question what else Cantor might be distorting.[43]

· Tapping into existing grassroots networks was also an important part of the Brat strategy. Werrell called the grassroots networks "the foundation to our success."[44] Local conservatives had been mobilized in 2012 in support of Republican presidential candidate Mitt Romney and again in 2013 in support of conservative Republican gubernatorial candidate Ken Cuccinelli. The Brat campaign benefitted from the fact that these were committed and trained campaign workers, "not fresh volunteers hired by a consulting firm."[45] According to Werrell, "This political climate, this network of people, existed with Romney and Cuccinelli. They were ready to win . . . we became their candidate."[46] Throughout the campaign, Brat relied heavily on traditional grassroots campaign tactics, especially personal phone calls from so-called Brat Pack volunteers, rather than "robo-calls" paid for with campaign funds.[47]

Brat benefitted as well from name recognition he received from national conservative pundits. In early January, Doc Thompson interviewed Brat on his radio show and begged him to defeat Cantor. On April 17, Ann Coulter announced that she would endorse Brat; Laura Ingraham followed soon after.[48] It was Ingraham that took the most interest in Brat. As *Politico* reported, "Ingraham featured Brat on her show several times, championing his anti-establishment message and attacking Cantor for what she called his 'immigration amnesty' policy—just when Republicans in Washington were fretting about the party's trouble attracting Hispanic voters."[49]

The Ingraham Rally

One week prior to primary election day, Ingraham appeared at a rally for Brat at Dominion Country Club in Glen Allen, Virginia. The rally, which also featured conservative former presidential candidate Alan Keyes, was expected to draw a modest crowd. The campaign hoped for 100 people. Instead, more than 650 people packed the country club, forcing the event to move from its original room within the club to the larger atrium. So many people arrived that latecomers had to park across the street in another subdivision. Inside the club, guests pressed against the balcony railing and strained to get a glimpse of Brat and Ingraham in the columned, semicircular room. As Photo 5.1 reveals, the event was standing room only.

Ingraham spoke for nearly 30 minutes. She opened by joking that attendees risked Internal Revenue Service audits and National Security Administration wiretaps. Then she went after Cantor, whom she said President Obama should have traded to the Taliban in exchange for U.S. soldier Bowe Bergdahl just days before the rally. "I wouldn't come down here unless I thought this was critically important, if I didn't support Dave 100 percent," Ingraham said. She criticized Cantor for serving the "donor class" instead of

Photo 5.1: Standing room only at Dave Brat's rally with Laura Ingraham

Photo credit: David Elliot Meyer

his constituents and slapped at him for his "insane idea of engaging this President," whom she alleged to have broken the law and lied to the American people.[50]

The Ingraham rally was widely perceived as a turning point for the Brat campaign. In the days following the rally, his campaign headquarters buzzed with activity as scores of new volunteers appeared to offer support. The Cantor campaign alleged that Ingraham's presence demonstrated that he was "running his campaign from Washington" and that "[t]his election will be decided by Virginia voters, not Washington D.C. elites"—ironic responses given the perceptions of Cantor's near-total absence from the district during the campaign.[51]

Brat had calculated that he would need just 25,000 to 30,000 votes to win the primary election—in 2012, just 44,000 voters had turned out in the contested Cantor-Bayne Republican primary—and during his speech at the rally with Laura Ingraham, he addressed the crowd:

> If we have 500 people in this room tonight, and I only need about 25,000 votes to win, do the math on that. You all go get 50 people. No, you can't get the 50 people in this room. You all go get 50 new people and I'm your new congressman.[52]

The Ingraham rally was a turning point for the Brat campaign. After her appearance, the campaign headquarters buzzed with unprecedented energy. "We've been getting checks and donations from Texas to Minnesota," one of Brat's volunteers shared with Elliot Meyer. "People just keep coming in, asking for [yard signs] and how they can help out."[53]

ELECTION DAY

Perhaps nothing summarizes the differences between the Cantor and Brat campaigns better than a description of their activities on June 10, primary election day. The morning of the primary election, Federal Election Commission filings confirm that Cantor paid $432 in catering costs at a Starbucks on Capitol Hill—reportedly one of his regular monthly gatherings with lobbyists who spent $2,500 for the privilege of attending.[54] Brat spent the morning at polling places throughout the district, greeting voters and encouraging them to cast their votes for him.

Turnout was significantly higher than anyone expected on that election day, with more than 65,000 votes cast. Shortly after the polls closed on election night, returns showed Brat well ahead of Cantor, and just an hour after poll closing, the Associated Press declared Brat to be the winner. Brat won 36,105 votes districtwide—far more than the 25,000 votes he had hoped to garner—compared with Cantor's 28,912 votes.[55] Eric Cantor had been defeated, and the loss sent shockwaves rippling throughout central Virginia and Washington, DC. Cantor conceded with a brief speech; Brat made a jubilant victory speech in which he thanked God, declared it "the happiest moment obviously in my life," and thanked his supporters, saying, "The reason we won this campaign is because dollars do not vote, you do."[56]

National media immediately began to report on the loss, declaring it to be the result of Cantor's willingness to work with the White House on immigration reform. Immigration and especially the idea of "amnesty" became the national media's narrative to explain why Cantor lost, although immigration reform was just one of the many issues that had been raised by the Brat campaign throughout the spring. But with the only significant national attention Brat's campaign had garnered coming from Laura Ingraham's vocal opposition to immigration reform both before and during the campaign event the week before, the national media seized on the subject as the explanation for the Cantor loss. They were, of course, wrong.

Higher-than-expected turnout was another part of the story. Turnout in primary elections, especially for the congressional midterms, tends to be low. In the 2014 primary, nearly 50 percent more voters went to the polls in the 2014 primary election than had voted in the 2012 primary election between Cantor and challenger Floyd Bayne. But while more voters went to the polls, Cantor had difficulty mustering a majority of votes in most of the precincts he won previously. In 2012's primary election, Cantor won an average of 65 percent of the two-party vote across the 181 precincts that remained in the Seventh District during the 2014 primary election. Cantor won on average just 44 percent of the two-party vote in these same precincts in 2014. More voters went to the polls, and in most cases, those voters supported Dave Brat.

In addition, Cantor received the fewest votes in 2014 from the 2010 precincts in which he previously had the greatest amount of electoral success. The same group of 181 precincts that had supported Cantor by nearly two to one over his Democratic challenger in 2010 were far less favorable to him in 2014's contested party primary. Cantor's poor showing is starkly evident when his precinct-by-precinct share of the vote in 2014 is compared against precinct-level general election results from 2010, the last congressional midterm election. As Figure 5.1 demonstrates, in the vast majority of precincts in which he won by a two-to-one or three-to-one margin in 2010, Cantor struggled to reach a 50 percent share of the vote against Dave Brat in 2014. Each small circle represents one precinct. The circles in the lower right-hand quadrant in Figure 5.1 represent precincts in which Eric Cantor

FIGURE 5.1
Shifting support for Eric Cantor from 2010 to 2014

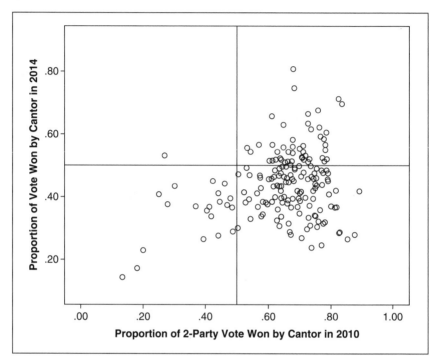

Each small circle represents one precinct. The circles in the lower right-hand quadrant represent precincts in which Eric Cantor won more than 50 percent of the vote for Congress in 2010 but less than 50 percent of the vote for Congress in the 2014 Republican primary.

Source: Compiled by authors from Virginia State Board of Elections results.

won more than 50 percent of the vote for Congress in 2010 but less than 50 percent of the vote for Congress in the 2014 Republican primary. It is clear that while a majority of precincts elected Cantor by a wide margin (greater than 55 percent) in 2010, very few of those same precincts mustered even majority support for him in 2014.

Democratic Crossover Voting

Another part of the explanation proffered by the Cantor camp and some media outlets was that Democrats had crossed party lines to support Brat. Analysis of this question began almost immediately following the election. When called out for their wildly inaccurate polling results, the polling firm hired by Cantor to poll for him during the primary election, McLaughlin and Associates, commissioned a postelection poll at its own expense. In the follow-up memorandum issued by McLaughlin on June 18, McLaughlin noted that the original late-May survey commissioned by the Cantor campaign had drawn its sample only from Seventh District residents who had voted in a recent primary election. To determine why the primary election results were so far removed from the predicted outcome, the mid-June sample was drawn from a more inclusive population that included voters in recent general elections or primary elections for either party.

The differences in the surveys were striking. The mid-June study revealed that a sizeable proportion of the voters that turned out in the primary election were Democrats or independents. McLaughlin concluded the following:

> It is now clear that Eric Cantor's national standing gave the race a lot of local interest among many more voters than just past Republican primary voters, including politically interested Independents and Democrats as well. Without a parallel Democrat primary, this election was very similar to a wide-open blanket-style primary. It created an organic turnout of new voters not included in our previous poll of past primary voters.[57]

McLaughlin estimated that 8,300 Democrats and independents turned out to vote in the Republican primary, enough to decide the election in Brat's favor.[58]

Of course, these are extrapolations from a relatively small number of survey respondents. Nevertheless, these results indicate that there is likely some truth to the claim that Democrats engaged in strategic crossover voting aimed at ousting Eric Cantor. Anecdotally, local Democrats boasted to friends and on social media that they had cast their votes for Brat, as part of the "ABC—Anybody But Cantor" movement throughout the district. Perhaps the most visible call for Democrats to cross party lines and vote in the Republican primary came from Democrat Ben "Cooter" Jones, Cantor's Democratic opponent in the 2002 general election, who also encouraged Democrats to turn out. In an open letter originally published by the *Huffington Post* the morning of the election, Jones wrote the following:

> [B]y voting for David Brat in the Seventh District Republican primary, we Democrats, independents, and Libertarians can make a big difference. . . . Cantor should not be rewarded with another term. Every Seventh District voter, Republican, Democrat, Libertarian and Independent can take an historic action on Tuesday, June 10.[59]

TABLE 5.1
2014 Republican primary precinct-level results by 2012 presidential election results

			Presidential winner in 2012		
			Obama	Romney	Total
2014 precinct winner	Brat	Number of precincts won	47	115	162
		Percent of precincts won	82.5	67.6	71.4
	Cantor	Number of precincts won	10	55	65
		Percent of precincts won	17.5	32.4	28.6
Total			57	170	227

$X^2 = 4.581$ (1df) $p = .032$
Source: Compiled by authors from Virginia State Board of Election.

While the literature on it has suggested that crossover voting, when it occurs, is done sincerely rather than strategically, evidence from the precinct-level election returns suggested that many Democrats did turn out. As we demonstrate in Table 5.1 using data compiled from the Virginia State Board of Elections, Brat won in a remarkable 82.5 percent of the Seventh District precincts that Obama won in 2012. This, combined with anecdotal and general election exit poll evidence, provides an indication of the extent to which Democrats turned out during the 2014 Republican primary and voted against Eric Cantor.

SUMMARY

When the media reported on Eric Cantor's loss in the June 10, 2014, Republican primary, most political observers were stunned that the Seventh District would reject the second-most powerful man in the U.S. House of Representatives. But few of Eric Cantor's constituents felt that they benefitted from Cantor's prominent position. Their view was that it made little difference whether they were represented by a member of the House leadership or by a virtual unknown since Cantor was so rarely seen in the district. On primary election day, the voters expressed their preference for the candidate that they had seen in their neighborhoods, at their local political gatherings, and at events throughout the district.

The painstaking gerrymandering, the efforts to control the local Republican meetings, and the slick, negative campaign against his opponent were not enough to propel Cantor to victory. All three of these tactics backfired on Cantor.

The more conservative voters who were added when district lines were redrawn did not know him and were unimpressed by his leadership role in Congress. His efforts to reclaim the Republican Party by stacking local meetings with establishment-backed candidates left him vulnerable to claims that he was elitist and antidemocratic. His campaign literature lacked a discernible message about his accomplishments and focused instead on painting his opponent as something he was not. The result was that longtime supporters questioned Cantor's honesty.

When the primary election results were tallied, the main media narrative was that Cantor was undone by his failure to take a hard-line stance against amnesty for those who had crossed America's borders illegally. But the slaying of Eric Cantor resulted from a much more complicated set of circumstances. To be sure, the conservative grass roots in the district were concerned about amnesty, but they were more concerned about what they perceived as Cantor's leadership of the Republican establishment's efforts to disenfranchise conservatives in the Seventh District. Their fury over slating led the local grass roots—which were highly organized and well trained after the Mitt Romney and Ken Cuccinelli campaigns—to work doggedly on behalf of David Brat. At the same time, local Democrats believed for the first time since his election in 2000 that they had an opportunity to unseat Eric Cantor. They too were highly motivated, and evidence suggested that they went to the polls in large numbers in order to express their discontent. These Democratic votes were not likely sufficient to tip the scales in favor of Brat on their own, but a large number of Democratic votes were cast for Brat as Democrats sought to unseat Cantor.

CHAPTER 6

The Aftermath

"We have seen a major uptick in the intensity of the grass roots and they are clearly reinvigorated."

—Ken Cuccinelli[1]

Immediately following Cantor's defeat, questions began to surface about whether Cantor would seek to run as an independent or write-in candidate in the November election. News of a Democratic Party nominee had not yet spread widely, and there was speculation that as voters came to learn how conservative Brat was, they would decide they actually preferred Cantor. It soon became clear that Virginia's election rules would make it difficult for Cantor to get his name on the ballot. Cantor himself seemed to foreclose the possibility almost immediately, although that did not stop the speculation from occurring. Cantor's announcement the day after his loss that he would step down as majority leader also prompted conjecture that he might be stepping down to pursue an independent bid for reelection. Within a few weeks, Cantor made it clear that despite vowing to serve as the Seventh District's representative until the end of the 113th Congress he would not serve out the remainder of his final term. This left the Seventh District without a representative in the U.S. House for nearly three months, from the time that Cantor stepped down on August 18 until his successor, Dave Brat, was sworn in on November 13, 2014.

In this chapter, we explore the chaotic aftermath of the Cantor–Brat primary election. Brat's victory set in motion a media narrative that served mostly to obscure rather than illuminate the issues that doomed Cantor's reelection bid. Both in the Seventh District and on Capitol Hill, Cantor's loss raised questions about his future plans and the future of the Republican leadership in the House of Representatives. Cantor's decision to step down from his post as majority leader sent ambitious Republican hopefuls scrambling to secure endorsements from their colleagues and from powerful outside groups. For eight days in mid-June, it was unclear whether the House Republicans would select a more moderate or a more conservative majority leader. When Cantor then decided to leave Congress with nearly five months remaining in his term, Virginia officials scrambled to figure out how to fill the remainder of Cantor's term. The campaigns to replace Cantor ramped up even more as it became clear that the candidates were competing not only for a seat in the 114th Congress but also to take office in November 2013 to replace Cantor. We detail this tumultuous period in this chapter, paying particular attention to the implications of Cantor's loss for the Republican Party leadership in the House and for the nascent grassroots conservative movements taking hold in states across the country.

THE MEDIA (AND EVERYONE ELSE) MISSED THE SIGNS

As we have documented already, one of the key messages of the Cantor loss is that incumbents who lose touch with the district cannot hope to win reelection. Almost no one within the district was enamored of Eric Cantor by the time the 2014 primary election rolled around. Conservatives in the district believed he had used them (in Virginia, and also elsewhere) to build a Republican majority, then had abandoned them when they insisted upon being heard in the House of Representatives. Establishment Republican voters felt that they were represented by an absentee member of Congress more interested in his own power than in his constituents. Long-suffering Democrats were ready to seize on any possible vulnerability in the hopes of removing the Republican leader from office.

Yet on election night, the most commonly expressed reaction to the Cantor loss was shock. Implicit in these messages of the Brat victory as "shocking" was the suggestion that there was no way that anyone could have seen it coming. What is more, the media's nonstop analysis of Cantor's failed reelection bid in the days and weeks after the fact meant that there was little time for pundits to engage in self-reflection or to analyze why they found themselves so surprised by the Brat victory. As the previous chapter made clear, there were plenty of signs, but they went ignored.

Part of why the media's political analysts and the Cantor campaign itself missed the big story of the impending Brat victory was because they over-relied on traditional sources and outmoded ways of thinking about elections. The Cantor team did what it had always done—for example, it focused on the *Richmond Times-Dispatch* and traditional media throughout the campaign—and assumed that the voters that had always supported Cantor would do so once again. In contrast, the Brat campaign was aggressively beating the bushes to identify potential new voters and to figure out how to tailor its messages to pique and hold their interest.

One of the Brat campaign's few expenditures was to test "rVotes," a voter-targeting system. rVotes was developed by political consultant Steve Adler, who had helped to develop the Voter Activation Network, a voter database preferred by Democratic candidates and consultants. According to *Campaigns & Elections* magazine, Adler constructed a voter-targeting universe for Brat based on data gathered from various tea party organizations. These databases extended existing microtargeting techniques to incorporate a variety of latent indictor codes for voters who would be a good pro-Brat/anti-Cantor voter, regardless of party. Adler told *Campaigns & Elections* the following:

> Now, suddenly [Brat] had access to hundreds if not thousands of different codes. Funky stuff like anything from "voter owns only American cars" to "known patriot group member" to "voter flies a flag" or "voter has an NRA sticker on their car." They were aggressively using the system to microtarget. [2]

Adler provided the service at a deep discount during the primary election in exchange for a more lucrative general election contract from Brat, assuming he won.

Brat was also aided by the significant presence of right-wing blogs in the Virginia Seventh District. Blogs such as Radtke's *Bull Elephant* or the *Virginia Right!* have come to be the go-to news source for disaffected conservatives who view the mainstream press in the district as in the back pocket of establishment interests. The Brat campaign understood this and worked from the beginning to be accessible to the citizen journalists who provide content for these sites. The Cantor campaign, in contrast, focused its outreach efforts on traditional media. It made little effort to court conservative activists—on the contrary, it appeared to go out of its way to marginalize them. The Republican establishment's slating efforts were part of this, to be sure, but beyond slating, the Cantor campaign did little to reach out to the local tea party-affiliated groups that were active in the district.

This "we've-always-done-it-this-way" attitude also affected the quality of the polling commissioned and relied on by the Cantor campaign to the candidate's detriment throughout the entirety of the race. Using sampling parameters set by the Cantor campaign, Cantor's pollster John McLaughlin predicted a large win. But as McLaughlin observed after the election, his team had been polling medium-propensity Republican voters—people who had voted in at least one of the last three GOP primaries. The sampling frame was built around generally loyal Republicans, who are most often older voters. Of course, if one is facing a potential revolt, surveys of loyalists are not likely to reveal the insurgents.[3]

As a corollary, we should note that the same danger that befell Cantor's pollster exists for the media, campaign consultants, and political observers in general. Relying on outdated campaigning and polling techniques can result in missed signs of trouble. Indeed, there is evidence that Virginia's incumbent U.S. senator Mark Warner ran into a similar problem with his polling, which suggested he would easily defeat Republican challenger Ed Gillespie in the 2014 general election. Just days before the election, *Real Clear Politics* predicted Warner would win by nearly a 10-point margin.[4] As a matter of fact, Warner only won reelection by 17,727 votes out of more than 2.1 million cast. Ironically, one explanation for why the pollsters were so far off in predicting the Cantor and Warner races is that the predicted incumbent wins by large margins suppressed turnout among those voters inclined to support the current officeholders. That is a difficult proposition to test, but it is clear that when a primary appears to be headed for low turnout, a selective voter-targeting and mobilization effort can break the turnout model for the polls and render them effectively meaningless.

Because Brat was employing sophisticated microtargeting techniques, his campaign had the opportunity to exploit two avenues for expanding the electorate outside the framework used by Cantor's pollster. The first was to go after Republicans who did not usually vote in the primary and to work to turn them out. The other was to take advantage of the open primary and expand the electorate to independents and Democrats and ask them to engage in strategic voting.

In the wake of Cantor's defeat, the reaction in the professional consulting community was summed up in the statement by Public Opinion Strategy's Neil Newhouse, who queried with amazement to a political consulting conference, "How do you not pick up on what is going on down in that district?"[5] But as obvious as it was in hindsight, Cantor's vulnerability went completely overlooked. That is why on election night pundits, politicians, and political scientists all were caught off guard by Cantor's loss.

IT'S (NOT) IMMIGRATION, STUPID

Compounding the error, in the immediate wake of the 2014 primary the media both locally and nationally (and, as a result, even internationally) offered problematic explanations for what had happened in the Seventh District. Having missed Cantor's pending implosion, nearly instantaneously political analysts from across the spectrum were called upon to explain it. Without missing a beat—within minutes of the election being called for Dave Brat—the media began proffering explanations for Cantor's loss. The dominant theme that emerged was that Cantor was insufficiently critical of President Barack Obama's plans to address illegal immigration and that his loss reflected the district's anger over Cantor's seeming openness to amnesty for illegal immigrants.

That was the only narrative that made sense to those who scrambled for answers: Brat was a little-known and poorly financed challenger whose most prominent supporter, Laura Ingraham, had made immigration her cause célèbre. Therefore, since Brat had won, Cantor's position on immigration reform surely was a significant part of the explanation. The disruption of Cantor's election night watch party by pro-reform immigration protestors contributed to the narrative that Cantor's upset was the result of immigration.[6] Of course, as we have shown, immigration reform was almost certainly not the reason for Brat's victory. The Cantor campaign's missteps, the highly motivated Brat campaign, and the generally pervasive sentiment within the Seventh District that Cantor had forgotten his constituents combined to bring about his defeat. But reality was less important to the pundits and Congress watchers who needed an instant explanation.

In the 1992 presidential election, the phrase "It's the economy, stupid" became the unofficial slogan of the Clinton campaign. The phrase was intended to make sure that the campaign did not lose sight of the most important issue on the minds of the voters; it also became a jab at then president George H. W. Bush, whom the Clinton campaign painted as out of touch with voters' economic concerns. In the days and weeks following Cantor's loss, the Clinton campaign slogan was trotted out repeatedly as an explanation for the surprising upset. As one media source wrote, "If it were up to former president Bill Clinton, he would put it simply; "It's IMMIGRATION, stupid.""[7]

The immigration explanation quickly gained traction and was disseminated widely. Unfortunately, it was wrong: "I think people that are making this about immigration really have no clue about the dynamics of the Seventh District and what's been going on here the last five years," Virginia Tea Party Patriots cofounder Jamie Radtke told a conservative radio program the morning after Cantor's loss. "To me when I hear those reports, it's national outsiders looking at this and trying to make an assessment," she said.[8] In a postelection survey, Cantor's pollster, McLaughlin and Associates, found that just 8 percent of voters cited immigration as the issue that was most important to them.[9] Moreover, the grass roots' anger at Cantor was palpable, but it was primarily related to his role in the slating efforts throughout the district a few months prior.

Even Brat's own campaign manager, Zachary Werrell, disagreed with the analyses that put immigration front and center among the explanations for Brat's win. In an interview a week after the primary, Werrell noted that Cantor's stance on immigration reform was not the reason that Brat won. "The media has it all wrong," said Werrell. "Amnesty was something that resonated with voters, but it wasn't a deciding factor at all."[10] Nevertheless, long after the primary contest had ended, media outlets as venerable as the *Washington Post* continued to advance the narrative that immigration reform had doomed Cantor.[11] In Werrell's estimation, the turning point in the campaign came in March at the Henrico mass meeting when the establishment candidate to chair the meeting, Don Boswell, lost to a member of the party's conservative wing, Russ

Moulton, and the establishment's efforts at slating were thwarted. Slating, not immigration, was the real story, but the media missed it.[12]

The consequences of the "Cantor-lost-because-of-immigration" narrative extended to Capitol Hill itself, with pro-reform members of Congress citing Cantor's loss as part of the reason that reform efforts were unlikely to proceed.[13] As University of Virginia political analyst Larry Sabato noted, "Everybody agrees that if immigration reform was on life support before, they're pulling out the plugs."[14] The concern for members of Congress, some of whom in the House of Representatives had yet to be renominated in their own primaries at the time of Cantor's loss, was that if they worked with President Barack Obama or congressional Democrats on immigration, they too would be ousted by their constituents, either in a primary contest or in the November general elections. Congress indeed failed to act on immigration reform legislation in the remaining months of the 113th Congress.

Congress's failure to act on comprehensive immigration reform legislation then led to President Barack Obama issuing an executive order in November 2014 to expand deferred action programs that prevent individuals who have entered the country illegally from being deported, provided that they have a child who is a lawful permanent resident of the United States and that they have themselves been law-abiding during their residency in the United States.[15] Although a U.S. district court judge issued an injunction preventing the order from being enforced in 2015, Obama's actions fueled conservative ire. Obama was accused of executive branch overreach, and conservative Republicans in Congress threatened to defund and shut down the U.S. Department of Homeland Security (and were very nearly successful in early 2015).

The immigration narrative, which dominated the explanation for Cantor's loss in the aftermath of the 2014 Seventh District primary election, had a direct impact on the public policy discussions taking place in Washington, DC, during the summer of 2014. But it was an armchair analysis, borne of the 24-hour news cycle and the pundit class's need to provide an explanation for one of the biggest upsets in political history—an upset that not a single pundit saw coming. In providing an explanation that focused on Cantor's policy positions, the media likely altered the dynamics of the debate in Congress over immigration reform. To be sure, immigration reform was not moving forward with much alacrity prior to Cantor's loss, but the media's focus on immigration to explain the loss made it all but certain that members would be afraid to be linked to the legislative proposal. More broadly, the focus on immigration suggested that substantive policy considerations dominated the 2014 primary election.

As the previous chapter demonstrated, the narrative that dominated conversations within the Seventh District during the primary was that of a member of Congress out of touch with his constituents and who attempted to marginalize those ideological members of his own party whom he felt were harming the prospects for the Republican Party in Virginia to reclaim a significant role in statewide races. In other words, political concerns, not policy ones, dominated the primary election and were to blame for Cantor's loss—but no one would know it to read the hastily compiled explanations repeated by the media immediately following the election.

There is one exception to this portrait of the media that we have painted here, and that is the conservative alternative media. The conservative blogs in the Seventh District as well as across the Commonwealth of Virginia were nearly spot-on in their assessment of Cantor's loss as being the consequence of the Washington insider's failure to adequately maintain relationships with his constituents and his work to marginalize the conservative grass roots. But these explanations, confined as they were primarily to right-wing blogs and social media sites, did not gain widespread traction. Just as they had been during the campaign, the grass roots were ignored in the Monday morning quarterbacking that took place following the primary election.

WILL HE OR WON'T HE?

The 24 hours following the close of the polls on primary election day was a busy time for the mainstream media's spin doctors who were covering the Cantor loss. As if constructing the immigration narrative wasn't enough, they found time as well to speculate about all the ways that Cantor might still be able to secure reelection to the House of Representatives. One suggestion was that Cantor could mount a challenge as an independent. Because the Seventh District is one in which Republicans enjoy a sizable numerical advantage over the Democrats, the thinking was that if Cantor ran as an independent, he would force Republican voters to make a choice about which faction of the party they preferred—the right-wing faction or the establishment faction. Doing so in the context of a general election, where turnout would likely be significantly higher and more moderate, would give Cantor a chance to retain his seat.

Ultimately, however, Virginia's "sore loser" law made a campaign as an independent impossible. The sore-loser provision is a clause in § 24.2-520 of the Code of Virginia, which provides that when a candidate files to run in a primary, he or she must include "a statement that, if defeated in the primary, [his or her] name is not to be printed on the ballots for that office in the succeeding general election."[16] Sore-loser laws are common throughout the United States; they are designed to prevent candidates who lose their party's primary from being able to mount a second attempt. In this way, they promote party discipline since where sore-loser laws exist, they prevent an unsuccessful challenger from trying again to keep the party's nominee from winning election to office.

Since Virginia's sore-loser law would prevent Cantor from mounting a challenge as an independent, a second possibility that was bandied about was that Cantor could mount a write-in campaign. Speculation about this option surfaced within hours of the majority leader's defeat. Sore-loser laws do not prohibit write-in campaigns since it is up to voters to write in the name of their preferred candidate. But there are significant coordination problems inherent to running write-in campaigns. Voters need to be educated about the write-in process and need to be willing to spend the extra time in the voting booth to write in the name of their preferred candidate. Moreover, write-in candidates, even those who are well known, may be unable to raise funds or hire sufficient staff to support their efforts.[17] As a result, such efforts are almost never successful. Still, Sen. Lisa Murkowski, the Republican from Alaska, won her seat via write-in campaign, and if voters in Alaska could accurately manage to write in "Murkowski" (which was a requirement in order for the vote to be counted), certainly there was hope that voters in Virginia's Seventh District could negotiate writing Cantor's name on the ballot.

Cantor concluded quickly that he would not mount a write-in campaign. *Yahoo News* reported that Cantor told his current and former staff members in a closed-door meeting the morning after the election, "I am not going to do a write-in. I am a Republican and proud of that."[18] In case there was any doubt and perhaps to silence the drumbeat of those calling for him to do a write-in campaign, Cantor made it clear that he was not going to be on the ballot in November; however, he stopped far short of endorsing Brat.

THE MAJORITY LEADER STEPS DOWN

Cantor's loss turned out to be just the first in a series of political bombshells. The big news at Cantor's press conference the day following his primary defeat was that he would step down as majority leader of the U.S. House of Representatives as of July 31, 2014. His announcement came after nearly five minutes of reflection on his career in Congress and, especially, as a member of the Republican Party. At his concession speech the night before, Cantor had seemed shell-shocked by the election outcome. The next day he was more composed and seemed much more relaxed as he again met the press. He told them, "[E]ach setback is an opportunity. . . . And while I may have suffered a personal setback last night, I couldn't be more optimistic about the future of this country. . . . I've had the privilege to serve and represent the people of Virginia's Seventh District."[19] Cantor went on to thank his staff and the support staff in Congress and to tout the successes of the Republican-led House of Representatives. He then made the announcement that he would vacate his leadership position:

While I intend to serve out my term as a member of Congress from the Seventh District of Virginia, effective July 31, I will be stepping down as majority leader. It is with great humility that I do so, knowing the tremendous honor it has been to hold this position.[20]

The date Cantor selected to conclude his service as majority leader coincided with the scheduled monthlong August congressional recess, which is primarily used as a work session back home in members' own districts. It gave the Republicans in Congress sufficient time to select his replacement, while providing time for Cantor to wrap up his work as party leader in an orderly fashion. With members departing at the end of July for several weeks at home, the transition to a new party leader would not seem as sudden.

Cantor's decision to step down as majority leader set off a frenzy among ambitious House Republicans. There were rumors that the candidates to succeed Cantor included fellow Young Gun and then House majority whip Kevin McCarthy, Texans Jeb Hensarling and Pete Sessions, and Ohioan Jim Jordan. In the end, however, only McCarthy and Idaho conservative Raul Labrador made bids for the majority leader post.[21] McCarthy won in the secret ballot vote, which was held in the Ways and Means Committee room on June 19.[22] The Republican conference's selection of McCarthy over Labrador suggested that the party leadership would continue largely along the same path, although Louisiana Republican Steve Scalise, a member of the conservative wing of the party, won the conference's election to replace McCarthy as majority whip. Cantor was in attendance for the leadership elections but "slipped out a back door" as the new leaders were announced.[23]

Although Cantor nominally remained majority leader until midnight at the conclusion of July 31, reports suggested that Cantor spent little time engaged with House business once McCarthy was selected to replace him. A report by the *Wire* explained further:

[Cantor] stopped attending GOP leadership meetings and . . . has missed nearly 20 percent of House floor votes since his defeat. McCarthy has been doing "double duty" for the last five weeks. . . . In addition to assuming many of Cantor's responsibilities, he has continued to do the job of whip.[24]

CANTOR'S RESIGNATION

On July 31, 2014, Cantor officially said his farewell to the leadership position. That same day he informed the *Richmond Times-Dispatch* that despite his pledge to serve out the remainder of his term the day after the primary election, he would be resigning his seat on August 18.

When Cantor announced his resignation in an exclusive interview with the *Richmond Times-Dispatch,* he also called on Virginia's governor, Terry McAuliffe, to hold a special election to elect someone to serve out the remainder of his term. Cantor's recommendation was that it should be held at the same time as the already-scheduled November 4 general election in order to minimize the expense associated with holding a special election. In addition, Cantor reasoned, by holding a special election in November, the winner could be sworn in immediately afterward, giving that person seniority over all other new members elected in November 2014.

News of Cantor's resignation pleased some voters and infuriated others. Most speculated that Cantor was in the middle of a deal to join a major bank or Wall Street firm and was stepping down in order to reduce the amount of time he would be prevented from lobbying his former colleagues. Former members of the House of Representatives are prohibited from lobbying their former colleagues for a year after leaving office, so resigning early meant that Cantor could reduce the amount of time he would be prohibited from engaging with his former coworkers.

But while Cantor's departure would make it easier for him to return to the Hill as a lobbyist of the 114th Congress, his decision to resign completely from Congress left the Seventh District without representation for nearly three months. Referring to the likelihood that Cantor was headed to a lucrative job in the private sector, Jamie Radtke at the *Bull Elephant* blog noted, "There is certainly nothing wrong with free market capitalism, although it would have been nice for Cantor to finish out his term and not complicate a critical November election."[25] Even Cantor supporters in the new media responded with frustration, as evident from political activist Justin Higgins's blog:

> Seniority and better office space is nice and all, but the idea that voters in Virginia's Seventh District will go without a voice for two and a half months is loathsome to me. As a Cantor booster, this closing decision has me a little perplexed.[26]

Rank-and-file voters within the district saw Cantor's decision to step down early as evidence of just how little he had actually cared about his constituents. A *Richmond Times-Dispatch* columnist noted that with his resignation, Cantor "gave his soon-to-be former constituents what they gave him: the back of a hand."[27]

Ultimately, Virginia's governor concurred with Cantor and called a special election to elect someone to serve out the remainder of Cantor's term to coincide with the November general election that was already scheduled. That decision meant that both parties would have to nominate candidates for the special election—it would not be automatic that Brat and Democrat Jack Trammell, the

7th District Democrats' general election nominee and one of Brat's colleagues at Randolph-Macon College, would be the nominees for the special election. In fact, the Brat campaign worried that the establishment wing of the Republican Party would nominate a candidate to run for the special election in order to embarrass Brat; this did not happen. Once the two parties had officially nominated Brat and Trammell, both campaigns scrambled to figure out how to make their cases to the voters twice. The Libertarian candidate on the November ballot, James Carr, cried foul because he did not have sufficient time to collect the signatures needed to get his name on the ballot for the special election.[28] Local election offices struggled to figure out how to explain to voters why they were seeing the same names on the ballot twice and worried that absentee voters especially would be confused and would not have the benefit of being able to ask someone for assistance.[29]

When the special election and general election were scheduled to occur at the same time, it touched off a round of prognosticating within the major party campaigns and among voters in the Seventh District, who recognized the possibility that several different scenarios could play out. The most likely scenario, based on partisan demographics, was that Brat would win both elections. But after his first media appearances following his victory in the primary went badly, Brat had been hard to find throughout the summer, and when he did make appearances, they were frequently at closed-door meetings where reporters were not invited. Moreover, the establishment wing of the party was not entirely comfortable with Brat as the party's candidate. Perhaps, it was speculated, some voters might use the special election as an opportunity to send Brat a message by voting for Trammell. If Trammell won the special election, it would mean that there would be no seniority advantage conferred if Brat won in the general election. An even less likely scenario was one in which Brat was the winner of the special election but Trammell won in the general election.

THE CONSEQUENCES

As election officials, politicians, and former constituents struggled toward the November 4 general and special elections, the *Wall Street Journal* reported on September 2 that Cantor had been hired as vice-chairman and board member at Moelis & Company, a "boutique" investment bank.[30] *Fortune* magazine described the terms of Cantor's hire as earning him between $1 and $2 million in salary, stock, and incentive payments—a huge increase over the $193,000 he was making as a member of Congress.[31] He was reportedly hired to open a Washington, DC, office of the firm.

The consequences for the other players in the 2014 Seventh District primary election story were not so rosy. Ultimately, as we discuss in the epilogue of this text, Brat won both elections in the Seventh District. But the need to be attentive both to the special election and the general election divided not only *his* time, but the time and resources of the other candidates vying for the seat. On Capitol Hill, Cantor's loss set off a struggle for power between the conservative and establishment wings of the Republican Party. Although the Republican conference in the House ultimately settled on Kevin McCarthy as the heir apparent to Cantor for the position of majority leader, the conference's selection of conservative Steve Scalise as majority whip demonstrated that the conservative faction within the party would not fade from view.

Still, when McCarthy defeated Labrador for the majority leader position, many conservatives lamented that the new leadership team would not be any more open to their views than was the old leadership team. According to the *Washington Post*, immediately following the leadership elections "the House's two new GOP leaders got a hint of how many other people—outside conservative groups, even other Republicans in Congress—want to lead their troops instead." At 4 p.m. immediately following the leadership elections, Sen. Ted Cruz (R-TX), who had repeatedly encouraged House conservatives to defy their leaders, sent an e-mail to a large group of conservative House Republicans. Cruz invited them to meet with him June 24 for an "off-the-record gathering" and "an evening of discussion and fellowship."[32]

Cantor's loss and the erroneous explanations that pervaded the media and political circles in its aftermath had effects on other 2014 races as well. Eighteen states held their primary elections after Virginia, and Cantor's loss likely gave hope to conservative activists in several contests. According to the *Washington Post*, this was true:

> The results from Virginia emboldened tea party advocates and enthusiasts, who suffered several high-profile defeats in intraparty contests this spring. It also put the establishment on notice that the long-running struggle inside the party will continue beyond this year's campaigns and into the 2016 elections.[33]

The Brookings Institute's "Primaries Project" speculated that the Cantor loss might even encourage local tea party groups to confront the national tea party organizations, citing the U.S. Senate primary race in Oklahoma between James Lankford and T. W. Shannon. In that race, 36 leaders of 23 conservative grassroots organizations penned two open letters to the "DC Tea Party Establishment" to complain about national leaders' endorsements of T. W. Shannon in the race.

Their June 19, 2014, open letter complained, in part, that the organizations offering endorsements were doing so in conflict with the local groups' preferences. The local groups noted the following (emphasis as in the original):

> **[E]ndorsements from the Senate Conservatives Fund, Governor Palin, Senators Cruz and Lee as well as others are at odds with many of the Tea Party and Grassroots Liberty organizations in Oklahoma.** . . . Oklahoma grassroots leaders and activists were not consulted regarding who the true conservative was prior to the endorsements.[34]

Conversely, Cantor's loss may also have galvanized establishment Republicans and perhaps some Democrats in places like Mississippi. Cantor's loss came one week after Republican Sen. Thad Cochran was forced into a runoff with tea party-backed Chris McDaniel after neither candidate garnered 50 percent of the vote during the June 3 Republican primary election. During the campaign period between the primary and the runoff, Cochran made deliberate overtures toward minority and union voters, who typically cast ballots in the Democratic primary. But under Mississippi law, any voter that did not vote in the Democratic primary on June 3 was eligible to vote in the Republican primary runoff, which was held June 24. As *CBS News* noted, "Cochran and McDaniel are both conservatives by just about any objective measure, but the race served as a proxy fight between tea party-aligned, anti-establishment conservatives and traditional conservatives."[35]

SUMMARY

Not only is the Seventh District primary an epic tale of a leader felled by the most unlikely of challengers, but it is also the story of how new and alternative media, expansive grassroots social networks, and the creative use of technology can undermine even the most tried-and-true methods of campaigning and of predicting election outcomes. Beyond the turmoil that characterized the immediate aftermath of the primary election, Cantor made a series of decisions following his loss that created significant challenges for the candidates, campaigns, and election officials in the Seventh District.

As we have shown in this chapter, the scramble in the immediate aftermath of the Seventh District primary by media outlets and political consultants to explain Cantor's loss and their own failure to see it coming compounded the already chaotic situation that was created by the upset. The immigration narrative in particular had significant policy consequences, as it further stalled immigration reform efforts on Capitol Hill. More broadly, by focusing on a salient public policy area as the explanation for Cantor's loss, the pundit class made it politically risky for members of Congress to engage in substantive policymaking while in Washington without fear of reprisal. As we have shown, however, the narrative simply does not hold up when submitted to even the slightest scrutiny.

CHAPTER 7

Conclusions

"So David triumphed over the Philistine with a sling and a stone; without a sword in his hand he struck down the Philistine and killed him."

—1 Samuel 17:50

In many quarters, Eric Cantor's loss to political neophyte Dave Brat was the end of an almost unfathomable story that played out in Virginia's Seventh Congressional District during the spring of 2014. Explanations abounded. Despite scrupulously avoiding the race during the election, national tea party leaders and supporters suddenly claimed that Cantor's loss was evidence that their message was being heard and that they are a force that cannot be ignored. Local Democrats whispered that their votes had been sufficient to oust Cantor and began planning for 2016. Next time, they declared, they would be more organized earlier in the process, and next time their candidate just might be able to pull off a victory—but this would require an epic swing of votes in the most conservative district in Virginia. Pundits cited the race as evidence of a restive electorate and blamed Cantor's immigration policy stance. In *The Partisan Divide,* former members of Congress Tom Davis and Martin Frost used the race as an example of the way that national factors can affect local congressional races. They alleged that Tip O'Neill's famous slogan, "All politics is local" no longer held true. Brat himself analyzed his victory as "basically a miracle."[1]

At the beginning of our telling of this story, we related other possible explanations for Eric Cantor's loss in his 2014 renomination bid. A few apply in part, but most don't, and the list of reasons that incumbents lose that do *not* apply to Eric Cantor's defeat is lengthy. There is robust literature on primary losses suffered by incumbents, and Cantor's loss does not quite fit into any extant explanation of why incumbents lose. His loss was not the consequence of his age, his race, a political scandal, redistricting, the presence of multiple challengers, or the type of nominating process used in Virginia. Perhaps, then, the tea party, immigration reform, Democrats who crossed over, and the nationalization of congressional elections or the national mood really undid Cantor. In the absence of a complete analysis of the Seventh District race, any one of these explanations might make sense. Or perhaps it *was* a miracle.

In the end, however, we think all of these explanations fall short. That is because all of them miss the most important factors in Cantor's defeat—namely, the loss of fit with his congressional district (due in part to his neglect and in part to redistricting, which changed the district's demography) and an accompanying inability to connect with his constituents. Some of that inability was the result of the significant responsibilities his leadership post conferred upon him, but much seems to be the result of a lack of interest in attending to his constituents' needs. Put simply, Eric Cantor lost his "homestyle." Put more broadly, Eric Cantor was defeated because he set political goals, pursued them, and succeeded. But he and his political team failed to match his progressive ambition to become a leader in Congress and to reassert control over the state party with a workable homestyle in Virginia's Seventh.

What remain as reasons to explain Cantor's loss after we have systematically eliminated all other reasons are these two explanations: a failed constituency relationship and a bad campaign. It is from this starting point that we draw the object lessons that emerge from our study of Eric Cantor's 2014 primary defeat.

TIP O'NEILL WAS RIGHT

At the outset, we note that former Democratic Speaker of the House Tip O'Neill was right and continues to be right—politics is very much about local circumstances, and it is local sentiment that slayed Eric Cantor. His loss reflects several fundamental truths of running and winning congressional election and reelection: Members of Congress who fail to attend to basic constituency service lose; members of Congress who are inattentive to the rules of the electoral game lose; members of Congress who run a bad campaign lose; and members of Congress who fail to adequately respond to or neutralize vocal opposition lose.

None of these principles are at all new. The scholarly work done on Congress and congressional elections dating back to the 1970s makes clear how important each of these principles is. Yet the story of Cantor's loss demonstrates the extent to which Cantor and the team of staffers around him failed to adequately attend to these most fundamental requisites of reelection. None of the other factors that were at play would have been sufficient to lead to Cantor's ouster had Cantor continued to provide the kind of constituency support and advocacy he had been known for in the earliest part of his career as a member of Virginia's House of Delegates.

Rather, as we have shown, Eric Cantor lost because he neglected to engage in the activities that ensure that candidates for public office will win elections. His loss illustrates a classic case of a member of Congress who forgot where he came from and who forgot that in order to do anything to influence policy or personal career success, he must first be reelected. The primary result serves to remind us that members of Congress must constantly be working to maintain their constituents' trust and confidence. In that respect, Cantor's loss serves as a warning to all members of Congress.

Cantor was insufficiently attentive to what has been called the personal vote—the portion of a candidate's support that comes from his or her personal qualities, legislative activities, and record.[2] In addition, his own unwillingness to accept earmarks to support his district reduced the mechanisms available to him to demonstrate that he was working on behalf of his constituents.[3] In the parlance of the literature on Congress, Cantor failed to put his constituents' satisfaction above his own desire to gain intra-Washington influence.[4] As his influence in Washington grew, his connection to the district waned; this made conditions ripe for a challenger to emerge from within his own party, even though the emergence of a qualified challenger under the circumstances extant in the district should not have occurred.[5]

In this concluding chapter, we address the ways in which Cantor's loss reinforces each of the axioms of congressional elections we mentioned above. In doing so, we both summarize the main points of this volume and demonstrate the extent to which Cantor's loss simply resulted from a failure to attend to the most basic principles of running for and winning elective office. Finally, this chapter addresses the way in which a lack of understanding of what happened in the Virginia Seventh District is likely to imperil candidate recruitment and public policymaking over the next several years. We present these as a series of lessons learned.

LESSON #1: HOMESTYLES MATTER

A "homestyle" is the way a lawmaker behaves back in the congressional district and how he or she relates to the district. It is what social scientist Erving Goffman called the "presentation of self."[6] The term, used in the 1970s by Richard Fenno to describe members of Congress's efforts to explain their DC activities to folks back home, encompasses the behaviors and relationships constructed by the member between him- or herself and his or her constituents, the allocation of staff resources to the district, and the content of the lawmaker's activities in the constituency. The incumbent's homestyle serves the relationship with the constituents while allowing the lawmaker to gain and exercise the discretion needed to pursue her or his other political goals. Homestyles might be built on person-to-person friendships with individuals or on transactional relationships. Some politicians have styles that are tied to a set of issues. Other members of Congress carve out a homestyle as a "leader" from a more hierarchical relationship to the constituency. The one thing all successful homestyles have in common is that they are invested in culture and identity and that they provide members the ability to connect with constituents in such a way that constituents come to believe that the lawmaker is "one of them."

Eric Cantor was vulnerable in 2014 because he lost his relationship with his constituents. He developed a homestyle that was not consistent with the district or his career goals—to the extent that he presented himself or his activities to his constituents at home, he did so in a way that constituents concluded they simply did not like.[7] This was not always the case, however. Cantor once had a functional homestyle more akin to Congressman B, the "popular local boy" that Fenno describes in *Home Style*. Cantor was born and raised in the Virginia Seventh, and with the exception of leaving to attend college and graduate school, Cantor resided for his entire adult life in the district. As a member of the Virginia House of Delegates, Cantor worked tirelessly to champion issues that were important to his constituents. As we noted in Chapter 5, his homestyle in the earliest years of his career in Congress was typical of what Fenno called the "expansionist" career phase. He came home often, which is especially easy for Virginia and Maryland lawmakers. His legislative efforts were focused on the district and aspects of the agenda of his predecessor, Tom Bliley. His constituents adored him, returning him to Congress in 2006 by a vote of nearly three to one.

But Cantor's rocket-like ascension through the House leadership ranks did not give his constituents time to adjust to changes in his homestyle. As his career quickly evolved and his goals changed, he did little to bring his constituents along with him. We noted previously that members of Congress have three goals: reelection, gaining power in Congress, and crafting "good" public policy. Members also strive to successfully pursue progressive ambition—efforts to advance themselves into positions of increasingly greater prestige and influence.[8] For Eric Cantor, the importance of power as a goal was evident. Just four years into his career and with only two reelections under his belt, he stopped pursuing or accepting earmarks and moved away from local legislation. He quickly shifted from building constituency relationships to minimally maintaining them in order to pursue institutional power. Together with colleagues Kevin McCarthy and Paul Ryan, he started pursuing a national political agenda. He formed a leadership political action committee (PAC), started recruiting candidates for Congress, and was keeping an eye peeled for emerging trends in the national party base, such as the tea party. By 2010, he had largely abandoned local legislation and local priorities as he fully grasped the reins of institutional power. He actively sought a leadership position and then continued up the leadership ladder. He was anointed as the heir apparent to (or potential leader for a coup against) Speaker John Boehner.

Unfortunately for Cantor, this shift in style was not one that assured him of sufficient discretion in DC to act as leader. As his attention turned to national politics, visits home and the cultivation of relationships within his primary and reelection constituencies should have become more important to him. Local legislation, too, should have been easier to pursue, but Cantor had abandoned earmarks and local legislation in general fairly early on in his career. The time and attention needed to successfully match one's homestyle with one's "Hillstyle" is challenging for congressional leaders, but that is usually because of the physical distance between a member's home and his or her office on Capitol Hill. Cantor had one of the easiest commutes of any member of Congress, yet he was seen less and less in the district; he and his staff allowed constituency relationships to decay in pursuit of DC relationships. The security entourage that he was required to travel with at all times further increased the physical and psychological distance between him and his constituents. Cantor was increasingly less well regarded by his constituents. A series of declining reelection vote totals versus unknown opponents should have sent a signal to Cantor and his political team that there were problems with his constituency relationships that might not be sufficiently surmountable by massive amounts of campaign spending and advertising—yet no alarms seem to have sounded.

Constituency service is one of the primary functions of Congress members. It also confers significant advantage for incumbents. This is because constituency service brings the member, through his or her staff usually, into direct contact with constituents within the context of solving a problem. More than 30 years ago, congressional scholars Bruce Cain, John Ferejohn, and Morris Fiorina noted, "All else being equal, a very favorable image as a good constituency representative is more important to the candidate in determining the vote than having the same party affiliation as the voter."[9] By the end of his congressional career, however, Cantor seemed to put little effort into constituency relations.

In the district, constituents chafed at unanswered letters and unreturned phone calls.[10] They resented that their only opportunities to engage with their congressman were at expensive breakfasts and fund raisers or at access-controlled "Cantor Advisory Council" meetings, which required advance registration. Meaningful opportunities for constituents to engage with Cantor were replaced with semiannual glossy mailers touting Cantor's work in areas such as education policy and immigration. There were even whispers that suggested Cantor's team was using local law enforcement to keep constituents away from him.[11] In fairness, Cantor's leadership position genuinely required his attention in Washington. But the lack of attentiveness to his constituents also reflected a pervasive attitude within the Cantor organization that there was simply no way he could lose.

The late David Carr, media and culture reporter for the *New York Times*, noted the following a few days after the election:

Even a cynical power broker like Frank Underwood on *House of Cards*—also part of the House leadership—knew that if you don't pay fealty to the voters who elected you, all the trappings of leadership can disappear at the whim of the people.[12]

And just two hours after the polls closed, Erick Erickson penned a column on the *RedState* blog, summing up the sentiment that was prevalent in the district:

> [Cantor] kept his attention off his district, constituents, and conservatives while he and his staff plotted to get the Speaker's chair. Cantor lost his race because he was running for Speaker of the House of Representatives while his constituents wanted a congressman.[13]

Eric Cantor did not adequately make the case to his constituents that his work in Washington was important or effective, regardless of whether it was specifically having a positive impact within the district itself. This failure to attend to even basic presentation of self provides a lesson for other members: Members of Congress must perpetually make the case to their constituents for why they should be reelected. Failing to do so almost always ensures that they will not be.

LESSON #2: THE INADEQUACY OF FIRST IMPRESSIONS

In the days and weeks that followed Cantor's loss, there was a rush to explain his defeat. It was a resurgent tea party and Cantor's willingness to compromise on immigration reform that did him in, at least according to the early analyses. But with the benefit of distance from the event, it is clear that neither of these initial explanations is accurate or complete. While local conservative activists in the Seventh District did indeed win a victory of sorts in Brat's defeat of Cantor, the national tea party groups stayed out of the race, and Brat himself made efforts to distance himself from the tea party movement.

As Virginia Tea Party Patriots cofounder Jamie Radtke told a conservative talk radio program the morning after Cantor's loss, "Brat's experience with the national organizations was the same one I experienced, where they cheerlead you behind the scenes, in quiet, but they won't come out publicly to support you."[14] Moreover, after Brat's primary victory, his hiring of Brian Gottstein and Amanda Chase alienated some local tea party-affiliated supporters who claimed that by hiring established (if not "establishment") political operatives, Brat was selling out the grass roots. Moreover, while active grassroots engagement by conservatives played a role in Cantor's primary loss, it was not likely the only factor that mattered.

Tea party challenges to incumbents garner media attention, but as a general rule, they are not effective in the primaries. Cantor's is one of the few incumbent losses ever credited to the tea party, and as we have shown, even that claim is dubious. He had been an ally to their cause and had never been targeted by any major tea party organizations. His challenger, Brat, actively avoided the tea party label. It is, therefore, only out of rhetorical convenience that we say that the tea party contributed to Cantor's loss and only to the extent that what we mean when we refer to the "tea party" is the loosely affiliated groups of disaffected conservatives living in the Seventh District. In every primary that preceded Cantor's, the tea party-favored candidate lost, which suggests that even in races where the national tea party organizations were involved, their involvement was insufficient to defeat the incumbents they challenged.[15] Nationally, Republicans won big gains in 2014, and "establishment" Republicans in particular competed favorably against more conservative challengers.

Likewise, Cantor's position on immigration did not doom his reelection. As we have shown, a majority of registered voters in the Seventh District *supported* immigration reform.[16] A survey conducted by Public Policy Polling (PPP) on the day of the primary election indicated that the percentage of Seventh District registered voters that supported reform was as high as 72 percent. These poll results were dismissed by many in the media for focusing on all registered voters. The *Washington Post* surmised the following:

> The automated poll from Democratic pollster Public Policy Polling shows voters in [Cantor's] district favor comprehensive immigration reform 72–23. But this is among all registered voters, not among those who voted Tuesday or even just among Republicans. We would hazard a guess that the electorate was dominated by the 23 percent.[17]

We are confident that the problem for Cantor wasn't immigration. The PPP survey taken on election day of Virginia Seventh District voters reveals that these voters would support either of two potential reforms of immigration before the House and that there was an overwhelming belief that the issue had to be dealt with by Congress. Republicans were even more supportive than the overall sample in support of these reform proposals, and the point estimate for those results is well above 50 percent among Republicans. Exit polls taken during the November general election likewise revealed that within Hanover County, the most conservative part of the Seventh Congressional District, just 21.1 percent of voters surveyed cited immigration in response to the question "What is the most important problem facing this country?"[18] These exit polls—the only ones available from the Cantor-Brat race—suggest that even among those who cast votes in the June primary, immigration reform was not the most important policy at issue in the race.

Just as tea party activists involved themselves in the Brat–Cantor race, some segment of the electorate might have been activated by anti-immigrant sentiment. But frustration about immigration reform efforts was a part of a general anticompromise sentiment that was directed at Cantor and took root in a general environment of distrust and diminished approval that preceded the issue. This is evident by widespread dissatisfaction with his performance as a member of the House leadership that we discuss in the next section. If it had not been immigration, it likely would have been some other hot-button political issue such as the debt ceiling or working with President Obama or Cantor's willingness to make some other pragmatic compromise that is part of the job of being a party leader during a period of divided government.

LESSON #3: THE OTHER CANDIDATE CAN BE STRATEGIC

In 9 of 11 southern states, including Virginia, crossover voting in primaries is legal. In the wake of the 2014 Republican primary in Virginia, Cantor's pollster accused Democrats of crossover voting to nominate Brat. Republicans have spent decades encouraging Democrats to leave their party and vote Republican and have used this practice to facilitate realignment.[19] So this seems to be a plausible explanation, although it does not excuse Cantor's campaign staff or his polling firm for the failure to identify the movement in the electorate.

Brat's campaign contends that it did not target Democrats. But it did engage in voter targeting, going after voters with certain profiles regardless of their party identification. Their use of rVotes, which we discussed in the previous chapter, gave them access to a sophisticated database of likely voters that allowed them to engage in specific targeting efforts—a real boon when campaign resources are scarce. While it is difficult to know with certainty just how many Democratic votes might have been gained through the use of this system, it is likely that some number of conservative Democrats would have ended up in Brat's target universe.

Thus, we concur with postprimary analyses that indicated that Democratic crossover voting likely did occur, but we agree that this crossover voting probably did not occur in sufficient numbers to have been entirely responsible for Brat's victory. As we demonstrated in Chapter 4, it is unlikely that enough Democrats crossed over to vote against Cantor to have been responsible for Cantor's defeat. But the exit poll data demonstrates that among the 20 percent of Democrats voting in Hanover County in the November general election who claimed they had voted in the Republican primary, 87.5 percent reported that they voted for

Brat. Independents who responded to exit polls in Hanover County claimed to have voted in the 2014 Republican primary in high enough numbers that they may have also been a factor. The Cantor–Brat race sharpens our understanding of the ways in which open primaries can lead to strategic voting and to exploitation by underdog candidates. The exit poll data collected during the November 2014 general election support the allegations made following the primary election that Seventh District Democrats and independents made a strategic choice to cross over in the 2014 Republican primary. Given that word of Democrat Jack Trammell's candidacy had not yet spread widely as of primary election day, it is likely that these crossover votes were aimed at removing Cantor from office rather than at setting up the possibility of a Democratic victory in the general election. Brat's own efforts to target like-minded voters regardless of party makes this even more likely.

LESSON #4: THE NEW SOUTHERN FACTIONALISM

A larger lesson that can be drawn from Cantor's loss has to do with the peculiar nature of the new factionalism in southern Republican politics. In the old South, and especially in Virginia, politics was often easily manipulated because the electorate was kept small through restrictions on legal voting rights. The old Democratic Party, which was the precursor of the current Republican Party in the South, used the tools available to it to suppress other political parties in addition to most people who were not white. The new politics of the old South does not explicitly exclude through restrictions on voting rights (although some recent efforts to exclude through voter identification laws, for example, have been consistent with these old traditions).

But the new southern politics does manifest in political parties that are ideologically defined and distinct, and, in the case of the GOP, through internal factionalism based upon identity politics that exclude rather than include people because of the ways in which the different internal factions perceive the issues. Evangelical voters, for example, seek a return to the moral governance of the public space. Libertarian voters want to reduce the tax code and also reduce the state, while pulling government increasingly out of the moral governance of the public space. Nationalists are concerned about immigration and national security. The tea party attracts a range of supporters through its 10th-Amendment rhetoric and has been accused by some of the Left of racist and xenophobic tendencies. The old southern factions studied by V. O. Key in the 1940s were about geography or rural-versus-urban or elites-versus-populists or built around families or cults of personality. In contrast, the new southern factionalism of the GOP is built around a variety of ideologically distinct conservative movements. They all have a populist bent that is a marked departure from the historic Republican Party.[20]

The other feature of all of these movements is the potential to organize and be effective in low-turnout elections. The case of Eric Cantor shows that through alternate and new media and with the use of a couple of distinct themes to draw on, a significant challenge can be raised in a GOP primary. A successful insurgency can best be achieved by expanding the electorate as Dave Brat did. Brat's successful campaign demonstrated that when a challenger can activate low-propensity party primary voters or can attract new voters, he or she can mount a successful challenge but one that will run below the radar of inattentive incumbents and may not be identified using the practices of conventional polling. Then, when political operatives and the media act on the bad data coming in—data that is not representative of the potential electorate—bad choices and bad narratives follow. This was the story of Virginia's Seventh Congressional District right up to, and even after, June 10, 2014.

Cantor was not targeted in the manner of most targeted incumbents. No large-money group or well-heeled movement was bankrolling Dave Brat. The financial component of the campaign was not an arms race, and had it become one, Cantor had seemingly inexhaustible assets to pull from. But the entry of voices from the conservative alternate new media—talk radio hosts and also the increasingly well-networked and antiestablishment, anticorporate conservative blogosphere—made Cantor's vulnerability known. The alternative new media played up Brat's virtues, fact-checked Cantor, and provided a source of competing content and campaign narrative for a small but activated opposition in Virginia's Seventh. When combined with the nimble voter identification system being used by Brat, a great deal of effect was realized for a modest expenditure of cash. These efforts were not generally covered by the mainstream media until late in the campaign, roughly four weeks out, and an examination of the coverage prior to the primary indicates that it was spare.

LESSON #5: CAMPAIGNS MATTER

If Eric Cantor was not going to have a good homestyle, he needed either to have bad opponents or campaigns that could overcome the shortcomings of his representative style. For over a decade, he had gotten by on the expenditure of massive amounts of money, scaring off credible opponents and generally overwhelming his district's media market with television and mail. As it turned out, the electoral numbers we observed regarding his previous reelection efforts were evidence of support that was wide but shallow.

The evidence from this last reelection effort indicates that Cantor was prone to running campaigns that assumed that name recognition, incumbency, and the ability to demonize his opponent would be sufficient to win. The efforts to characterize David Brat as a liberal college professor were designed to activate a set of stereotypes in the minds of voters—that Brat was a liberal tax-and-spend Republican in Name Only and an elitist from an ivory tower to boot. Even when the campaign was brought up short by fact-check organizations that declared the "liberal college professor" label untrue, Cantor's campaign continued to use it. Cantor's lack of connection with his constituents was so complete that he presumed that his constituents—who, as we noted in Chapter 2, have more education than the national average—would not know or would not care that he was lying to them.

Cantor's efforts to paint his opponent as a liberal fell flat with the electorate. And they came amidst media coverage of a variety of divisive issues where Cantor's need to act as a leader or to try to craft passable legislation created conflicts with the issues in the campaign. In short, the Cantor campaign was a brute force campaign. What it lacked was a convincing message and a candidate who cultivated trust in the electorate. Put simply, Cantor could control his TV and mail, but instead of crafting a message that would resonate with voters, his campaign filled its communication with content that was easily called into question by journalists and also many conservatives. Nor could Cantor or his campaign team control either the new media or the mainstream press. Both of these presented narratives of the campaign that were unfixable by any amount of campaign spending. Better data—and a better understanding of who was the potential electorate—would have allowed Cantor to tailor his message and to get out in front on campaign issues. Instead, the Brat campaign knocked him back on his heels early on and then continuously hammered the message that Cantor was beholden to big business and working to marginalize individual voices. Cantor was running from behind throughout the entire campaign—he simply was too disconnected to realize it.

Cantor's behavior during the primary election is much more explainable if we conclude that he truly believed that he would win the primary race regardless of what happened during the campaign. Had he been certain of victory in June and then again in the November general election, his role in the slating efforts which proved so damaging to his candidacy would have made perfect sense. The Virginia GOP was at a crossroads at the end of 2013 when Terry McAuliffe's election as governor and the election or reelection of Democrats to every statewide elected office left Cantor as the most senior Republican elected official within the commonwealth. There is some evidence that Cantor viewed his most important role during spring 2014 as reconceiving the party and helping to position it so that it would have a chance to win in future statewide races. But he miscalculated his likelihood of winning and did not take his opponent or the primary election seriously. Campaigns do matter, and Cantor neglected the race playing out for his own seat.

LESSON #6: THE BIG SORT AND THE DANGER OF THE NEW HOMOGENEITY

As we noted in the book's introduction, the particular type of primary election system employed by Virginia, the open primary, is no more or less likely to lead to an incumbent defeat than any other. But not accounting for the nature of the primary system in planning for a reelection campaign is a rookie mistake. Yet that seems to be exactly what Cantor did—not just in terms of his 2014 reelection campaign but even with regard to his efforts to redistrict political moderation out of his district.

When Eric Cantor's constituency relationships soured, they did so in the worst possible way, given his district and his institutional position. In Chapter 5, we noted that Cantor had grown unpopular throughout Virginia. He was the leading state (and a leading national) Republican in a southern state enjoying increased Democratic success. He occupied the most Republican district in the commonwealth, a district so packed with Republicans that it should have freed him up to act as a strong leader in his party. He did not have to worry about holding on to that elusive "median voter" who dominates the politics of competitive districts. With even modest efforts at staying connected with the district, he should have been able to place reelection concerns at the back of his mind.

American legislative districts, especially those held by Republicans of the American South, are more politically and demographically homogenous than they have been at any other point in the last century. This is a general trend of political and social sorting in the United States, driven by the choices people make about where to live—what journalist Bill Bishop calls "the Big Sort." And, increasingly, lifestyles and politics go together and are self-reinforcing. Much of the racial, ethnic, and gender diversity of America is politically and geographically concentrated in urban areas that consistently cast votes for Democrats. Republicans win almost exclusively in overwhelmingly white suburban and rural constituencies (at rates of 75 percent or better) and are nominated in primaries that are dominated by white voters (except in Florida, where pockets of the Hispanic vote go to Republican candidates). The general election is largely irrelevant in most legislative districts. Among Republican districts in the South, Virginia's Seventh is among the safest and the whitest.[21]

But lurking beneath this new homogeneity is a fractured and evolving Republican Party, especially in the South. The GOP in Virginia and other southern states has enjoyed an influx of new voters, largely whites, who hail mainly from the suburbs or rural areas. They exhibit a diversity of conservative identities, including evangelical protestants, states' rights advocates, defense-oriented patriots, Libertarians, and nationalists who are often anti-immigrant or anti-Muslim. They are also characterized by a strong populist streak that shares the business sector goal of lower taxes but is also very much anti-big business and in conflict with traditional marketplace Republicans. All of this drama and conflict has been playing out in GOP primaries over the last three election cycles. This polyglot of conservative voters, some of whom fuel tea party organizations, is frustrated with the GOP leadership within Congress and in state and national party organizations. When Republican politicians are unable to marshal these forces and hold them together, there is a possibility that they will fall victim to increased factionalization within the GOP electorate and lose their efforts at renomination in the process.

Eric Cantor, by making his district more homogenous, increased his vulnerability to factions within the party. These factions could manifest in three ways: as a segment of the primary electorate that had a policy disagreement with the incumbent; as a segment of the primary electorate that had a leadership problem; and as a segment of nonpartisans or Democrats entering the primary electorate under rules generally used throughout the South, to engage in strategic voting to beat an incumbent they don't like. Of these three possible vulnerabilities, we see evidence that all three manifested and helped to undo Cantor. Some Seventh District Republicans were opposed to Cantor for policy reasons. Others opposed him for focusing too much on the trappings of leadership in the House and not enough on the district. Democrats and independents who disliked Cantor were being encouraged by various quarters to go to the polls to vote for Brat; the lack of a Democratic primary removed all impediment to strategic crossover voting.

LESSON #7: THE TEA PARTY IS NOT MONOLITHIC

One of the most important lessons of Cantor's loss is that the tea party cannot be thought of in the same way we think about traditional political parties. Nor is the tea party a true social movement because its supporters are not unified around a single goal. While there are national tea party organizations, such as Sarah Palin's Tea Party Express, FreedomWorks, and the Tea Party Patriots, these national organizations do not even agree between and amongst themselves what their goals are. FreedomWorks notes that its "members all share three common traits: a desire for less government, lower taxes, and more economic freedom."[22] The Tea Party Express states that it stands for six principles, including those that FreedomWorks espouses, plus opposition to bailouts, Obamacare, and "out-of-control spending."[23] The Tea Party Patriots support personal and economic freedom and a "debt-free future" and add immigration, First and Second Amendment rights, and "voter integrity" to the list of issues they care most about.[24]

As the Seventh District race demonstrated, there are also a variety of local groups that assert "tea party" beliefs but may or may not be linked to any national organization. These local groups can make a difference in the outcome's of local races, including those for U.S. House of Representatives, primarily through mobilizing engaged, grassroots supporters. In Cantor's case, the national tea party groups stayed out of the race. Thus, to the extent that the tea party played a role in securing Cantor's defeat, it was as a weak identifier for a large number of active members of the conservative grass roots and not because of any connection whatsoever with national tea party organizations—all of whom elected to sit out the race. As the example from the 2014 U.S. Senate primary in Oklahoma demonstrates, when both national and local tea party groups wade into the political debate, they do not necessarily see eye to eye. In the Oklahoma Senate primary, the local groups went as far as to tell the national groups to stay out of it in the interest of not confusing voters about which candidate was the true conservative.

Moving forward, it seems unlikely that the tea party will be able to coalesce as a national movement capable of wielding influence in local contests. Victories like the one that local groups believe that they scored in Virginia's Seventh District offer hope to the local conservative grass roots and make it clear that they do not need the national organizations in order to effect change in an election. Thus, an important lesson from the Cantor case is that candidates must be attentive to the particular circumstances within their districts. Republican candidates especially should not assume that they understand the tea party simply because they have encountered it in national settings.

LESSON #8: LEADERSHIP AND RISK

Eric Cantor might have avoided trouble had his leadership and that of congressional Republicans been perceived favorably by his constituents, but the opposite was the case. Eric Cantor was not just an unpopular politician; he was specifically unpopular in his role as majority leader.

A poll of 488 voters taken by PPP on the day of the primary election in Virginia's Seventh District demonstrated the extent to which Cantor was in trouble. First, among all voters polled, his job approval was just 30 percent compared with 63 percent disapproval. His approval was upside-down among Republicans (43 percent–49 percent) and especially bad among independents (26 percent–66 percent), who were the second-largest bloc of voters. This lack of popularity was clearly a function of his position as House leader. Second, primary voters in the district were unimpressed by the Republican House leadership. When queried about the job the Republican House leadership was doing, the approval rating was just 26 percent compared with 67 percent disapproval. Among Republicans it was 41 percent–50 percent, and it was just 16 percent–77 percent among independents. Cantor's efforts and activities as leader were not satisfactory and doubtlessly contributed to his personal job approval as the district's representative.

Legislative leadership is historically difficult because leadership cannot "take a walk" on a vote because of their constituencies. Instead, they have to bear the brunt of votes and provide issue leadership that is in the party's interest or in the national interest, even if doing so goes against the district's interest. A safe district presumably tempers any backlash over controversial-but-necessary roll call votes and issue stands.[25]

In the new world of ideologically polarized Republican politics, GOP leaders in particular face electoral challenges from two directions. They cannot make their own districts too party competitive, lest a divisive issue cost them swing voters on the left. But they cannot make them too safe because the possibility of a primary challenge can come from so many ideological directions. This need to defend themselves within their party and also the general election constituency drives home the need for an active, engaged campaign apparatus that is integrated with a workable homestyle.

Eric Cantor's campaign had money, expertise, and campaign content with great production values. But the campaign and its consultants missed a firestorm that was brewing. They missed the firestorm because they were not looking where the votes were located, and they were not attending to the sources of vulnerability. Leaders must be at the forefront of campaign innovation, both for themselves and their fellow members—and so must their consultants. Cantor's efforts in these areas consisted primarily of raising and distributing significant amounts of campaign cash through ERICPAC.

Finally, leaders have to accept that they cannot be popular with all factions in their party. Cantor tried to be popular with the tea party when he was minority leader in an effort to co-opt the conservative wing of the Republican Party and leverage it to access majority party status in the House of Representatives. When he successfully accomplished that, he then tried to maneuver the party rules to exclude them. Tea party sympathizers are distrustful of big money and big banking; Eric Cantor was politically tied to both. Cantor had helped build a party majority based on not cooperating with President Obama, yet his leadership rhetoric in 2013 and 2014 was geared at working with the White House on several issues. He wanted to govern but also to hold the allegiance of the antigoverning faction of his own party.[26] In the end, Cantor learned that it is better to be a known and trusted enemy who is honest about differences than a dishonest "friend." Cantor's case illustrates a new danger to legislative leaders—that of the challenge from an ideological flank *within* the party.

LESSON #9: LESSONS FOR POLITICAL SCIENTISTS AND THE PUNDIT CLASS

It is impossible to review the events surrounding Cantor's 2014 primary loss without considering all the ways that the biggest political story of 2014 was completely missed by the media and political scientists. As we noted in Chapter 1, not a single news story ran in the national media suggesting that the Brat-Cantor race was one to watch. Cantor's reelection was considered to be such a foregone conclusion that almost no one was paying attention to it. The only polling done during the race was by the two campaigns themselves. There were no exit polls on primary election day. Cantor himself was so convinced he would win that he spent the morning at Starbucks in Washington, DC, meeting with lobbyists—and picking up the tab for their breakfast.

Hindsight is always 20/20, but it is amazing that every single pollster, pundit, Congress watcher and political scientist around the country missed the importance of the race. The exception was Elliot Meyer, the undergraduate coauthor of this text, who predicted that Brat was going to win several weeks before it happened.[27] Meyer was lucky, to be sure, but his participant observation of the Brat campaign proceeded in the very best tradition of Fenno's "soaking and poking" in order to get the real story. Within the discipline of political science, too little energy has been expended recently on linking theory to practical politics. If there is a lesson for political scientists who study Congress and elections, it is that they need to get out into the field and be present at the events they are studying. They need to talk to the people who participate in politics—not just candidates and paid campaign staffers, but the legions of volunteers and rank-and-file partisans whose efforts have enormous effects on election outcomes.

There is an important lesson here, too, about the need for more careful press coverage of congressional campaigns. A few days after the primary, the late *New York Times* media reporter David Carr took his colleagues in the national media to task for missing the impending Cantor loss. Carr acknowledged that the sheer number of congressional races—435, plus a third of the U.S. Senate every two years—makes it challenging for members of the press to focus on too many of them. But Carr also noted that journalists—not unlike political scientists—have been mesmerized by the endless amount of data available to them at their desks in the newsroom. [28]

PARTING THOUGHTS

Cantor's loss cannot be explained by the factors that typically result in an incumbent's defeat, nor can it be explained by any of the explanations offered in the aftermath of the election itself. Rather, Cantor's loss resulted from wholly predictable circumstances that would have been apparent had anyone been looking. Cantor's loss resulted primarily from a loss of fit with his district and the failure on his part to engage in the kinds of representational behaviors that constituents reward with their votes.

In the end, we do not believe that Cantor's loss portends a crisis in the Republican Party, in the political process, or in our system of congressional government. All of these have been experiencing turmoil that dates back far earlier than 2014. Nor does Cantor's loss reflect a nationalization of local races, despite claims to the contrary. His loss does not even offer significant insights into the role of the tea party going forward since to the extent the tea party played a role, it was through the individualized efforts of local, conservative, grassroots activists. The tea party remains a decentralized collection of grassroots entities only loosely connected through a shared conservative ideology, making it is impossible to offer sweeping claims about the movement's ability to affect any particular race.

What Cantor's loss does offer is a powerful reminder that no matter how well funded a candidate might be, no matter how many trappings of power a leader might have gained, and no matter how much the political system favors the status quo, most members of Congress who lose do so because their constituents judge them to be inadequate to the task of representation, not because of forces beyond their own control.

The 2014 General Election and a Look toward 2016

> *"I used to believe that anyone would be an improvement over the woeful Eric Cantor as my congressman. In this season of Lent, for that idea, too, I repent."*
>
> —Comment in the *Richmond Times-Dispatch* online forum, February 26, 2015[1]

In many respects, Cantor's primary loss was just the start of the surprises in the Seventh District during 2014. Almost as soon as Brat won, he was sequestered from the media, reducing his visibility in the district. On election night, news spread that Brat would face one of his colleagues in the November general election. Within a matter of weeks, the district's Republican Central Committee sent several hundred thousand dollars to the party's national offices. What had been an unusual primary election season was turning into an unusual general election.

In this brief epilogue, we summarize the general election race, discuss Brat's first few months in office, and offer a look ahead to 2016. The unique circumstances of Brat's election, combined with the potential of significant geographic and demographic changes to the district prior to the 2016 election, mean that the Seventh District remains one to watch.

BRAT VERSUS TRAMMELL

If the story of Dave Brat's 2014 Seventh District primary upset over Eric Cantor wasn't surprising enough, the morning of the primary election, Seventh District voters learned that the winner of the Cantor–Brat race would face newly nominated Democrat Jack Trammell in the November 2014 general election. Trammell, like Brat, was employed at Randolph-Macon College. The two men had known each other for nearly 15 years; they were teammates on the faculty intramural basketball team.[2] College professors are not typically candidates for Congress; the Brat–Trammell race may be the only time in history that two faculty members from the same institution squared off against each other in a contest for a seat in Congress.

Trammell's nomination came as a surprise to nearly everyone. The Seventh District Democrats had originally planned to nominate a candidate on May 2, 2014, at a nominating convention. However, when no candidates filed to run by that date, the event was canceled. Virginia's unique rules governing the parties' nominating processes meant that in the absence of interest from any prospective candidates, the central committee could select a candidate by a simple vote of the committee members.[3] Trammell was nominated by the Seventh District's Democratic Central Committee on June 8, 2014, and filed his candidate paperwork with the Virginia State Board of Elections the following day, just one day before the Republican primary. Word of his candidacy did not spread widely until election night, as local and national reporters deconstructed virtually every aspect of the Cantor loss in real time. Just four days later, in his first speech to local Democrats at Ashland Coffee and Tea in Ashland, Virginia, Hanover County's Democratic chairman, Gordon Silver, presented Trammell to supporters with the following introduction:

> This is our candidate. What a surprise! A week ago, we didn't have a candidate for the Seventh Congressional District. Sunday night, the Seventh Congressional District Committee voted for him to be our official candidate for the Democratic nomination. We still didn't have any idea who . . . I mean . . . you were a sacrificial lamb. And now, all of a sudden, you're David against Goliath. And as a professor, we're sure you can send the Brat packing.[4]

Trammell had been expecting to face Cantor and was just as surprised as everyone else on primary election night when the race was called and Brat had been nominated. In an interview a few months after the election, Trammell recalled a conversation between the two candidates:

> I totally thought I was a sacrificial lamb for the Cantor race. On the day of the primary, I called Dave on his cell phone to tell him I'd been nominated. Dave was his normal, bubbly self. He was very talkative. "Well, congratulations on that!" he said. He said, "Hey, I want you to know I'm at the retirement home and Hermitage High School. We're doing exit polling and I am doing really well." I just figured it was Dave being Dave.[5]

Brat's victory changed the calculus not only for Trammell and his supporters but also for Republicans throughout the Seventh District who had been expecting to support Cantor once again in a November general election. Almost immediately following the election, the Brat campaign was forced to retreat and retrench. There were several reasons for this: First, Brat's performance in national media in the 24 hours following his victory over Cantor raised concerns locally and nationally about whether Brat was ready for the national spotlight. When asked by MSNBC political analyst Chuck Todd about his policy positions the morning after his victory, Brat struggled to provide answers, even to questions that his economics background should have left him well prepared to discuss. For example, when asked whether the United States should have a minimum wage, Brat responded, "I don't have a well-crafted response on that." When asked about the ongoing conflict in Syria, Brat gave the following response:

> Hey, Chuck, I thought we were just going to chat today about the celebratory aspects. I'd love to go through all this, but my mind is just . . . I didn't get much sleep last night. I love all the policy questions, I'm happy to do them more, but I just wanted to talk about the victory here. And I wanted to thank everybody that worked so hard on my campaign. I'm happy to take policy issues at any time, but I just wanted to call out thanks to everybody today.[6]

Then, just a few days following Brat's national debut, it was announced that his campaign manager, Zachary Werrell, was being replaced by former Cantor political director Amanda Chase.[7] That announcement came on the heels of revelations that Werrell had posted derogatory comments about minorities on social media. Brat also hired Brian Gottstein to serve as his communications director. Gottstein's conservative credentials were burnished during his stint in the same position for attorney general and gubernatorial candidate Ken Cuccinelli.[8]

The Brat campaign took another hit within three weeks following the primary when the Seventh District Republican Central Committee met and decided to send $300,000 of the money in its treasury to national Republican Party organizations—the Republican National Committee (RNC) and the National Republican Congressional Committee (NRCC)—rather than spend the money in the district to support Brat and Ed Gillespie, who was challenging incumbent Democratic senator Mark Warner for his seat in the U.S. Senate.[9] The Seventh District Committee allocated just $12,866 to the Republican Party of Virginia to support the purchase of software needed by the Brat campaign,[10] and the campaign received a total of only $10,000 from the Seventh District Republican Committee itself.[11] The decision to spend less than 3 percent of its funds to assist Brat reflected the sentiment expressed by a Republican leader in Orange County, Virginia—which had supported Cantor in the primary election—who noted, "Right or wrong, there are some hard feelings [toward Brat.]"[12]

The Brat campaign used the committee's decision to send the majority of its money to the national party organizations as a fund-raising call to arms, sending an e-mail to supporters the next day that read (in part) as the following:

> Those funds could have been used to equip our grassroots army to take our message to voters across the Seventh District. This situation . . . means we need more help from our most ardent supporters to make up the difference. . . . So, will you help me by donating today?[13]

All of this occurred just as the Trammell campaign was gearing up. Trammell hired Beth Cope, an Atlanta-based political operative, to manage his campaign against Brat. That hire raised some eyebrows; Cope had recently managed a losing campaign in a Democratic primary in Georgia and had few, if any, ties to the Seventh District.[14] The Democratic Congressional Campaign Committee had offered Trammell support and had recommended campaign staff to him, but Trammell "just felt comfortable" with Cope.[15]

Even with a novice candidate and a campaign staff from outside the district, Democrats were optimistic that Trammell posed a real threat to Brat. The early Brat gaffes and loss of party funds emboldened local Democrats, who for the first time in decades thought they might have a chance to win in the Seventh District. Trammell recalled the excited atmosphere:

> People in my campaign early on were ecstatic because they thought, OK, now a Democrat can beat Dave Brat. So there was excitement—sort of a circus atmosphere. Even I thought, "I can beat Dave Brat." Of course, I have to eat some crow now, but that was the mood at the time.[16]

Trammell was not the only one sizing up the race in that way. The *Washington Post* wrote, "With Cantor's loss, Trammell suddenly finds himself on a much more level playing field—facing, in Brat, a fellow Randolph-Macon professor and a candidate with a much leaner bankroll than Cantor's."[17]

On social media, Trammell quickly outpaced Brat for the number of "likes" on Facebook, and he began to use Twitter as a way to reach supporters. But despite the Trammell campaign's ebullience, it was still running from behind. Brat already had a campaign office and cadre of volunteers—the Brat Pack—that had extensive experience from the primary campaign. His victory gained him national prominence, which in turn led to increased fund-raising ability. In the meantime, Trammell was still largely unknown. He received early help from prominent Democrats in central Virginia, including Lieutenant Governor Ralph Northam and Virginia's junior senator, Tim Kaine, but in his early appearances, he seemed shell-shocked by the attention. In his first public events, he expressed how "overwhelmed" he felt; two weeks after his candidacy became official, he told an audience of donors and Democratic leaders that it had already "been quite a ride."[18]

Just as Trammell had to grow comfortable with running for office, he needed to raise funds—and quickly. Within the first month of his candidacy, he successfully raised $155,000.[19] Trammell's Federal Election Commission financial summary reveals that he received $534,279 in contributions, most of which came from individuals.[20] Approximately $30,000 of the total funds he raised came from political action committees (PACs) and local party committees. His campaign disclosure form revealed that he spent almost every penny of the funds he raised. By comparison, Brat's campaign finance disclosure forms reveal that he raised and spent approximately $800,000 during the general election cycle.[21] Like Trammell, Brat received contributions from the Republican Party and several PACs.

Save for the fact that the two candidates were both employed by the same small college, the general election proceeded in fairly traditional form. Both men made appearances at local festivals and events throughout summer and fall 2014. They both made use of yard signs and word of mouth; both held town hall–style events. Neither candidate had sufficient funds to mount much of a campaign using electronic media, although each man was able to run one television spot toward the end of the campaign.

There were some differences between the two campaigns, however. The Brat campaign focused on large events with controlled access—a rally with nationally syndicated radio personality Laura Ingraham and U.S. senator Jeff Sessions on September 27 and an event with Ed Gillespie and Kentucky senator Rand Paul on October 15. In the meantime, the Brat Pack canvassed homes and businesses throughout the Seventh District. According to exit poll data collected during the general election, 45.6 percent of voters reported being contacted by the Brat campaign compared with just 19 percent reporting being contacted by the Trammell campaign.[22]

For his part, Trammell focused a significant amount of effort on fundraising and held several smaller functions in private venues that featured appearances by Senator Kaine. The Trammell campaign also worked closely with U.S. senator Mark Warner, who was himself campaigning for reelection, forming a coordinated campaign staff. Trammell's ability to tap into the resources available via the Warner campaign helped him to overcome his fundraising and manpower challenges, particularly early on in the campaign. Both Trammell and Brat took leaves of absence from their jobs at Randolph-Macon College to campaign.

Other than crossing paths at large events and festivals throughout the district, there were few occasions for voters to hear from both candidates at the same time. Despite the frustration Brat had expressed during the primary election over Cantor's refusal to agree to a debate, Brat was criticized during the general election campaign for being unwilling to debate Trammell and the Libertarian candidate James Carr. Brat declined invitations from the AARP and a local civic association, both of which had hoped to schedule a debate among all three candidates. These decisions left local political activists frustrated and contributed to an anti-Brat narrative that ran throughout the media during the general election phase.[23]

Brat and Trammell did debate once—at Randolph-Macon College—on October 28, but Carr was not invited to participate. Reports circulated that the Brat campaign would not agree to the debate if Carr were included. Carr and Brat's communications director Gottstein sparred over the allegations in the comment section of a *Virginia Right!* blog post:

> **Gottstein:** I am sorry that Mr. Carr has resorted to fabricating stories to get attention from the media. While the media has willingly promoted the false narrative that Dr. Brat's opponents have created, where they say he won't appear publicly with them, Dr. Brat is committed to doing three debates or forums in this campaign.
>
> **Carr:** Mr. Gottstein, I have not fabricated anything. My statements . . . are based on feedback we've received from organizers. . . . Of course, Mr. Brat could easily prove that I am wrong and publicly request that RMC [Randolph-Macon College] add me to the debate.[24]

That did not happen, and the three candidates appeared on stage together just once during the campaign—at a Goochland County Chamber of Commerce forum on October 23.[25]

On Election Day, November 4, Brat defeated Trammell easily, 60.8 percent to 36.9 percent. Carr mustered just slightly more than 2 percent of the vote.[26] Exit poll data showed that just as was the case in the 2014 November elections, generally, the local electorate was more white, more male, and more Republican than general demographic trends would suggest. But it was not especially connected to the tea party. Even in the conservative stronghold of Hanover County, fewer than 5 percent of those who turned out to vote identified themselves as members of a tea party organization—and nearly half of all voters surveyed indicated that they either did not support or flat-out opposed the tea party.

BRAT'S EARLY CAREER IN CONGRESS

Dave Brat was sworn in the waning months of the 113th Congress on November 12, 2014, by virtue of having won not just one but two elections in November. When Cantor announced his resignation from the House of Representatives, he asked Virginia's governor, Terry McAuliffe, to hold a second, special election on November 4 to allow the winner to serve the remainder of Cantor's final term in office. Brat won the special election as well on November 4, so he was able to enter Congress two months ahead of other new members elected in November 2014.

In December 2014, Brat and his House colleagues Mick Mulvaney (R-SC) and Matt Salmon (R-AZ) led an effort to try to amend the so-called CRomnibus appropriations bill—a bill to provide appropriations to all executive branch departments except the Department of Homeland Security through September 2015 and to provide short-term funds to the Department of Homeland Security through a continuing resolution (the "CR" in CRomnibus).[27] Brat and his colleagues wanted to amend the bill to strip away any funding to implement President Obama's executive actions on immigration, which had been announced in late November. But the House leadership would not permit the amendment.[28] As a result, one of the first votes Brat cast when the 114th Congress opened on January 3, 2015, was against John Boehner's candidacy for Speaker of the House. Twenty-five Republicans defected from Boehner, voting for another Republican instead. Brat was the only Republican to vote for South Carolina's Republican Jeff Duncan for Speaker.[29] The *Chesterfield Observer,* one of the local newspapers in the Seventh District, analyzed Brat's vote:

> It was a bold move by Brat, given his status as a freshman lawmaker and the conventional wisdom that Boehner had the backing to easily retain the post he has held since 2011. Congressional newbies historically have been expected to not make waves and fall in line with the leaders of their respective caucuses.[30]

During the 114th Congress (2015–2016), Brat was appointed to serve as a member of the House Budget Committee, the Committee on Education and the Workforce, and the Small Business Committee. His committee assignments reflected his background in economics and his professional career in education. In the early months of his service in Congress, Brat continued to focus on opposing President Obama's executive actions on immigration and on budget matters in the House of Representatives. He joined the "Hell No" caucus, a group of Republican members of the House of Representatives that simply refuses to support the House

Republican leadership. ("Membership" in this caucus is conferred by the media and simply requires that a Republican member of Congress consistently refuse to vote for the Republican leadership's priorities.)[31] Brat also joined the House Freedom Caucus, a group of conservative lawmakers that essentially formalized the "Hell No" group into a cohesive force within the Congress. The stated goal of the group is to provide a conservative voice in the lawmaking process.

Early reviews of Brat's performance have been mixed and, predictably, depend upon the political perspective of the reviewer. Brat has made good on his campaign promise to hold public meetings and to make himself available to his constituents by holding meetings once per month in locations throughout the district. This has pleased many of his constituents, particularly those that felt that Cantor had abandoned the district. In February 2015, he opened a district office in Spotsylvania County, Virginia, moving the office that previously had been located in Culpeper to a more central location that offers greater access to constituents in the northernmost parts of his district.[32] In addition, Brat has made good on his campaign promise not to vote for any measure that would increase federal deficits.

At the same time, not all of Brat's constituents have been pleased with his early actions. His vote to eliminate federal subsidies for Amtrak's passenger rail service, which most observers believe would shutter passenger rail in the United States, raised eyebrows in the Seventh District. Amtrak traverses the Seventh, and many of the district's residents make significant use of the rail service via multiple Amtrak stations located within the district.[33] Additionally, Brat's political commentary, which has been published periodically in local newspapers, has drawn criticism. Among the most frequent critiques is the extent to which Brat relies on talking points from conservative think tanks. His comments during the House Education and Workforce Committee's February 11, 2015, markup on H.R. 5, the Student Success Act, were circulated widely on the Internet and elicited groans from various quarters. During the markup, Brat made the following comment:

> The greatest thinkers in Western civ were not products of education policy. Socrates trained Plato in on a rock, and then Plato trained in Aristotle roughly speaking on a rock. So, huge funding is not necessary to achieve the greatest minds and the greatest intellects in history.[34]

A LOOK AHEAD TO 2016

Almost immediately following the November election, speculation began to swirl whether establishment Republicans would attempt to unseat Brat in 2016.

Speculation deepened in January 2015 when Eric Cantor headlined a meeting of the Virginia Conservative Network, which, despite its name, was a gathering primarily of Virginia's establishment wing of the Republican Party. The *Washington Post* reported that Brat not only was not invited, but he did not know about the event, even though it was held in the Seventh District.[35] The conservative *Bull Elephant* blog covered the event and its apparent snub of Dave Brat by writing, "Oddly absent from the event was Rep. Dave Brat, in whose district the meeting was held. According to Brat's office, the Congressman was not invited."[36]

The blog post also noted that the meeting focused on how mainstream Republican candidates could reclaim positions in Virginia government and within the Republican Party. According to the blog, while the meeting was advertised as promoting party unity, there was little emphasis on doing so. Instead, according to the *Bull Elephant*, the meeting focused on organizing to ensure that "pro-establishment" Republicans would win future contests in Virginia, "starting with key local GOP committees and culminating in 2016 elections for District chairmanships and the State Central Committee."[37]

Trammell, too, has heard rumblings that Brat will be challenged in the 2016 Republican primary. "I have been told by Republicans that the establishment is going to come back and try to unseat Brat," said Trammell in March 2015. He continued with the following thoughts:

> His next election cycle is likely to look a little different. If he wins it again, it will be for different reasons. If you burn bridges with traditional Republicans, if the tea party loses interest, he could really be in trouble. But Dave is the type of personality who doesn't seem to worry about things—"We'll figure it out." It is going to be very interesting. He's already fund raising.[38]

Indeed, on March 25, 2015, Brat e-mailed a fund-raising solicitation to his Brat-for-Congress mailing list. In it, he claimed that because he had voted against preserving funds in the federal budget for the Department of Homeland Security in order to protest President Obama's executive orders on immigration, he was being targeted by the Republican leadership in the House. His appeal for funds claimed, "In retribution for refusing to accept the GOP surrender to President Obama's illegal amnesty scheme, I'm being blasted by $400,000 worth of media attack ads and telephone campaigns." Brat called upon his supporters to donate cash, quickly, to help him respond to the attack ads being run against him. The postscript to his appeal added (the boldface text appeared in the original): "**Please step forward today with your urgent contribution**—whatever you can afford will be a big help!"[39]

The claims in Brat's fund-raising e-mail were exaggerated. His reference to the House leadership spending $400,000 to attack him for his votes was tenuous at best. The American Action Network, a conservative activist group, did spend $400,000 on advertising aimed at encouraging recalcitrant conservative members to vote in favor of funding for the Department of Homeland Security.[40] But Brat was not targeted specifically. Nor did House Speaker John Boehner have direct control over the advertising, although former Boehner staffers do have prominent roles with the American Action Network.[41]

The fundraising e-mail's reference to President Obama taking executive action to raise taxes likewise was exaggerated. Brat was making reference to White House Press Secretary John Earnest's response at a press conference on March 2, 2015, during which Earnest was asked about whether the president was interested in using his executive authority to close corporate-tax loopholes to generate revenue for infrastructure projects.[42] Earnest noted that the president was "very interested" in moving forward on his tax proposals and had not ruled out doing so through executive action, but Earnest also made it clear that the president was not planning to act in the near term, saying, "Now, I don't want to leave you with the impression that there is some imminent announcement—there's not, at least that I know of."[43]

Whether Brat is challenged in 2016 by an establishment candidate will depend in part upon decisions that the Republican Party makes late in 2015 concerning its method of selecting its nominee for the 2016 congressional election. Local conservative activists and groups have made it clear that they are opposed to primary elections, which they see as an attempt by the party establishment to "drive out the grass roots."[44] Given the success they had in 2013 with forcing a convention, it is likely that local conservative activists will try to force a convention in 2016 as well. The *Roanoke Times* reported on March 24, 2015, that the Republican Party of Virginia was already considering not holding a primary election to select electors to the Republican National Convention in summer 2016. The editorial board explained that consideration this way:

> Virginia Republicans are thinking about not having a primary at all, and instead picking delegates to the national convention through other means—such as a convention or a "firehouse primary." The technical details of those options vary, but the key points are these: They're not elections, and they're run by the party, not the State Board of Elections, which handles actual primaries.[45]

In addition to the possibility of a challenge in the nominating process from an establishment candidate, Brat's first reelection effort will be shaped by two other important factors. First, even if Brat is not challenged for the nomination in 2016 or if he successfully fends off a challenger, he will be running for reelection in a presidential election year. Turnout will be significantly higher in 2016 than it was in the 2014 congressional midterm. In addition, Democratic turnout is likely to be significantly higher than it was in 2014. In the two most recent presidential elections, 2008 and 2012, Democrats won by a sizable margin—more than six percent in 2008 and just under 4 percent in 2012. And in 2013's statewide gubernatorial election, Democrat Terry McAuliffe narrowly defeated Republican Ken Cuccinelli. If the Seventh District Democrats field a viable challenger, Brat may find that he needs to do more to secure a victory in the general election than was necessary in 2014.

However, as the district is currently constituted, even with a viable Democrat in the race, Brat would be a strong favorite to win. As we noted in Chapter 1, the partisan makeup of the district, especially since the 2011 redistricting, makes the Seventh District particularly inhospitable to Democrats. But it is entirely possible that the Seventh District in which Brat must run for reelection will be different from the Seventh District as it was drawn in 2014. This is the second factor that is likely to affect Brat's reelection chances. In the Virginia redistricting case, *Page et al. v. Virginia State Board of Elections et al.*, a three-judge panel of the U.S. District Court for the Eastern District of Virginia found that the redistricting plan adopted by the Virginia General Assembly following the 2010 U.S. Census unconstitutionally diluted the influence of African American voters in other congressional districts by increasing the proportion of African American voters in the Third District beyond what was required to avoid diluting the existing majority-minority district.[46] Although the district court determined that the 2014 boundaries of the Third Congressional District were unconstitutional, it also recognized that the timing of its decision—just one month before the November 2014 general election—made it impracticable to require the Commonwealth of Virginia to redraw its congressional district lines before the 2014 November election. Instead, it gave the state legislature a deadline of April 1, 2015, to redraw the lines in a constitutional fashion.[47] Congressional Republicans appealed the decision, and on February 23, 2015, the district court amended its earlier decision to give Virginia more time to redraw the boundaries—either until September 1, 2015, or until "60 days after the U.S. Supreme Court rules on a pending appeal from [Virginia's] congressional Republicans."[48]

On March 25, 2015, the U.S. Supreme Court overturned an Alabama district court's decision that had invalidated congressional district boundaries in that state as being racially gerrymandered. The Supreme Court's action in that case, *Alabama Legislative Black Caucus et al. v. Alabama et al.*, suggested that it would uphold the finding that Virginia's legislative districts were unconstitutional. Thus, it is indeed likely that the Third District will be redrawn prior to the 2016 congressional elections. Virginia Governor Terry McAuliffe called the Virginia General Assembly into special session in August 2015 for this purpose. However, the General Assembly refused to act; the re-drawing of Virginia's Third District boundaries is now back in federal court, and it is entirely possible that the courts will redraw the lines.

This matters to Brat's reelection chances because the Third District is adjacent to the Seventh District. Many observers believe that when the Third District is redrawn, it will result in shifting some of the most conservative areas of the Seventh District back into the Third, since those parts of the district primarily house white voters and are contiguous to the Third District. This is because the Seventh is much more conservative and homogeneous than the Fourth Congressional District, which is also contiguous to the Third. Congressman Randy Forbes has represented the Fourth District since June 2001 and has substantially more seniority than does Congressman Brat. It is likely, therefore, that Forbes will be insulated from the changes that are likely to be made. As Jack Trammell noted, "I think redistricting would hurt Dave more than it would hurt the others."[49]

THE LAST WORD, FOR NOW

At the time of this writing, in late-2015, pundits and the national media have already begun to focus on the 2016 presidential election. To the extent that anyone is talking about elections for Congress in 2016, the discussion is focused primarily on the U.S. Senate, where Republicans face an uphill battle to hold on to their chamber majority in an election cycle that will test more of their incumbents than the Democrats'. Moreover, these Republicans will be trying to hold their own against the backdrop of presidential election-level turnout.

The House of Representatives is all but certain to remain under Republican control after 2016. Decades of partisan gerrymandering make it unlikely that Democrats will be able to capture enough seats to regain the majority. Barring significant changes to the boundaries and demography of Virginia's Seventh District, it is likely that a Republican will continue to hold that seat, just as the Republicans have done for decades. But whether that Republican is Dave Brat is less certain. There are already rumors of a primary challenge to Congressman Brat and whispers of a Trammell–Brat rematch. It remains to be seen whether either of these circumstances comes to pass.

What is clear, however, is that Virginia Republicans are at a crossroads. Without fundamental changes to the commonwealth's system of nominating candidates for public office, an activist, conservative grass roots will continue to pull the party rightward. This may have significant consequences for the party's ability to win statewide in 2016 and 2017, when the state holds its next gubernatorial election. Eric Cantor seemed to recognize this. Whatever else might be said about him, his actions during spring 2014 make sense when viewed in the context of what he (wrongly) perceived his most important fight to be—over the direction of Virginia's Republican Party. Ironically, it was Cantor himself through his Young Guns recruitment strategy and early embrace of the tea party that fueled the factionalization of the Republican Party. The question moving forward is whether the Republican Party will be able to wrest back control of its own electoral fortunes.

Notes

NOTES TO PREFACE

1. "Dick Tuck Biography," dicktuck.com, accessed April 4, 2015, http://dicktuck .com/bio.html.

NOTES TO CHAPTER 1

1. Jeff Singer, "2014 in Election Upsets: The Fall of Eric Cantor," *Daily Kos* (blog), January 1, 2015, http://www.dailykos.com/story/2015/01/01/1351933/-2014-in-election-upsets-The-fall-of-Eric-nbspCantor#.

2. R. Michael Alvarez and Betsy Sinclair, "Electoral Institutions and Legislative Behavior: The Effects of the Primary Processes," *Political Research Quarterly* 65, no. 3 (September 2012): 544–557.

3. Elisabeth R. Gerber and Rebecca B. Morton, "Primary Election Systems and Representation," *Journal of Law, Economics, & Organization* 14, no. 2 (October 1998): 322.

4. Karen M. Kaufmann, James G. Gimpel, and Adam H. Hoffman, "A Promise Fulfilled? Open Primaries and Representation," *Journal of Politics* 65, no. 2 (May 2003): 457–476; Barbara Norrander, "Nomination Choices: Caucus and Primary Outcomes, 1976–1988," *American Journal of Political Science* 37, no. 2 (May 1993): 343–364.

5. Gerber and Morton, "Primary Election Systems and Representation," 1998.

6. Barry C. Burden, "Candidate Positioning in U.S. Congressional Elections," *British Journal of Political Science* 34 (March 2004): 211–227.

7. Section 24.2-509 reads, "The duly constituted authorities of the state political party shall have the right to determine the method by which a party nomination for a member of the United States Senate or for any statewide office shall be made. The duly constituted authorities of the political party for the district, county, city, or town in which any other office is to be filled shall have the right to determine the method by which a party nomination for that office shall be made."

8. Anita Kumar, "Ken Cuccinelli, Seeing Governor's Seat, Stands to Get an Edge with Va. GOP's Switch to Convention," *Washington Post*, June 15, 2012, http://www.washington-post.com/local/dc-politics/ken-cuccinelli-seeing-governors-seat-stands-to-get-an-edge-with-va-gops-switch-to-convention/2012/06/15/gJQASkByfV_story.html.

9. Sean Gorman, "Sarvis Says Over 40 Percent of Virginia's General Assembly Seats Go Uncontested Each Election," *PolitiFact Virginia* (blog), *Richmond Times-Dispatch*, September 14, 2014, http://www.politifact.com/virginia/statements/2014/sep/14/robert-sarvis/sarvis-says-over-40-percent-virginias-general-asse/.

10. Paul L. Hain and James E. Piereson, "Lawyers and Politics Revisited: Structural Advantages of Lawyer-Politicians," *American Journal of Political Science* 19 (February 1975): 41–51.

11. David T. Canon, *Actors, Athletes, and Astronauts: Political Amateurs in the United States Congress* (Chicago: University of Chicago Press, 1990).

12. See, for example, Gerber and Morton, "Primary Election Systems and Representation," 1998, 304–324; also Alvarez and Sinclair, "Electoral Institutions and Legislative Behavior," 2012.

13. Tom Davis, Martin Frost, and Richard Cohen, "All Politics Is No Longer Local: These Days, Party Identity Trumps All," *Politico*, February 1, 2015, http://www.politico.com/magazine/story/2015/02/politics-is-no-longer-local-114800_Page3.html#ixzz3SDIIu5us.

14. Canon, *Actors, Athletes, and Astronauts*, 1990.

15. For example, Gary Jacobson, "The Republican Resurgence," *Political Science Quarterly* 126 (Spring 2011): 27–52.

16. R. Douglas Arnold, *The Logic of Congressional Action* (New Haven, CT: Yale University Press, 1990).

17. davenj1, "How Is the Tea Party Doing Thus Far?" *RedState* (blog), August 10, 2012, http://www.redstate.com/diary/davenj1/2012/08/10/how-is-the-tea-party-doing-thus-far/; Samuel Smith, "Is the Tea Party Winning or Losing?" *Christian Post*, August 21, 2014, http://www.christianpost.com/news/is-the-tea-party-winning-or-losing-125130/.

18. Louis Sandy Maisel, *From Obscurity to Oblivion: Running in the Congressional Primary* (Knoxville: University of Tennessee Press, 1986).

NOTES TO CHAPTER 2

1. Jonathan Chait, "Eric Cantor's Shocking, Richly Deserved Defeat," *New York Magazine,* June 10, 2014, http://nymag.com/daily/intelligencer/2014/06/eric-cantors-shocking-richly-deserved-defeat.html.

2. James Hohmann and Jake Sherman, "Behind Eric Cantor's Campaign Meltdown," *Politico*, June 15, 2014, http://www.politico.com/story/2014/06/2014-virginia-primary-eric-cantor-campaign-107815.html.

3. Peter Galuszka, "Brewing Discontent: Eric Cantor's Loss Shocked Just About Everyone. But Why?" *Chesterfield Monthly*, August 2, 2014, http://www.chesterfieldmonthly.com/news/brewing-discontent.

4. Catalina Camia, "Graham, Cantor Fight Tea Party Foes in Primaries Today," *USA Today,* June 10, 2014, http://www.usatoday.com/story/news/politics/elections/2014/06/10/lindsey-graham-primary-south-carolina-june-10/10256951/.

5. Spencer S. Hsu, "As Veteran Lawmakers Retire, Region Braces for Clout Fallout," *Washington Post*, June 2, 2014.

6. *Center for Responsive Politics* Staff, "2014 Overview—Incumbent Advantages," *Center for Responsive Politics,* April 6, 2015, https://www.opensecrets.org/overview/incumbs.php; James E. Campbell, "The Return of the Incumbents: The Nature of the Incumbency Advantage," *Western Political Quarterly* 36, no. 3 (September 1983), 434–444.

7. Morris Fiorina, *Congress: Keystone of the Washington Establishment* (New Haven, CT: Yale University Press, 1977).

8. John R. Johannes and John C. McAdams, "The Congressional Incumbency Effect: Is It Casework, Policy Compatibility, or Something Else? An Examination of the 1978 Election," *American Journal of Political Science* 25, no. 3 (August 1981): 512–542.

9. Thomas E. Mann, *Unsafe at Any Margin* (Washington, DC: American Enterprise Institute, 1978).

10. Gary C. Jacobson, "Polarized Politics and the 2004 Congressional and Presidential Elections," *Political Science Quarterly* 120, no. 2 (Summer 2005): 199–218; Charles Cook, "Did 2004 Transform U.S. Politics?" *Washington Quarterly* 28, no. 2 (Spring 2005): 173–186.

11. *New York Times* Staff, "Election 2004: Who Won Where," *New York Times,* November 9, 2004, http://www.nytimes.com/ref/elections2004/2004SD.html.

12. Sheryl Gay Stolberg, "Daschle, Democratic Senate Leader, Is Beaten," *New York Times,* November 3, 2004, http://www.nytimes.com/2004/11/03/politics/campaign/03dakotacnd_.html.

13. Kenton Bird, "Tom Foley's Last Campaign," *Pacific Northwest Quarterly* 95, no. 1 (Winter 2003/2004): 3–15, http://www.jstor.org/stable/40491705.

14. Bird, "Tom Foley's Last Campaign," 2003, 10.

15. Bird, "Tom Foley's Last Campaign," 2003, 3.

16. Ken Gold, "The Redistribution Factor in Cantor's Defeat," *Government Affairs Institute at Georgetown University,* June 12, 2014, http://gai.georgetown.edu/the-redistricting-factor-in-cantors-defeat/.

17. David A. Graham, "Six Theories for Eric Cantor's Loss," *Atlantic,* June 11, 2014, http://www.theatlantic.com/politics/archive/2014/06/six-theories-for-eric-cantors-loss/372552/?single_page=true.

18. V. O. Key, *Southern Politics in State and Nation* (New York: Knopf, 1949).

19. Donald R. Matthews and James Prothro, *Negroes and the New Southern Politics* (New York: Harcourt, 1966); Alec Lamis, *The Two-Party South,* 2nd ed. (New York: Oxford, 1990); Clay Risen, *The Bill of the Century: The Epic Battle for the Civil Rights Act* (New York: Bloomsbury, 2014).

20. Lamis, *The Two-Party South,* 2nd ed., 1990.

21. Lamis, *The Two-Party South,* 2nd ed., 1990; Mark J. Rozell, "Virginia," in *The New Politics of the Old South,* eds. Charles S. Bullock III and Mark J. Rozell (Boulder, CO: Rowman & Littlefield, 1998), 135–154.

22. John C. Green et al., "The Soul of the South," in *The New Politics of the Old South,* 2nd ed., eds. Charles S. Bullock III and Mark J. Rozell (Boulder, CO: Roman and Littlefield, 2003), 283–304.

23. Charles S. Bullock III, Donna R. Hoffman, and Ronald Keith Gaddie, "Regional Variations in the Realignment of American Politics, 1944–2004," *Social Science Quarterly* 87 (September 2006): 494–518.

24. Charles S. Bullock III, Donna R. Hoffman, and Ronald Keith Gaddie, "The Consolidation of the Southern White Vote," *Political Research Quarterly* 58 (June 2005): 231–243.

25. Bullock and Rozell, *The New Politics of the Old South, 1998.*

26. Charles S. Bullock III and David J. Shafer, "Party Targeting and Electoral Success," *Legislative Studies Quarterly* 22, no. 4 (November 1997): 573–584.

27. See Charles S. Bullock III, *Key States, High Stakes: Sarah Palin, the Tea Party, and the 2010 Elections* (Boulder, CO: Rowman & Littlefield, 2010).

28. Bullock and Shafer, "Party Targeting and Electoral Success," 1997, 575.

29. All of the data reported in this section are available from "My Congressional District," U.S. Census Bureau, http://www.census.gov and "Labor Force Statistics," Bureau of Labor Statistics, U.S. Department of Labor, accessed January 31, 2015, http://data.bls.gov/timeseries/LNS14000000.

30. Polidata, "Partisan Voting Index, Districts of the 113th Congress," *Cook Political Report,* 2013, http://cookpolitical.com/file/2013-04-47.pdf.

31. Jeffrey Toobin, "Drawing the Line: Will Tom DeLay's Redistricting in Texas Cost Him His Seat?" *New Yorker,* March 6, 2006, http://www.newyorker.com/magazine/2006/03/06/drawing-the-line-3.

32. Richard E. Cohen, "Va. House Delegation Protects Itself," *Politico,* March 14, 2011, http://www.politico.com/news/stories/0311/51212.html#ixzz3LtCzHJCp.

33. Olympia Meola, "GOP Panel Picks Peter Farrell to Run for Janis' House Seat," *Richmond Times-Dispatch,* August 23, 2011, http://www.richmond.com/news/article_10a5c94e-2782-5633-843f-ab17cf29d5c9.html.

34. Bob Holsworth, as quoted in Galuszka, "Brewing Discontent," 2014.

35. Betsy Woodruff, "Eric Cantor's Challenger from the Right," *National Review,* January 6, 2014, http://www.nationalreview.com/article/367690/eric-cantors-challenger-right-betsy-woodruff.

36. "What We Believe," *Dave Brat for Congress—7th District of Virginia,* http://davebrat.com/what-we-believe/; see also "Virginia Republican Creed," Republican Party of Virginia, http://rpv.org/about/virginia-republican-creed/.

37. Lee Anderson, "Q&A with Zach Werrell '13," *Haverford College (PA) Clerk,* October 19, 2014, http://haverfordclerk.com/qa-with-zach-werrell-13.

38. *CBS News* Staff, "Tea Party-Backed David Brat on Win over Cantor," *CBS News,* June 11, 2014, http://www.cbsnews.com/videos/tea-party-backed-david-brat-on-win-over-cantor/.

39. Chip Reid, "Meet the Young Campaign Whiz Who Helped Oust Eric Cantor," *CBS This Morning,* June 20, 2014, http://www.cbsnews.com/news/dave-brats-23-year-old-campaign-manager-zachary-werrell/.

40. Garance Franke-Ruta, "Dave Brat Campaign Manager Scrubs Facebook Page After Election," *Yahoo News,* June 11, 2014, http://news.yahoo.com/brat-campaign-manager-scrubs-facebook-page-after-election-173536113.html.

41. Section 24.2-509 reads, "The duly constituted authorities of the state political party shall have the right to determine the method by which a party nomination for a member of the United States Senate or for any statewide office shall be made. The duly constituted authorities of the political party for the district, county, city, or town in which any other office is to be filled shall have the right to determine the method by which a party nomination for that office shall be made."

42. John Holland, "Amid Boos, GOP Ices Tea Party with Beach Slate Vote," *Virginian-Pilot (Hampton Roads, VA),* March 11, 2014, http://hamptonroads.com/2014/03/amid-boos-gop-ices-tea-party-beach-slate-vote.

43. Jeff E. Schapiro, "Schapiro: Republicans in Parliamentary Hand-to-Hand Combat," *Richmond Times-Dispatch,* March 30, 2014, http://www.richmond.com/news/virginia/government-politics/jeff-schapiro/article_9da0544e-e815-55ca-af31-5f3ee45a8ecb.html.

44. Jenna Portnoy and Robert Costa, "Eric Cantor's Tea Party Opponent in Va. Primary May Be Picking Up Momentum," *Washington Post,* May 13, 2014, http://www.washingtonpost.com/local/virginia-politics/eric-cantors-tea-party-opponent-in-va-primary-may-be-picking-up-momentum/2014/05/13/1a2d92d0-d9d7-11e3-b745-87d39690c5c0_story.html.

45. "Eric Cantor Addresses the 7th District Republican Convention," YouTube video, 7:26, posted by Gray Delany, May 12, 2014, https://www.youtube.com/watch?v=bkp2M1sMGUw.

46. lowkell, "Huge Loss for Eric Cantor . . . His Top Lieutenant Linwood Cobb Is Toppled," *Daily Kos* (blog), May 10, 2014, http://www.dailykos.com/story/2014/05/10/1298428/Huge-loss-for-Eric-Cantor-his-top-lieutenant-Linwood-Cobb-is-toppled#.

47. Jenna Portnoy, "Cantor Faces Tea Party Fury in His Backyard," *Washington Post,* May 10, 2014, http://www.washingtonpost.com/local/virginia-politics/cantor-faces-tea-party-fury-in-his-back-yard/2014/05/10/0f9df00c-d884-11e3-8a78-8fe50322a72c_story.html.

48. See "About the Bull Elephant," *Bull Elephant* (blog), http://thebullelephant.com/about-thebullelephant-com/.

49. Jamie Radtke, "Update (Audio): Radtke's Nomination Speech for Fred Gruber—Winner of 7th District GOP Today!" *Bull Elephant* (blog), May 10, 2014, http://thebullelephant.com/nomination-speech-fred-gruber-winner-7th-district-gop-today/.

50. Devin Burghart, "Tea Party Membership Map, 2010–2012," *Institute for Research and Education on Human Rights,* last modified March 7, 2013, accessed February 20, 2015, http://www.irehr.org/issue-areas/tea-party-nationalism/the-data/tea-party-membership-map.

51. See Virginia Tea Party Patriots Federation, http://virginiateapartypatriots.com.

52. "Slogans for Signs and Messaging," *Virginia Committee of Correspondence* (blog), accessed December 16, 2014, http://www.virginiacommitteesofcorrespondence.com/slogans.html.

53. Sean Hannity, "Dave Brat Reacts to Upset Win over Eric Cantor in Virginia Republican Primary," *Fox News,* June 11, 2014, transcript and video, http://www.foxnews.com/on-air/hannity/transcript/2014/06/11/dave-brat-reacts-upset-win-over-eric-cantor-virginia-republican-primary.

NOTES TO CHAPTER 3

1. Eric Cantor, as quoted in Jim Ridolphi, "Cantor Hints at Shutdown in R-MC Talk," *Mechanicsville (VA) Local,* April 6, 2011, http://issuu.com/mechlocal/docs/040611rsma.

2. Kurt F. Stone, "Eric Ivan Cantor," *The Jews of Capitol Hill: A Compendium of Jewish Congressional Members* (Lanham, MD: Scarecrow Press, 2010).

3. Allison Hoffman, "The Gentleman from Virginia: The Rise and Fall of Eric Cantor," *Tablet Magazine,* February 8, 2011, http://www.tabletmag.com/news-and-politics/58200/the-gentleman-from-virginia/print/.

4. Robert S. Greenberger, "Can Eric Cantor Save the GOP?" *Moment Magazine,* March/April 2009, http://www.momentmag.com/can-eric-cantor-save-the-gop-2/.

5. Hoffman, "The Gentleman," 2011.

6. Kate Andrews, "Eric Cantor's Climb Up the Hill," *RichmondMag.com,* September 2, 2007, http://richmondmagazine.com/news/eric-cantors-climb-up-the-hill/; see also Hoffman, "The Gentleman," 2011.

7. Liz Halloran, "Eric Cantor: The 'Young Gun' in the Debt Standoff," *National Public Radio,* July 14, 2011, http://www.npr.org/2011/07/15/137856269/eric-cantor-the-young-gun-in-the-debt-standoff.

8. Ibid.

9. Hoffman, "The Gentleman," 2011.

10. Former staff member of Weinstein Jewish Community Center, conversation with the author Lauren Bell, March 10, 2015.

11. Herbert T. Ezekiel and Gaston Lichtenstein, *The History of the Jews in Richmond from 1769 to 1917* (Spotsylvania, VA: Sergeant Kirkland's Museum and Historical Society, 1998).

12. Robert N. Rosen, *The Jewish Confederates* (Columbia: University of South Carolina Press, 2000).

13. Ezekiel and Lichtenstein, *The History of the Jews,* 1998.

14. Myron Berman, "Richmond, Virginia," in *Encyclopedia of Southern Jewish Communities,* eds. Janet Bordelon and Stuart Rockoff, Goldring Woldenberg Institute of Southern Jewish Life, accessed June 2, 2015, http://www.isjl.org/virginia-richmond-encyclopedia.html.

15. "Beth Ahabah Civic Leaders—Thalhimer Family," Beth Ahabah Congregation, accessed March 15, 2015, https://bethahabah.org/civic-leaders/.

16. Berman, "Richmond, Virginia," 2015.

17. Ibid.

18. Bill Glose, "Where Richmond Shopped for 150 Years," *Virginia Living,* December 2010, http://www.virginialiving.com/arts-events/arts/where-richmond-shopped-for-150-years/.

19. "Beth Ahabah Museum and Archives: History of Jewish Richmond," *Beth Ahabah Museum and Archives,* https://bethahabah.org/bama/history/.

20. Times Wire Service, "May Department Stores to Buy Thalhimers for $325 Million," *Los Angeles Times,* October 9, 1990, http://articles.latimes.com/1990-10-09/business/fi-2331_1_may-department-stores.

21. The Fourth District has been a repeated target of efforts to increase the African American population in the hopes of crafting a second majority-minority congressional district from the commonwealth, besides the low-country Third District. Litigation in 2002 and 2003 failed to compel the creation of a second majority–African American district, and subsequent efforts after the 2010 census also failed.

22. David Singer and Lawrence Grossman, "Jewish Population of the United States, 2002," *American Jewish Yearbook, 2003*, (New York: American Jewish Committee, 2003), http://www.ajcarchives.org/ajc_data/files/2003_6_usdemographic.pdf.

23. Va. Const. art. IV, § 6.

24. Peverill Squire, "Measuring State Legislative Professionalism: The Squire Index Revisited," *State Politics & Policy Quarterly* 7, no. 2 (Summer 2007): 211–227.

25. Jeffrey R. Lax and Justin H. Phillips, "The Democratic Deficit in the States," *American Journal of Political Science* 56, no. 1 (January 2012): 148–166.

26. "Commercial Real Estate Sector Lost Big Ally in Eric Cantor," *Commercial Real Estate Direct*, June 12, 2014, http://www.crenews.com/general_news/general/commercial-real-estate-finance-sector-lost-big-ally-in-eric-cantor.html.

27. Andrews, "Eric Cantor's Climb Up the Hill," 2007.

28. Ibid.

29. Hoffman, "The Gentleman," 2011.

30. Joseph Aistrup and Ronald Keith Gaddie, "Candidate Recruitment and the New Southern Party System" (presented at the Annual Meeting of the Midwest Political Science Association, Chicago, IL, April 2001).

31. "Why Support Redistricting Reform?" League of Women Voters of Virginia, accessed March 12, 2015, http://lwv-va.org/redistrict.html.

32. Larry Sabato and Colin Allen, "Not Much to Remember, Not Much to Forget," *Bacon's Rebellion* (blog), May 10, 2004, http://www.baconsrebellion.com/Issues04/01-05/2003_election.htm.

33. Virginia House of Delegates Member Listing, s.v. "Eric I. Cantor," Virginia General Assembly.gov, http://dela.state.va.us/dela/MemBios.nsf/735bd5cd47938ad585256c23006d3f8a/3119609ff2853be785256b35005fb751?OpenDocument.

34. See Robert J. Huckshorn and Robert C. Spencer, *The Politics of Defeat: Campaigning for Congress* (Amherst: University of Massachusetts Press, 1971); Ronald Keith Gaddie, *Born to Run: Origins of the Political Career* (Boulder, CO: Rowman & Littlefield, 2004).

35. Hoffman, "The Gentleman," 2011.

36. Ibid.

37. Tyler Whitley, "Legal Feud Enters 7th Fray; Blake, Cantor File Lawsuits over Various Land Deals," *Richmond Times-Dispatch,* June 8, 2000.

38. Jeff E. Schapiro, "Politics Supreme for Cantor," *Richmond Times-Dispatch*, October 12, 2011.

39. Editorial, "Seventh Heaven," *Richmond Times-Dispatch,* June 4, 2000.

40. Hoffman, "The Gentleman," 2011.

41. Laura Gittleman, "Alma Native Now in the Red Hot Heat of Publicity," *Morning Sun,* June 11, 2014, http://www.themorningsun.com/government-and-politics/20140611/alma-native-now-in-the-red-hot-heat-of-publicity.

42. Doug Belden, "Virginia Tea party Victor Dave Brat Has Minnesota Ties," *St. Paul (MN) Pioneer Press,* June 10, 2014.

43. Gittleman, "Alma Native," 2014.

44. David A. Brat, *curriculum vitae.*

45. Ibid.

46. Ibid.

47. Turner, Brian. "Distinguished Alumni: A Rich History of Political Engagement," *Randolph-Macon College Online,* accessed 2014, http://www.rmc.edu/departments/political-science/distinguished-alumni.

48. "Distinguished Alumni," 2014.

49. Brat, *curriculum vitae.*

50. Kylie Mohr, "The Inside Scoop on Dave Brat from His Students," *CNN,* June 14, 2014, http://sotu.blogs.cnn.com/2014/06/14/the-inside-scoop-on-dave-brat-from-his-students/.

51. Ashley Codianni, "Professors Vying for Cantor's Seat Get Rave Reviews from Students," *Mashable,* June 15, 2014, http://mashable.com/2014/06/15/randolph-macon-students/.

52. David Brat, course syllabus, ECON 202: Principles of Economics, Randolph-Macon College, Summer 2009.

53. "VFIC Ethics Program," Virginia Foundation for Independent Colleges, http://www.vfic.org/programs/ethics.html.

54. Brat, *curriculum vitae.*

55. Allison Brophy Champion, "Seventh District Congressional Race: Brat Bring [*sic*] Economics, Ethics Background," *Culpeper (VA) Star-Exponent,* October 19, 2014, http://www.dailyprogress.com/starexponent/news/th-district-congressional-race-brat-bring-economics-ethics-background/article_1aabdd8c-5747-11e4-90ff-001a4bcf6878.html.

56. Larry Abramson, "Colleges Receive Grants, but Are Strings Attached?" *National Public Radio,* May 13, 2011, http://www.npr.org/2011/05/13/136285599/colleges-receive-gifts-with-strings-attached.

57. Robert Patterson, "R-MC Board of Associates Hosts Business Lecture," *Randolph-Macon College Online,* November 20, 2009, http://www.rmc.edu/news-and-calendar/current-news/2009/11/20/r-mc-board-of-associates-hosts-business-lecture.

58. Brat, *curriculum vitae.*

59. Filing of Six-Year Revenue Plan by Governor, Va. Code 2.2-1503 (2011), https://leg1.state.va.us/cgi-bin/legp504.exe?000+cod+2.2-1503.

60. Virginia Public Building Authority Act of 1981, Va. Code 2.2-2260 (2009), https://leg1.state.va.us/cgi-bin/legp504.exe?000+cod+2.2-2260.

61. Galuszka, "Brewing Discontent," 2014.

62. Ibid.

63. Meola, "GOP Panel Picks Peter Farrell," 2011.

64. Holsworth, as quoted in Galuszka, "Brewing Discontent," 2014.

65. Andrews, "Eric Cantor's Climb Up the Hill," 2007.

66. Jennifer Steinhauer, "Once Snubbed, He Turns the Tables," *New York Times,* June 12, 2014.

NOTES TO CHAPTER 4

1. Barry Wolk, "Farewell, Eric . . . We Hardly Knew Ye (The Saga of CantorPalooza)," *Daily Kos* (blog), June 15, 2014, http://www.dailykos.com/story/2014/06/15/1307042/-Farewell-Eric-We-Hardly-Knew-Ye-The-Saga-of-CantorPalooza#.

2. Richard F. Fenno Jr., *Congress at the Grassroots: Representational Change in the South, 1970–1998* (Chapel Hill: The University of North Carolina Press, 2000), 9.

3. John R. Hibbing, *Congressional Careers: Contours of Life in the U.S. House of Representatives* (Chapel Hill: The University of North Carolina Press, 1991), 26.

4. Richard F. Fenno Jr., *Congressmen in Committees* (Boston: Little, Brown, 1973).

5. Hibbing, *Congressional Careers,* 1991, 26.

6. Glenn R. Parker, *Institutional Change, Discretion, and the Making of the Modern Congress: An Economic Interpretation* (Ann Arbor: University of Michigan Press, 1992).

7. Richard F. Fenno Jr., "U.S. House Members in Their Constituencies: An Exploration," *American Political Science Review* 71, no. 3 (September 1977): 883–917.

8. Donald Matthews, *U.S. Senators and Their World* (New York: W. W. Norton, 1973).

9. Richard F. Fenno Jr., *Home Style: House Members in Their Districts* (New York: Little, Brown, 1978).

10. See U.S. Congressman Dave Brat, "Contact," http://brat.house.gov/contact.

11. Ibid.

12. Ibid.

13. Arnold, *The Logic of Congressional Action,* 1990.

14. Fenno, *Congress at the Grassroots, 2000,* 4. Emphasis as in the original.

15. William D. Anderson, Janet M. Box-Steffensmeier, and Valeria Sinclair-Chapman, "The Keys to Legislative Success in the U.S. House of Representatives," *Legislative Studies Quarterly* 28, no. 3 (August 2003): 357–386.

16. Kenneth S. Stroupe Jr., "Gerrymandering's Long History in Virginia: Will This Decade Mark the End?" *Virginia News Letter* 85, no. 1 (February 2009), http://www.cooper-center.org/sites/default/files/publications/vanl0209_0.pdf.

17. Karen M. Kroll, "A Civics Lesson on the Back of a Dollar Bill?" *Christian Science Monitor,* December 16, 2003, http://www.csmonitor.com/2003/1216/p12s02-legn.html.

18. Editorial, "Liberty Bill," *Richmond Times-Dispatch,* April 6, 2001.

19. Kiran Krishnamurthy, "Hills Are a Hive for the Tons of Movies: Depository Being Built in Culpeper Will Hold Audio-Video Treasures," *Richmond Times-Dispatch,* November 28, 2004.

20. Editorial, "Week's End," *Richmond Times-Dispatch,* December 4, 2004.

21. Editorial, "Trash Removal," *Richmond Times-Dispatch,* May 10, 2001.

22. Tyler Whitley, "Cantor Creates Antiterrorism Unit," *Richmond Times-Dispatch*, November 28, 2001.

23. Anderson, Box-Steffensmeier, and Sinclair-Chapman, "The Keys," 2003, 369.

24. Editorial, "Vote for Cantor," *Richmond Times-Dispatch*, October 12, 2002.

25. H.R. Res. 612, 108th Cong. (2004).

26. Jeff E. Shapiro, "The Politics of Faith for Cantor," *Richmond Times-Dispatch*, March 23, 2003.

27. Michael Paul Williams, "Selective Paternalism Grates on Urban Officials," *Richmond Times-Dispatch*, April 2, 2003.

28. "Realtors Join Habitat Blitz Build Event," *Richmond Times-Dispatch*, March 14, 2004.

29. Todd Culbertson, "Ahead of the Curve," *Richmond Times-Dispatch*, September 1, 2004.

30. Editorial, "Election 2004," *Richmond Times-Dispatch*, October 14, 2004.

31. Paul Ryan, Eric Cantor, and Kevin McCarthy, *Young Guns: A New Generation of Conservative Leaders* (New York: Simon & Schuster, 2010), 23.

32. Ryan, Cantor, and McCarthy, *Young Guns*, 2010, 25.

33. Darren Samuelsohn, "Eric Cantor's Legacy," *Politico*, June 12, 2014, http://www.politico.com/story/2014/06/eric-cantor-legacy-legislative-record-107795.html; Andrews, "Eric Cantor's Climb Up the Hill," 2007.

34. *Center for Responsive Politics* Staff, "Every Republican Is Crucial PAC Summary Data," *Center for Responsive Politics*, https://www.opensecrets.org/pacs/lookup2.php?strID=C00384701&cycle=2006.

35. Ryan, Cantor, and McCarthy, *Young Guns*, 2010, 155.

36. Brady Dennis, Alec McGillis, and Lori Montgomery, "Origins of the Debt Showdown," *Washington Post*, August 5, 2011.

37. Ryan, Cantor, and McCarthy, *Young Guns*, 2010, 169.

38. Dennis, McGillis, and Montgomery, "Origins," 2011.

39. Matt Taibbi, "The Truth about the Tea Party," *Rolling Stone*, September 28, 2010, http://www.rollingstone.com/politics/news/matt-taibbi-on-the-tea-party-20100928.

40. Molly Ball, "How the GOP Establishment Tea-Partied the Tea Party," *Atlantic*, November 6, 2013, http://www.theatlantic.com/politics/archive/2013/11/how-the-gop-establishment-tea-partied-the-tea-party/281208/.

41. Jonathan Rauch, "Group Think: Inside the Tea Party's Collective Brain," *National Journal*, September 11, 2010, http://www.jonathanrauch.com/jrauch_articles/2010/09/group-think-inside-the-tea-partys-collective-brain.html.

42. Jane Mayer, "Covert Operations: The Billionaire Brothers Who Are Waging a War against Obama," *New Yorker*, August 30, 2010, http://www.newyorker.com/magazine/2010/08/30/covert-operations.

43. Russ Choma, "Unreported Spending Helped Stoke Discontent with Cantor," *Center for Responsive Politics*, June 19, 2014, http://www.opensecrets.org/news/2014/06/unreported-spending-helped-stoke-discontent-with-cantor/.

44. Ryan Lizza, "The House of Pain," *New Yorker*, March 4, 2013, http://www.newyorker.com/magazine/2013/03/04/the-house-of-pain.

45. Anderson, Box-Steffensmeier, and Sinclair-Chapman, "The Keys," 2003, 370.

46. Anderson, Box-Steffensmeier, and Sinclair-Chapman, "The Keys," 2003.

47. Randy Forbes, comments at "Coffee and Conversation," Randolph-Macon College, November 10, 2014; Matt Laslo, "Cantor's Loss Leaves Virginia Legislators Reeling over Decline in Influence," WAMU 88.5 *American University Radio*, June 20, 2014, http://wamu.org/news/14/06/20/cantors_loss_leave_virginia_legislators_reeling_over_loss_of_influence

48. Eric Cantor, "A Step Toward Curing Washington's Spending Disease—Eliminating Earmarks," *Politico,* October 13, 2010, http://www.politico.com/news/stories/1010/43514.html#ixzz3bOReHiRG.

49. Lesley Stahl, "The Majority Leader: Rep. Eric Cantor," *60 Minutes,* January 3, 2012, http://www.cbsnews.com/news/the-majority-leader-rep-eric-cantor/.

50. D. Andrew Austin and Mindy R. Levit, "The Debt Limit: History and Recent Increases," *Congressional Research Service Report for Congress,* October 15, 2013, https://www.fas.org/sgp/crs/misc/RL31967.pdf.

51. Dennis, McGillis, and Montgomery, "Origins," 2011.

52. Ibid.

53. Charles Riley, "S&P Downgrades U.S. Credit Rating," *CNN Money,* August 6, 2011, http://money.cnn.com/2011/08/05/news/economy/downgrade_rumors/.

54. Warren Fiske, "Cantor Has Shifted His Stand on Offsetting Disaster Aid with Cuts," *Richmond Times-Dispatch,* September 5, 2011.

55. Jennifer Bendery, "House Republicans Torn over Paying for Storm Aid Package," *Huffington Post,* May 26, 2011, http://www.huffingtonpost.com/2011/05/26/missouri-tornado-storm-aid-republicans-divided_n_867613.html.

56. Naftali Bendavid, "Cantor: No Playing Politics on Disaster Aid," *Washington Wire* (blog), *Wall Street Journal,* September 7, 2011, http://blogs.wsj.com/washwire/2011/09/07/cantor-no-playing-politics-on-disaster-aid/.

57. Jennifer Steinhauer, "Dispute on Disaster Aid Threatens Bill to Avert Government Shutdown," *New York Times,* September 21, 2011.

58. Ibid.

59. Brian Beutler, "Cantor Presses FEMA On Status of Disaster Aid for His District," *Talking Points Memo,* September 27, 2011, http://talkingpointsmemo.com/dc/cantor-presses-fema-on-status-of-disaster-aid-for-his-district; also Bendavid, "Cantor: No Playing Politics on Disaster Aid," 2011.

60. Laura Vozzella, "Cantor Debates Challenger," *Washington Post*, October 3, 2012.

61. Joshua, "Tea across the State," *Virginia Conservative* (blog), May 20, 2012, http://virginiaconservative.wordpress.com/2012/05/20/tea-across-the-state/.

62. Ibid.

63. See Politicians and Elections, "Personal Finances: Richest Members of Congress, 2013," *Center for Responsive Politics,* http://www.opensecrets.org/pfds/.

64. Fiorina, *Congress: Keystone,* 1977.

65. Johannes and McAdams, "The Congressional Incumbency Effect," 1981.

66. Mann, *Unsafe at Any Margin,* 1978, 103.

67. Public Policy Polling, "Congress Less Popular Than Cockroaches, Traffic Jams," news release, January 8, 2013, http://www.publicpolicypolling.com/pdf/2011/PPP_Release_Natl_010813_.pdf.

68. Editorial, "Cantor Voted in His Own Interests," *Richmond Times-Dispatch*, January 12, 2013.

69. Public Policy Polling, "Warner Safe for Reelection," news release, May 30, 2013, http://www.publicpolicypolling.com/pdf/2011/PPP_Release_VA_53013.pdf.

70. David Sherfinski, "Poll: Approval Ratings in Va. Drop across Party Lines," *Washington Times*, September 18, 2012, http://www.washingtontimes.com/news/2012/sep/18/poll-approval-ratings-va-drop-across-party-lines/.

71. Jeff Schapiro, "Cantor Is Running Out of Time and Options," *Richmond Times-Dispatch*, September 18, 2012, http://vgea.org/wp-content/uploads/2012/10/sept182013 RTDSchapiroCantorsRunningOutOfTimeAndOptions.pdf

72. Dave Brat, conversation with the author, April 10, 2014.

73. John Pudner, "What a Difference a Year Makes," e-mail to undisclosed recipients, January 9, 2015.

74. Hibbing, *Congressional Careers*, 1991, 36–37.

75. Jeff E. Schapiro, "Brat Gives Voters Way to Vent in New Kent," *Richmond Times-Dispatch*, May 25, 2014.

76. Laura Kebede, "Cantor Holds Google Hangout; Va. Congressman Engages in Online Q&A with Richmond-Area Students," *Richmond Times-Dispatch*, November 15, 2013.

77. Sean Trende, "What Cantor's Loss and Graham's Win Mean," *Real Clear Politics*, http://www.realclearpolitics.com/articles/2014/06/11/what_cantors_loss_and_grahams_win_mean_122944.html.

78. Stephen Kull, "Congress Should Listen to the People," *Richmond Times-Dispatch*, October 31, 2014.

79. Olympia Meola, "Cantor Will Skip Weekend GOP Event," *Richmond Times-Dispatch*, October 4, 2013.

NOTES TO CHAPTER 5

1. Paul Kane, "Cantor Loss Throws Congress into Disarray," *Washington Post*, June 10, 2014, http://www.washingtonpost.com/politics/cantor-loss-throws-congress-into-disarray/2014/06/10/210250e2-f0e2-11e3-914c-1fbd0614e2d4_story.html.

2. Public Policy Polling, "Democrats Lead Republicans in Upcoming Virginia Races," news release, January 10, 2013, http://www.publicpolicypolling.com/pdf/2011/PPP_Release_VA_719.pdf; Public Policy Polling, "Warner Leads 2014 Senate Race," news release, July 19, 2013, http://www.publicpolicypolling.com/pdf/2011/PPP_Release_Virginia_110.pdf.

3. Ibid.

4. Charles S. Bullock III, Ronald Keith Gaddie, and Ben Smith, "White Voters, Black Representative, and Candidates of Choice," *American Review of Politics* 26 (Fall 2005): 267–289.

5. Paul Bedard, "Free Ride? Democrats Failing to Field Challenger to Eric Cantor," *Washington Examiner*, April 14, 2014, http://www.washingtonexaminer.com/free-ride-democrats-fail-to-field-challenger-to-eric-cantor/article/2547192.

6. Jeff Branscome, "Spotsy Democrats Grill Congressional Hopeful," fredericksburg.com of the *Free Lance-Star*, February 24, 2014, http://www.fredericksburg.com/news/spotsy-democrats-grill-congressional-hopeful/article_0e9f0d1c-a0d4-5df3-b8fa-fa8ab-2f2c96e.html.

7. Burden, "Candidate Positioning in U.S. Congressional Elections," 2004.

8. Federal Election Commission, "Report of Receipts and Disbursements—Cantor for Congress," accessed June 2, 2015, http://docquery.fec.gov/cgi-bin/dcdev/forms/C00355461/918852/.

9. Federal Election Commission, "Report of Receipts and Disbursements—Friends of Dave Brat, Inc.," accessed June 2, 2015, http://docquery.fec.gov/cgi-bin/dcdev/forms/C00554949/934126/.

10. Peter Greenwald, a teacher in the Chesterfield County public schools, announced that he would challenge Cantor for the nomination on November 18, 2013; he officially kicked off his campaign on November 23. He remained in the race until March 30, 2014, when he officially endorsed Brat as a "true conservative" in a post to his Facebook page (https://www.facebook.com/GreenwaldForCongress).

11. Tom White, "Proof Eric Cantor Is a Desperate, Despicable Liar," *Virginia Right!* (blog), February 27, 2014, http://www.varight.com/opinion/proof-eric-cantor-is-a-desperate-despicable-liar/.

12. James A. Bacon, "Weasel Watch: Eric Cantor," *Bacon's Rebellion* (blog), May 11, 2014, http://www.baconsrebellion.com/2014/05/weasel-watch-eric-cantor.html.; Federal Election Commission, "Campaign Finance Disclosure Portal: Details for Candidate ID H4VA07143," accessed June 2, 2015, http://www.fec.gov/fecviewer/CandidateCommitteeDetail.do?candidateCommitteeId=H4VA07143&tabIndex=1.

13. John Dixon, "Eric Cantor: Lies and Deceptions," *Hanover Conservative Caucus* (blog), May 11, 2014, http://hanoverconservativecaucus.blogspot.com/2014/05/eric-cantor-lies-and-deceptions.html.

14. David Brat, speech to supporters at Bass Pro Shops, Ashland, Virginia, April 24, 2014.

15. *Almanac of American Politics* Staff, "Representative Dave Brat (Member Profile)," *Almanac*, online database adapted from the *2014 Almanac of American Politics*, January 2015, http://www.nationaljournal.com/almanac/member/4530.

16. Jeff E. Schapiro, "In New Kent, Brat Backers Hope to Hold Cantor Accountable," *Richmond Times-Dispatch*, May 24, 2014, http://www.richmond.com/news/virginia/government-politics/article_dff230e0-d76a-599d-992e-3bb000efe560.html.

17. Dixon, "Eric Cantor: Lies and Deceptions," 2014.

18. Brat campaign volunteer, conversation with Elliot Meyer, June 17, 2014.

19. Dave Brat, "Eric Cantor Fails to Lead on Benghazi," *Augusta Free Press (Waynesboro, VA)*, May 2, 2014, http://augustafreepress.com/dave-brat-eric-cantor-fails-lead-benghazi/.

20. Jake Sherman, "Cantor Unleashes Red Meat Mailings," *Politico*, June 2, 2014, http://www.politico.com/story/2014/06/eric-cantor-hillary-clinton-barack-obama-ads-

mailings-dave-brat-june-10-primary-107316.html; see an image of the mailer, http://images.politico.com/global/2014/06/02/ericcantormail01.html.

21. See an image of the mailer, http://images.politico.com/global/2014/06/02/ccf05302014_00000.html.

22. The Republican Party of Virginia's "Plan," its governing document, describes this proportional method as follows: Republican Voting Strength is "a uniform ratio of the votes cast in a political subdivision for the Republican candidates for Governor and President to the total votes cast in the entire Election District for the Republican candidates for Governor and President in the last preceding Gubernatorial and Presidential elections. In all proceedings for nominations for statewide office, the relevant Unit shall be entitled to one (1) delegate vote for each 250 votes. In all proceedings at the District level, the relevant Unit shall be entitled to one (1) delegate vote for each 100 to 500 votes. In all proceedings at the local and Legislative District level, the relevant political subdivision shall be entitled to one (1) delegate vote for each 25 to 500 votes. The exact number shall be decided by the appropriate Official Committee and included in the call"; "Republican Party Plan," http://rpv.org/wp-content/uploads/2014/06/Party-Plan-Amended-March-2014.pdf, 4.

23. Jon Ward, "'Richmond Hubris' Drove Eric Cantor's War with Grassroots, Led to His Demise," *Huffington Post,* June 11, 2014, http://www.huffingtonpost.com/2014/06/11/eric-cantor-demise_n_5482910.html.

24. James Hohmann, "Why Ken Cuccinelli Is Losing the Virginia Governor's Race," *Politico,* September 16, 2013, http://www.politico.com/story/2013/09/ken-cuccinelli-virginia-governors-mcauliffe-96834.html; Ben Jacobs, "Ken Cuccinelli Loses Narrowly to Terry McAuliffe for Virginia Governor," *Daily Beast,* November 6, 2013, http://www.thedailybeast.com/articles/2013/11/06/ken-cuccinelli-loses-narrowly-to-terry-mcauliffe-for-virginia-governor.html.

25. Ward, "'Richmond Hubris' Drove Eric Cantor's War," 2014.

26. Jeff E. Schapiro, "Republicans in Parliamentary Hand-to-Hand Combat," *Richmond Times-Dispatch,* March 30, 2014, http://www.richmond.com/news/virginia/government-politics/jeff-schapiro/article_9da0544e-e815-55ca-af31-5f3ee45a8ecb.html.

27. Holland, "Amid Boos, GOP Ices Tea Party with Beach Slate Vote," 2014.

28. Matthew Boyle, "Conservative Grassroots Shocks Team Cantor in His Own District with Surprise Intra-Party Victory," *Breitbart,* March 30, 2014, http://www.breitbart.com/big-government/2014/03/30/conservative-grassroots-shocks-team-cantor-in-his-own-district-with-surprise-intra-party-victory/; Schapiro, "Republicans in Parliamentary Hand-to-Hand Combat," 2014.

29. D. J. Spiker, "Don't Piss Off the Grassroots," *Bearing Drift* (blog), June 10, 2014, http://bearingdrift.com/2014/06/11/dont-piss-off-the-grassroots/.

30. Portnoy and Acosta, "Eric Cantor's Tea Party Opponent," 2014.

31. Sean Sullivan, "Cantor Internal Poll Claims 34-Point Lead over Primary Opponent Brat," *Washington Post,* June 6, 2014, http://www.washingtonpost.com/blogs/post-politics/wp/2014/06/06/cantor-internal-poll-claims-34-point-lead-over-primary-opponent-brat/.

32. Neil Munro, "Shock Poll Shows Eric Cantor Struggling in the Primary," *Daily Caller,* June 6, 2014, http://dailycaller.com/2014/06/06/shock-poll-shows-eric-cantor-struggling-in-primary/.

33. Galuszka, "Brewing Discontent," 2014; Peter Galuszka, "McDonnell Fallout Highlights Republican Party's Leadership Woes in Virginia," *Style Weekly,* September 9, 2014, http://www.styleweekly.com/richmond/mcdonnell-fallout-highlights-republican-partys-leadership-woes-in-virginia/Content?oid=2116322.

34. Galuszka, "Brewing Discontent," 2014.

35. Jim McConnell, "Brat Makes Early Statement: 'Principles Have to Matter,'" *Chesterfield Observer,* January 28, 2015, http://m.chesterfieldobserver.com/news/2015-01-28/News/Brat_makes_early_statement_Principles_have_to_matt.html.

36. David Brat, speech to supporters at Bass Pro Shops, Ashland, Virginia, April 24, 2014.

37. Ibid.

38. Elliot Meyer, field notes, 2014.

39. Anderson, "Q&A with Zach Werrell," 2014.

40. Zach Werrell, interview by Elliot Meyer, June 17, 2014.

41. Eric Steigleder, "The Race in the 7th District: Eric Cantor Can Be Beaten," *Blue Virginia* (blog), November 25, 2012, http://www.bluevirginia.us/diary/8214/the-race-in-the-7th-district-eric-cantor-can-be-beaten.

42. Brian Umana, "I'm a Democrat and I Helped the Tea Party Unseat Eric Cantor," *Washington Post,* June 13, 2014, http://www.washingtonpost.com/posteverything/wp/2014/06/13/im-a-democrat-and-i-helped-the-tea-party-unseat-eric-cantor/.

43. Zach Werrell, interview by Elliot Meyer, June 17, 2014.

44. Ibid.

45. Ibid.

46. Ibid.

47. Ibid.

48. Jamie Radtke, "Ann Coulter Endorses Dave Brat against Eric Cantor," *Bull Elephant* (blog), April 16, 2014, http://thebullelephant.com/ann-coulter-endorses-dave-brat-eric-cantor/.

49. *Politico* Staff. "The *Politico* 50—Number 21: David Brat and Laura Ingraham," *Politico,* accessed February 4, 2015, http://www.politico.com/magazine/politico50/2014/#.VNJgIUI1AyE.

50. Elliot Meyer, field notes, June 3, 2014; "Laura Ingraham and Dave Brat at Dominon [*sic*] Club," YouTube video, 59:21, posted by Dave Brat for Congress, June 4, 2014, https://www.youtube.com/watch?v=tg5zRKcWj68.

51. Olivia Meola, "Ingraham Attends Rally for Brat," *Richmond Times-Dispatch,* June 4, 2014, http://www.richmond.com/news/virginia/article_42d6db58-1932-5a85-9b42-6431d6c35e64.html.

52. "Laura Ingraham and Dave Brat at Domino [*sic*] Club," 2014.

53. Brat campaign volunteer, interview with Elliot Meyer, June 5, 2014.

54. Federal Election Commission, "Details for Candidate ID: H0VA07042," accessed

April 4, 2015, http://www.fec.gov/fecviewer/CandidateCommitteeDetail.do?candidateCo
mmitteeId=H0VA07042&tabIndex=1.

55. Virginia Department of Elections, "Official Results—Primary Election—June 10, 2014," Virginia.gov, accessed April 4, 2015, http://elections.virginia.gov/Files/ ElectionResults/2014/June-Primaries/resultsSW7217.html?type=CON&map=CTY.

56. "Dave Brat Defeats Cantor Victory Speech," You Tube video, 11:02, posted by Rshill7, June 11, 2014, https://www.youtube.com/watch?v=ye5SIiQRy0Y.

57. John McLaughlin, "VA 7 C.D. Post-Primary Survey" memorandum to "All Interested Parties," June 18, 2014, http://mclaughlinonline.com/pols/wp-content/ uploads/2014/06/VA-CD-07-Primary-Post-Elect-Memo-6-18-14.pdf.

58. Ibid.

59. Huff Post Politics, "Cooter Has a Plan to Unseat Eric Cantor. It's So Crazy, It Just Might Work," *Huffington Post*, June 7, 2014, http://www.huffingtonpost.com/2014/06/06/ ben-cooter-jones_n_5463196.html.

NOTES TO CHAPTER 6

1. Eric Eisenstadt, "Election 2014: Eric Cantor's Loss Jolts Political Landscape," *Politico*, June 21, 2014, http://www.politico.com/story/2014/06/2014-elections-eric-cantor-dave-brat-tea-party-republicans-108143.html#ixzz3WM990Uzd.

2. Sean J. Miller, "Brat Consultant: Campaign Widened GOP Primary Universe," *Campaigns & Elections*, June 10, 2014, http://campaignsandelections.com/campaign-insider/157/brat-consultant-campaign-widened-gop-primary-universe; Steve Adler, "How a Tiny GOP Data Firm Helped David Brat Win," *Campaigns & Elections*, June 24, 2014, http://campaignsandelections.com/magazine/1699/how-a-tiny-gop-data-firm-helped-david-brat-win; Sean J. Miller, "Romney Pollster: Cantor 'Lost Touch,'" *Campaigns & Elections*, June 10, 2014, http://campaignsandelections.com/campaign-insider/155/rom-ney-pollster-cantor-lost-touch; Sean J. Miller, "Six Stories That Rocked the Consulting World in 2014," *Campaigns & Elections*, December 30, 2014, http://campaignsandelections. com/campaign-insider/2378/6-stories-that-rocked-the-consulting-world-in-2014.

3. Sean J. Miller, "Cantor's Loss Leaves Pollsters Stunned," *Campaigns & Elections*, June 10, 2014, http://campaignsandelections.com/campaign-insider/158/cantor-s-loss-leaves-pollsters-stunned.

4. *Real Clear* Politics Staff. "Virginia Senate—Gillespie vs. Warner," *Real Clear Politics*, accessed April 4, 2014, http://www.realclearpolitics.com/epolls/2014/senate/va/virginia_ senate_gillespie_vs_warner-4255.html.

5. Miller, "Romney Pollster: Cantor 'Lost Touch,'" June 10, 2014.

6. Laura Vozzella, "Chaos Erupts at Cantor's Election Night Headquarters after His Departure," *Washington Post*, June 10, 2014, http://www.washingtonpost.com/local/vir-ginia-politics/chaos-erupts-at-cantor-election-night-headquarters-after-his-departure/201 4/06/10/5710c56e-f106-11e3-bf76-447a5df6411f_story.html.

7. Viki Mason, "'It's Immigration, Stupid,'" *U.S. Finance Post*, June 11, 2014, http:// usfinancepost.com/its-immigration-stupid-19757.html.

8. Jamie Radtke, interview by WMAL.com, June 11, 2014.

9. McLaughlin, "VA 7 C.D. Post-Primary Survey," 2014.

10. Zach Werrell, interview by Elliot Meyer, June 17, 2014.

11. Rachel Weiner, "Virginia's Rep. Dave Brat to Oppose Boehner's Reelection as House Speaker," *Washington Post,* January 5, 2015, http://www.washingtonpost.com/local/virginia-politics/virginias-rep-dave-brat-to-oppose-boehners-reelection-as-house-speaker/2015/01/05/5e40bc0a-94e3-11e4-aabd-d0b93ff613d5_story.html.

12. Zach Werrell, interview by Elliot Meyer, June 17, 2014.

13. David Nakamura and Ed O'Keefe, "Immigration Reform Effectively Dead until Obama Leaves Office, Both Sides Say," *Washington Post,* June 26, 2014, http://www.washingtonpost.com/politics/immigration-reform-deal-now-unlikely-until-after-obama-leaves-office-both-sides-say/2014/06/26/945d1210-fc96-11e3-b1f4-8e77c632c07b_story.html.

14. Olympia Meola and Jim Nolan, "Cantor Ousted in 'One of the Most Stunning Upsets in Modern American Political History,'" *Richmond Times-Dispatch,* June 11, 2014, http://www.richmond.com/news/virginia/government-politics/article_f8cada8e-423d-5f92-8264-ca1cbf0f14a2.html.

15. State of Texas et al. v. United States of America et al., Case 1:14-cv-00254 (February 16, 2015), http://pdfserver.amlaw.com/nlj/texas_immigration_20150216.pdf.

16. Declaration of Candidacy Required, Va. Code 24.2-520 (2001).

17. Aaron Blake, "The Tortured History of Write-In Candidates," *Washington Post,* September 21, 2010, http://voices.washingtonpost.com/thefix/senate/the-tortured-history-of-write-.html.

18. Oliver Knox, Meredith Shiner, and Chris Moody, "Cantor Loss Touches Off 'Game of Thrones' House GOP Struggle," *Yahoo News,* June 11, 2014, http://news.yahoo.com/defeated-cantor-says-he-won-t-try-a-write-in-campaign-161637338.html;_ylt=AwrSyCTqgphTeXEAzgbQtDMD.

19. Paul Kane et al., "Eric Cantor to Step Down as Majority Leader at End of July," *Washington Post,* July 11, 2014, http://www.washingtonpost.com/politics/eric-cantor-returns-to-the-capitol-says-he-will-discuss-his-plans-later-wednesday/2014/06/11/0d1abcac-f166-11e3-bf76-447a5df6411f_story.html?hpid=z1.

20. Ibid.

21. Robert Costa, "For Rep. Raúl Labrador, Running for House Leadership Position Is a Noble Effort," *Washington Post,* June 17, 2014, http://www.washingtonpost.com/politics/for-rep-raul-labrador-running-for-house-leadership-position-is-a-noble-effort/2014/06/17/aa0642ee-f63d-11e3-a606-946fd632f9f1_story.html.

22. Matt Fuller, "Kevin McCarthy Elected Majority Leader," *Roll Call* (blog), June 19, 2014, http://blogs.rollcall.com/218/kevin-mccarthy-elected-majority-leader/.

23. Robert Costa, Jackie Kucinich, and David A. Fahrenthold, "Kevin McCarthy of Calif. Selected Majority Leader, Steve Scalise of La. Whip on Busy Day," *Washington Post,* June 19, 2014, http://www.washingtonpost.com/politics/2014/06/19/ccc0b35e-f7e2-11e3-a606-946fd632f9f1_story.html.

24. Russell Berman, "Rep. McCarthy Turns Into House Majority Leader at the Stroke of Midnight," *Wire: News from the Atlantic,* July 31, 2014, http://www.thewire.com/politics/2014/07/rep-mccarthy-turns-into-house-majority-leader-at-the-stroke-of-midnight/375342/.

25. Jamie Radtke, "Two Elections for Same Office, on Same Day," *Bull Elephant* (blog), August 8, 2014, http://thebullelephant.com/two-elections-office-day/.

26. Justin Higgins, "Eric Cantor's Somewhat Baffling Resignation," *JHPolitics*, August 1, 2014, http://jhpolitics.com/2014/08/eric-cantors-somewhat-baffling-resignation/.

27. Jeff E. Schapiro, "Cantor Games the System, Even on Way Out," *Richmond Times-Dispatch*, August 6, 2014.

28. David Sherfinski, "As Eric Cantor Steps Down, Virginia Election Officials Worry about Voter Confusion," *Washington Times*, August 11, 2014, http://www.washingtontimes.com/news/2014/aug/11/as-eric-cantor-steps-down-virginia-election-offici/?page=all.

29. Ibid.

30. Dana Cimilluca and Patrick O'Connor, "Eric Cantor to Join Wall Street Investment Bank," *Wall Street Journal*, September 2, 2014, http://www.wsj.com/articles/eric-cantor-to-join-wall-street-investment-bank-1409630638.

31. John Kell, "Eric Cantor Joins Investment Bank Moelis," *Fortune*, September 2, 2014, http://fortune.com/2014/09/02/cantor-moelis/.

32. Costa, "For Rep. Raúl Labrador," 2014.

33. Dan Balz and Phillip Rucker, "GOP Strategists Try to Assess Impact of Cantor Loss on Other Primaries," *Washington Post*, June 10, 2014, http://www.washingtonpost.com/politics/gop-strategists-try-to-assess-impact-of-cantor-loss-on-other-primaries/2014/06/10/07e9a0e2-f10a-11e3-914c-1fbd0614e2d4_story.html.

34. TheOKieBlaze, "An Open Letter to the DC Tea Party Establishment," *Scribd* (digital library), June 19, 2014, http://www.scribd.com/doc/230525806/An-Open-Letter-to-the-DC-Tea-Party-Establishment.

35. Stephanie Condon and Steve Chaggaris, "Thad Cochran Fends Off Tea Party in Mississippi Runoff," *CBS News*, June 25, 2014, http://www.cbsnews.com/news/thad-cochran-fends-off-tea-party-in-mississippi-runoff/.

NOTES TO CHAPTER 7

1. Drew Sandholm, "Brat: Cantor Defeat Was 'Basically a Miracle,'" *CNBC*, June 11, 2014, http://www.cnbc.com/id/101750452.

2. Bruce E. Cain, John A. Ferejohn, and Morris P. Fiorina, "The Constituency Service Basis of the Personal Vote for U.S. Representatives and British Members of Parliament," *American Political Science Review*, 78, no. 1 (March 1984): 110–125, http://web.stanford.edu/~mfiorina/Fiorina%20Web%20Files/ConstituencyService.pdf.

3. Scott A. Frisch and Sean Q. Kelly, *Cheese Factories on the Moon: Why Earmarks Are Good for American Democracy* (Boulder, CO: Paradigm, 2011).

4. John W. Kingdon, "Models of Legislative Voting," *Journal of Politics* 39, no. 3 (August 1977): 563–595.

5. Thomas A. Kazee, *Who Runs for Congress? Ambition, Context, and Candidate Emergence* (Washington, DC: Congressional Quarterly Press, 1994); Michael L. Mezey, "Ambition Theory and the Office of Congressman," *Journal of Politics* 32, no. 3 (August 1970): 563–579.

6. Erving Goffman, *The Presentation of Self in Everyday Life* (Garden City, NY: Doubleday, 1959).

7. Fenno, *Home Style*, 1977; Parker, *Institutional Change, Discretion, and the Making of Modern Congress*, 1992.

8. Richard F. Fenno Jr., *Senators on the Campaign Trail* (Norman: University of Oklahoma Press, 1996); Gaddie, *Born to Run*, 2004.

9. Cain, Ferejohn, and Fiorina, "The Constituency Service Basis of the Personal Vote," 1984.

10. Trende, "What Cantor's Loss and Graham's Win Mean," 2014.

11. Kellie Doyle, "Congressman Cantor Continues to Hide from People Like Me—the Unemployed," *Blue Virginia* (blog), August 26, 2011, http://www.bluevirginia.us/diary/4735/congressman-cantor-continues-to-hide-from-people-like-me-the-unemployed; Chris Bowers, "Police Remove Eric Cantor Protestors from a Hotel Ballroom They Rented," *Daily Kos* (blog), September 1, 2011, http://www.dailykos.com/story/2011/09/01/1012506/-Police-remove-Eric-Cantor-protesters-from-a-hotel-ballroom-they-rented#.

12. David Carr, "Reporter's Beltway Blind Spot in a Congressman's Defeat," *New York Times*, June 15, 2014.

13. Erick Erickson, "Why Eric Cantor Lost," *RedState* (blog), June 10, 2014, http://www.redstate.com/2014/06/10/why-eric-cantor-lost/.

14. "Jamie Radtke on WMAL 6-11-14," YouTube video, 6:14, posted by WMAL Washington, June 11, 2014, https://www.youtube.com/watch?v=nQltZeyYsgM.

15. Dean Clancy, "The Tea Party Is a Victim of Its Own Success," *TJS Politics Blog, U.S. News and World Report*, May 21, 2014, http://www.usnews.com/opinion/blogs/opinion-blog/2014/05/21/primaries-show-tea-party-is-a-victim-of-its-own-success.

16. Full results of the Public Policy Polling survey are available at "Virginia 7th Congressional District Survey Results," Public Policy Polling, June 10, 2014, http://www.americansunitedforchange.org/page/-/VA7Results61114.pdf.

17. Aaron Blake, "Make No Mistake: Immigration Reform Hurt Eric Cantor," *Washington Post*, June 11, 2014, http://www.washingtonpost.com/blogs/the-fix/wp/2014/06/11/yes-immigration-reform-hurt-eric-cantor/.

18. The *Hanover (VA) Herald-Progress* newspaper and local radio station WHAN partnered with Randolph-Macon College to conduct an exit poll of 396 voters from precincts in Hanover County, Virginia, on November 4, 2014 (sampling error=+/-4.8 percent). According to the results, immigration ranked fourth with regard to the most important problem facing the United States:

Economy/jobs 41.7

Taxes 32.3

Health care 33.1

Immigration 21.0

Social Security/Medicare 19.7

Education 16.2

Same-sex marriage 9.6

Gun control 9.0

Other moral issues 6.8

Abortion 6.3

The values presented are the percentage of respondents claiming each issue was the most important one facing the United States. Percentages do not sum to 100 because, despite instructions to select only one choice, many respondents selected several issues; also David Ashton, "R-MC Takes to the Field for Exit Polling," *Yellow Jacket (Randolph-Macon College newspaper)*, November 26, 2014, http://rmcnews.org/?p=427.

19. For more on the overall realignment of southern politics and the emergence of the GOP majority, we direct you to Earl Black and Merle Black, *The Rise of Southern Republicans* (Cambridge: Belknap Press, 2002); Peter Applebome, *Dixie Rising: How the South Is Shaping American Values, Politics, and Culture* (New York: Harcourt Brace and Jovanovich, 1993); Joseph Aistrup, *The Southern Strategy Revisited* (Lexington: University Press of Kentucky, 1996); Charles S. Bullock III and Mark J. Rozell, eds., *The Oxford Handbook of Southern Politics* (New York: Oxford University Press, 2012).

20. Key, *Southern Politics in State and Nation*, 1949.

21. Thomas Brunell contends that one-party homogenous districts are better for representation because more voters get a representative that they are generally satisfied with, compared with voters in swing districts. See Thomas Brunell, *Redistricting and Representation: Why Competitive Elections Are Bad for America* (New York: Routledge, 2008).

22. FreedomWorks Staff, "About Us," FreedomWorks.org, http://www.freedomworks.org/about/about-freedomworks.

23. Tea Party Express Staff, "Mission Statement," Tea Party Express.org, http://www.teapartyexpress.org/.

24. Tea Party Patriots Staff, "Our Vision," Tea Party Patriots.org, http://www.teapartypatriots.org/ourvision/personal-freedom/.

25. John Kingdon posited that a lawmaker who takes a string of votes that run contra to the constituency is at greater risk to lose reelection. See John W. Kingdon, *Congressmen's Voting Decisions*, 3rd. ed. (Ann Arbor: University of Michigan Press, 1989).

26. See Kate Zernike, *Boiling Mad: Inside Tea Party America* (New York: Times Books, 2010); Bullock, *Key States, High Stakes*, 2010.

27. Meyer's prediction of Brat's win was reported soon after the primary election by the Canadian Press. See Alex Panetta, "A U.S. Student Predicted Electoral 'Tsunami,'" *Metro News*, June 28, 2014, http://metronews.ca/news/world/1081193/a-u-s-student-predicted-electoral-tsunami/.

28. David Carr, "Reporters' Beltway Blind Spot in a Congressman's Defeat," *New York Times*, June 16, 2014.

NOTES TO EPILOGUE

1. See comment posted by Brooke Wilson in response to Dave Brat, "Op-Ed: DHS Bill—Constitution Hangs in the Balance," *Richmond Times-Dispatch*, February 26, 2015, http://www.richmond.com/opinion/their-opinion/guest-columnists/article_9d532883-1d29-585c-aa43-3d268b20dc75.html.

2. L. Carol Ritchie, "College Colleagues Will Face Off for Eric Cantor's Seat," *National Public Radio*, June 11, 2014, http://www.npr.org/blogs/itsallpolitics/2014/06/11/320848217/college-colleagues-face-off-for-eric-cantors-seat.

3. "VA-07: Jack Trammell's Path to the Democratic Nomination," *Ballot News*, June 11, 2014, http://www.ballotnews.org/congress/va-07-jack-trammells-path-to-the-democratic-nomination/.

4. "Jack Trammell Gives Debut Speech Before Hanover County Democrats," *Richmonder* (blog), June 14, 2014, http://www.the-richmonder.com/2014/06/jack-trammell-gives-debut-speech-before.html.

5. Jack Trammell, interview by Lauren Bell, Ashland, Virginia, March 19, 2015.

6. "Chuck Todd Interview with Dave Brat," YouTube video, 6:44, posted by dcexaminer, June 11, 2014, https://www.youtube.com/watch?v=cqjkbfbGqdE.

7. Betsy Woodruff, "Dave Brat Doesn't Have a 23-Year-Old Campaign Manager Anymore," *Washington Examiner,* June 19, 2014, http://www.washingtonexaminer.com/dave-brat-doesnt-have-a-23-year-old-campaign-manager-anymore/article/2549959.

8. Emily Cahn, "Dave Brat Hires Communications Aide in Virginia," *Roll Call* (blog), June 16, 2014, http://www.rollcall.com/news/dave_brat_hires_communications_aide_in_virginia-233913-1.html.

9. Jamie Radtke, "Cantor Supporters Bleed the 7th District GOP Bank Account," *Bull Elephant* (blog), July 1, 2014, http://thebullelephant.com/cantor-supporters-drain-7th-district-gop-bank-account/.

10. Ibid.

11. Federal Election Commission, "Party Committees Contributions—Brat, David Alan," accessed March 22, 2014, http://www.fec.gov/fecviewer/CandidateCommitteeDetail.do.

12. Gary Robertson, "Rare Competition: Election Cycle Offers Two Intriguing Races in Republican Strongholds," *Virginia Business,* September 30, 2014, http://www.virginiabusiness.com/news/article/rare-competition.

13. Dave Brat for Congress, "7th District Funds Not Staying in 7th; Going to Nat'l GOP—We Need Your Help!" e-mail to undisclosed recipients, June 28, 2014.

14. Jim Galloway, "Atlanta Dem to Manage Campaign against Republican Who Beat Eric Cantor," *Atlanta Journal Constitution* (blog), June 27, 2014, http://politics.blog.ajc.com/2014/06/27/atlanta-dem-to-manage-campaign-against-republican-who-beat-eric-cantor/#__federated=1.

15. Jack Trammell, conversation with Lauren Bell, Ashland, Virginia, November 20, 2015.

16. Jack Trammell, interview by Lauren Bell, Ashland, Virginia, March 19, 2015.

17. Mike diBonis, "Meet Jack Trammell, the Democrat Who Will Face David Brat, the Man Who Beat Eric Cantor," *Washington Post,* June 11, 2014, http://www.washingtonpost.com/local/virginia-politics/meet-jack-trammell-the-democrat-who-will-face-david-brat-the-man-who-beat-eric-cantor/2014/06/10/df00f972-f10a-11e3-914c-1fbd0614e2d4_story.html.

18. See "Jack Trammell Gives Debut Speech Before Hanover County Democrats," 2014; see also "Jack Trammell, June 24, 2014," *Richmonder* (blog), http://www.the-richmonder.com/2014_06_01_archive.html.

19. Federal Election Commission, "FEC Disclosure Form 3 for Trammell for Congress," accessed March 26, 2015, http://docquery.fec.gov/cgi-bin/dcdev/forms/C00565218/939681/.

20. Federal Election Commission, "Details for Candidate ID: H4VA07150," accessed March 22, 2015, http://www.fec.gov/fecviewer/CandidateCommitteeDetail.do.

21. Federal Election Commission, "Details for Committee ID: C00554949," accessed March 22, 2015, http://www.fec.gov/fecviewer/CandCmteTransaction.do.

22. Hanover County Exit Poll Results, November 4, 2014 (*Hanover Herald-Progress,* WHAN radio, and Randolph-Macon College); Ashton, 2014.

23. Markus Schmidt, "Brat Dodges Debate Challenges, Opponents Say," *Richmond Times-Dispatch,* September 16, 2014, http://www.richmond.com/news/virginia/government-politics/article_457c0ccb-cb3f-5b5b-90b0-ab13b7ec19da.html.

24. Ellwood Sanders, "I Spoke with Dr. David Brat Today. He Did Not Keep Carr Out of the RM-C Debate," *Virginia Right!* (blog), September 22, 2014, http://www.varight.com/news/i-spoke-with-dr-david-brat-today-he-did-not-keep-carr-out-of-the-rm-c-debate/.

25. Markus Schmidt, "Brat, Trammell, Carr Field Questions at Goochland Forum," *Richmond Times-Dispatch,* October 23, 2014, http://www.richmond.com/news/virginia/government-politics/article_b4b40d12-b47f-5c59-b9fb-8f2cd9fce054.html.

26. Virginia Department of Elections. "2014 Election Results," Virginia.gov, November 4, 2014, http://elections.virginia.gov/index.php/resultsreports/election-results/2014-election-results/2014-nov-general/11042014_final.html.

27. Rebecca Shabad, "What Is the 'Cromnibus?'" *Hill,* December 3, 2014, http://thehill.com/policy/finance/225783-what-is-the-cromnibus.

28. David Brat, "Next House Speaker Must Tackle Trillion-Dollar Problems," *Breitbart,* January 4, 2015, http://www.breitbart.com/big-government/2015/01/04/exclusive-david-brat-next-house-speaker-must-tackle-trillion-dollar-problems/.

29. Allison Brophy Champion, "Brat Goes It Alone with Speaker Vote," *Culpeper (VA) Star-Exponent,* January 6, 2015, http://www.dailyprogress.com/starexponent/news/brat-goes-it-alone-with-speaker-vote/article_d701e9ee-95f0-11e4-af2f-d787b7cc2364.html.

30. McConnell, "Brat Makes Early Statement," 2015.

31. For a discussion of the "Hell No" caucus, see David Weigel, "Who Are These Guys? Eight Votes That Explain Who House Republicans Really Are," *Slate,* October 10, 2013, http://www.slate.com/articles/news_and_politics/politics/2013/10/house_republicans_the_hell_no_caucus_and_moderates_which_house_gop_members.html; see also Chris Cillizza, "The Fix's Complete Guide to Understanding House Republicans," *Washington Post,* July 9, 2013, http://www.washingtonpost.com/blogs/the-fix/wp/2013/07/09/the-fixs-complete-guide-to-understanding-house-republicans/.

32. Jeff Branscome, "Brat Receives a Spirited Welcome in Spotsylvania: 7th District Congressman Opens Office in County," *Fredericksburg (VA) Free-Lance Star,* February 7, 2015, http://www.fredericksburg.com/news/local/spotsylvania/brat-receives-a-spirited-welcome-in-spotsylvania/article_bf5e9a1c-49b6-5c55-ba0d-a769f4601c79.html.

33. Daniel Sherrier, "Editorial: Federal Funding for Amtrak," *Hanover (VA) Herald-Progress,* March 11, 2015, http://www.herald-progress.com/?p=21098.

34. "Full Committee Markup—H.R. 5, Student Success Act," YouTube video, 9:10, posted by EdWorkforce, February 11, 2015, https://www.youtube.com/watch?v=CFPcWxbBLXg.

35. Jenna Portnoy, "Cantor Speaks to Establishment Republicans in Va. about How to Win," *Washington Post,* January 17, 2015, http://www.washingtonpost.com/local/virginia-politics/cantor-speaks-to-virginia-republicans-about-how-to-win-elections-again/2015/01/17/19b7962e-9e90-11e4-96cc-e858eba91ced_story.html/.

36. Steve Albertson, "Cantor, Comstock Launch Mainstream Organization for 'Reforming the Elephant,'" *Bull Elephant* (blog), January 20, 2015, http://thebullelephant.com/cantor-comstock-launch-mainstream-organization-for-reclaiming-the-elephant/.

37. Ibid.

38. Jack Trammell, interview by Lauren Bell, Ashland, Virginia, March 19, 2015.

39. Congressman David Brat, e-mail to undisclosed recipients, March 25, 2015.

40. Jake Sherman and John Bresnahan, "GOP Group Targets House Conservatives on DHS Fight," *Politico,* March 2, 2015, http://www.politico.com/story/2015/03/american-action-network-targets-house-conservatives-dhs-funding-115668.html.

41. Matthew Boyle, "Boehner Tells House Republicans: 'We All Need to Be Team Players and Support Each Other," *Breitbart,* March 3, 2015, http://www.breitbart.com/big-government/2015/03/03/boehner-tells-house-republicans-we-all-need-to-be-team-players-and-support-each-other/.

42. Office of the Press Secretary, "Press Briefing by Press Secretary Josh Earnest, 3/2/15," *The White House,* March 2, 2015, https://www.whitehouse.gov/the-press-office/2015/03/02/press-briefing-press-secretary-josh-earnest-3215.

43. Ibid.

44. Ron Hedlund's Facebook page, posted January 12, 2015, https://www.facebook.com/ron.hedlund.

45. Editorial, "Our View: Will There Be a Republican Presidential Primary in Virginia?" *Roanoke Times,* March 24, 2015, http://www.roanoke.com/opinion/editorials/our-view-will-there-be-a-republican-presidential-primary-in/article_bd716115-acc4-5e71-9eff-22b7451ca1be.html.

46. Dawn Curry Page et al. v. Virginia State Board of Elections et al., Civil Action No. 3:13cv678, 2014, http://redistricting.lls.edu/files/VA%20page%2020141007%20opinion.pdf.

47. Ibid.

48. Jenna Portnoy, "Va. Lawmakers Get More Time to Redraw Districts," *Washington Post,* February 23, 2015, http://www.washingtonpost.com/local/virginia-politics/federal-court-gives-va-legislature-more-time-to-redraw-districts/2015/02/23/458cb46a-bb8b-11e4-8668-4e7ba8439ca6_story.html.

49. Jack Trammell, interview by Lauren Bell, March 19, 2015.

Bibliography

Aistrup, Joseph, and Ronald Keith Gaddie. "Candidate Recruitment and the New Southern Party System." Presented at the Annual Meeting of the Midwest Political Science Association, Chicago, IL, April 2001.

Almanac of American Politics Staff. "Representative Dave Brat (Member Profile)." *Almanac*, online database adapted from the *2014 Almanac of American Politics*. January 2015. http://www.nationaljournal.com/almanac/member/4530.

Alvarez, R. Michael, and Betsy Sinclair. "Electoral Institutions and Legislative Behavior: The Effects of the Primary Processes." *Political Research Quarterly* 65, no. 3 (September 2012): 544–557.

Anderson, William D., Janet M. Box-Steffensmeier, and Valeria Sinclair-Chapman. "The Keys to Legislative Success in the U.S. House of Representatives." *Legislative Studies Quarterly* 28, no. 3 (August 2003): 357–386.

Arnold, R. Douglas. *The Logic of Congressional Action.* New Haven, CT: Yale University Press, 1990.

Austin, D. Andrew, and Mindy R. Levit. "The Debt Limit: History and Recent Increases." *Congressional Research Service Report for Congress.* October 15, 2013. https://www.fas.org/sgp/crs/misc/RL31967.pdf.

Berman, Myron. *Richmond's Jewry: Shabbat in Shockoe, 1769–1976.* Charlottesville: University Press of Virginia, 1979. Essential source for "Richmond, Virginia." In *Encyclopedia of Southern Jewish Communities.* Edited by Janet Bordelon and Stuart Rockoff. Accessed June 2, 2015. http://www.isjl.org/virginia-richmond-encyclopedia.html.

Bird, Kenton. "Tom Foley's Last Campaign." *Pacific Northwest Quarterly* 95, no. 1 (Winter 2003/2004): 3–15. http://www.jstor.org/stable/40491705.

Boatright, Robert G. *Congressional Primary Elections.* New York: Routledge, 2014.

_____. *Getting Primaried: The Changing Politics of Congressional Primary Challenges.* Ann Arbor: University of Michigan Press, 2013.

Brunell, Thomas. *Redistricting and Representation: Why Competitive Elections Are Bad for America.* New York: Routledge, 2008.

Bullock, Charles S., III. *Key States, High Stakes: Sarah Palin, the Tea Party, and the 2010 Elections.* Boulder, CO: Rowman & Littlefield, 2010.

Bullock, Charles S., III, and David J. Shafer. "Party Targeting and Electoral Success." *Legislative Studies Quarterly* 22, no. 4 (November 1997): 573–584.

Bullock, Charles S., III, Donna R. Hoffman, and Ronald Keith Gaddie. "Regional Variations in the Realignment of American Politics, 1944–2004." *Social Science Quarterly* 87 (September 2006): 494–518.

———. "The Consolidation of the Southern White Vote." *Political Research Quarterly* 58 (June 2005): 231–243.

Bullock, Charles S., III, Ronald Keith Gaddie, and Ben Smith. "White Voters, Black Representative, and Candidates of Choice." *American Review of Politics* 26 (Fall 2005): 267–289.

Burden, Barry C. "Candidate Positioning in U.S. Congressional Elections." *British Journal of Political Science* 34 (March 2004): 211–227.

Burghart, Devin. "Tea Party Membership Map." *Institute for Research and Education on Human Rights*. Last modified March 7, 2013. Accessed February 20, 2015. http://www.irehr.org/issue-areas/tea-party-nationalism/the-data/tea-party-membership-map.

Cain, Bruce E., John A. Ferejohn, and Morris P. Fiorina. "The Constituency Service Basis of the Personal Vote for U.S. Representatives and British Members of Parliament." *American Political Science Review* 78, no. 1 (March 1984): 110–125. http://web.stanford.edu/~mfiorina/Fiorina%20Web%20Files/ConstituencyService.pdf.

Campbell, James E. "The Return of the Incumbents: The Nature of the Incumbency Advantage." *Western Political Quarterly* 36, no. 3 (September 1983): 434–444.

Canon, David T. *Actors, Athletes, and Astronauts: Political Amateurs in the United States Congress.* Chicago: University of Chicago Press, 1990.

Center for Responsive Politics Staff. "Every Republican Is Crucial PAC Summary Data." *Center for Responsive Politics*. Accessed June 2, 2015. https://www.opensecrets.org/pacs/lookup2.php?strID=C00384701&cycle=2006.

Cook, Charles. "Did 2004 Transform U.S. Politics?" *Washington Quarterly* 28, no. 2 (Spring 2005): 173–186.

Dave Brat for Congress. "Laura Ingraham and Dave Brat at Dominon [*sic*] Club." YouTube video, 59:21. Posted June 4, 2014. https://www.youtube.com/watch?v=tg5zRKcWj68.

Davis, Tom, Martin Frost, and Richard E. Cohen. *The Partisan Divide: Congress in Crisis.* Campbell, CA: Premiere, 2014.

dcexaminer. "Chuck Todd Interview with Dave Brat." YouTube video, 6:44. Posted June 11, 2014. https://www.youtube.com/watch?v=cqjkbfbGqdE.

Denzau, Arthur T. and Michael Munger. "Legislators and Interest Groups: How Unorganized Interests Get Represented." *American Political Science Review* 80, no. 1 (March 1986): 89–106.

EdWorkforce. "Full Committee Markup—H.R. 5, Student Success Act." YouTube video, 9:10. Posted February 11, 2015. https://www.youtube.com/watch?v=CFPcWxbBLXg.

Ezekiel, Herbert T., and Gaston Lichtenstein. *The History of the Jews in Richmond from 1769 to 1917.* Spotsylvania, VA: Sergeant Kirkland's Museum and Historical Society, 1998.

Fenno, Richard F., Jr. *Congress at the Grassroots: Representational Change in the South, 1970–1998.* Chapel Hill: University of North Carolina Press, 2000.

———. *Congressmen in Committees.* Boston: Little, Brown, 1973.

———. *Home Style: House Members in Their Districts.* New York: Little, Brown, 1978.

_____. *Senators on the Campaign Trail.* Norman: University of Oklahoma Press, 1996.

_____. "U.S. House Members in Their Constituencies: An Exploration." *American Political Science Review* 71, no. 3 (September 1977): 883–917.

Fiorina, Morris. *Congress: Keystone of the Washington Establishment.* New Haven, CT: Yale University Press, 1977.

Frisch, Scott A., and Sean Q. Kelly. *Cheese Factories on the Moon: Why Earmarks Are Good for American Democracy.* Boulder, CO: Paradigm, 2011.

Gaddie, Ronald Keith. *Born to Run: Origins of the Political Career.* Boulder, CO: Rowman & Littlefield, 2004.

Gerber, Elisabeth R., and Rebecca B. Morton. "Primary Election Systems and Representation." *Journal of Law, Economics, & Organization* 14, no. 2 (October 1998): 304–324.

Glose, Bill. "Where Richmond Shopped for 150 Years." *Virginia Living.* December 2010. http://www.virginialiving.com/arts-events/arts/where-richmond-shopped-for-150-years/.

Goffman, Erving. *The Presentation of Self in Everyday Life.* Garden City, NY: Doubleday, 1959.

Gold, Ken. "The Redistribution Factor in Cantor's Defeat." *Government Affairs Institute at Georgetown University.* June 12, 2014. http://gai.georgetown.edu/the-redistricting-factor-in-cantors-defeat/.

Green, John C., Lyman A. Kellstedt, Corwin E. Smidt, and James L. Guth. "The Soul of the South." In *The New Politics of the Old South,* 2nd ed., edited by Charles S. Bullock III and Mark J. Rozell, 283–304. Boulder, CO: Rowman & Littlefield, 1998.

Greenberger, Robert S. "Can Eric Cantor Save the GOP?" *Moment Magazine.* March/April 2009. http://www.momentmag.com/can-eric-cantor-save-the-gop-2/.

Hain, Paul L., and James E. Piereson. "Lawyers and Politics Revisited: Structural Advantages of Lawyer-Politicians." *American Journal of Political Science* 19 (February 1975): 41–51.

Hibbing, John R. *Congressional Careers: Contours of Life in the U.S. House of Representatives.* Chapel Hill: University of North Carolina Press, 1991.

Huckshorn, Robert J., and Robert C. Spencer. *The Politics of Defeat: Campaigning for Congress.* Amherst: University of Massachusetts Press, 1971.

Jacobson, Gary C. "Polarized Politics and the 2004 Congressional and Presidential Elections." *Political Science Quarterly* 120, no. 2 (Summer 2005): 199–218.

_____. "The Republican Insurgence." *Political Science Quarterly* 126 (Spring 2011): 27–52.

Johannes, John R., and John C. McAdams. "The Congressional Incumbency Effect: Is It Casework, Policy Compatibility, or Something Else? An Examination of the 1978 Election." *American Journal of Political Science* 25, no. 3 (1981): 512–542.

Kaufmann, Karen M., James G. Gimpel, and Adam H. Hoffman. "A Promise Fulfilled? Open Primaries and Representation." *Journal of Politics* 65, no. 2 (May 2003): 457–476.

Kazee, Thomas A. *Who Runs for Congress? Ambition, Context, and Candidate Emergence.* Washington, DC: Congressional Quarterly Press, 1994.

Key, V. O. *Southern Politics in State and Nation.* New York: Knopf, 1949.

Kingdon, John W. *Congressmen's Voting Decisions,* 3rd ed. Ann Arbor: University of Michigan Press, 1989.

Kingdon, John W. "Models of Legislative Voting." *Journal of Politics* 39, no. 3 (August 1977): 563–595.

Lamis, Alec. *The Two-Party South,* 2nd ed. New York: Oxford, 1990.

Lax, Jeffrey R., and Justin H. Phillips. "The Democratic Deficit in the States." *American Journal of Political Science* 56, no. 1 (January 2012): 148–166.

Lizza, Ryan. "The House of Pain." *New Yorker Magazine.* March 4, 2013. http://www.newyorker.com/magazine/2013/03/04/the-house-of-pain.

Maisel, Louis Sandy. *From Obscurity to Oblivion: Running in the Congressional Primary.* Knoxville: University of Tennessee Press, 1986.

Mann, Thomas E. *Unsafe at Any Margin.* Washington, DC: American Enterprise Institute, 1978.

Matthews, Donald R. *U.S. Senators and Their World.* New York: W. W. Norton, 1973.

Matthews, Donald R., and James Prothro. *Negroes and the New Southern Politics.* New York: Harcourt, 1996.

Mayer, Jane. "Covert Operations: The Billionaire Brothers Who Are Waging a War against Obama." *New Yorker Magazine.* August 30, 2010. http://www.newyorker.com/magazine/2010/08/30/covert-operations.

Mayhew, David R. *Congress: The Electoral Connection.* New Haven, CT: Yale University Press, 1974.

Mezey, Michael L. "Ambition Theory and the Office of Congressman." *Journal of Politics* 32, no. 3 (August 1970): 563–579.

Norrander, Barbara. "Nomination Choices: Caucus and Primary Outcomes, 1976–1988." *American Journal of Political Science* 37, no. 2 (May 1993): 343–364.

Parker, Glenn R. *Institutional Change, Discretion, and the Making of the Modern Congress: An Economic Interpretation.* Ann Arbor: University of Michigan Press, 1992.

Polidata. "Partisan Voting Index, Districts of the 113th Congress." *Cook Political Report.* 2013. http://cookpolitical.com/file/2013-04-47.pdf.

Risen, Clay. *The Bill of the Century: The Epic Battle for the Civil Rights Act.* New York: Bloomsbury, 2014.

Rosen, Robert N. *The Jewish Confederates.* Columbia: University of South Carolina Press, 2000.

Rozell, Mark J. "Virginia." In *The New Politics of the Old South,* edited by Charles S. Bullock III and Mark J. Rozell, 135–154. Boulder, CO: Rowman & Littlefield, 1998.

Rshill7. "Dave Brat Defeats Cantor Victory Speech." You Tube video, 11:02. Posted by June 11, 2014. https://www.youtube.com/watch?v=ye5SIiQRy0Y.

Ryan, Paul, Eric Cantor, and Kevin McCarthy. *Young Guns: A New Generation of Conservative Leaders.* New York: Simon & Schuster, 2010.

Singer, David, and Lawrence Grossman. "Jewish Population of the United States, 2002." *American Jewish Yearbook, 2003.* New York: American Jewish Committee, 2003. http://www.ajcarchives.org/ajc_data/files/2003_6_usdemographic.pdf.

Stone, Kurt F. "Eric Ivan Cantor." *The Jews of Capitol Hill: A Compendium of Jewish Congressional Members.* Lanham, MD: Scarecrow Press, 2010.

Stroupe, Kenneth S., Jr. "Gerrymandering's Long History in Virginia: Will This Decade Mark the End?" *Virginia News Letter* 85, no. 1 (February 2009). http://www.cooper-center.org/sites/default/files/publications/vanl0209_0.pdf.

Squire, Peverill. "Measuring State Legislative Professionalism: The Squire Index Revisited." *State Politics & Policy Quarterly* 7, no. 2 (Summer 2007): 211–227.

Taibbi, Matt. "The Truth about the Tea Party." *Rolling Stone.* September 28, 2010. http://www.rollingstone.com/politics/news/matt-taibbi-on-the-tea-party-20100928.

Toobin, Jeffrey. "Drawing the Line: Will Tom DeLay's Redistricting in Texas Cost Him His Seat?" *New Yorker Magazine.* March 6, 2006. http://www.newyorker.com/magazine/2006/03/06/drawing-the-line-3.

Virginia Department of Elections. "Official Results—Primary Election—June 10, 2014." Virginia. gov. Accessed April 4, 2015. http://elections.virginia.gov/Files/ElectionResults/2014/June-Primaries/resultsSW7217.html?type=CON&map=CTY.

WMAL Washington. "Jamie Radtke on WMAL 6-11-14." YouTube video, 6:14. Posted June 11, 2014. https://www.youtube.com/watch?v=nQltZeyYsgM.

Zernike, Kate. *Boiling Mad: Inside Tea Party America.* New York: Times Books, 2010.

Index